DELTIC

One of the handsome English Electric Type '3' diesels (1,750 hp), later Class '37' (English Electric).

BRITISH LOCOMOTIVES
OF THE 20th CENTURY
O.S.Nock

Volume 3 1960~the present day

PSL Patrick Stephens, Wellingborough

First published March 1985
Reprinted October 1985

British Library Cataloguing in Publication Data

Nock, O. S.
    British locomotives of the 20th century.
    Vol. 3. 1960–The present day
    1. Locomotives—Great Britain—History—
    I. Title
    625.2'6'0941   TJ603.4.G7

ISBN 0-85059-681-5

*Patrick Stephens Limited is part of the
Thorsons Publishing Group*

Photoset in 10 on 10 pt Baskerville by MJL Typesetting,
Hitchin, Herts. Printed in Great Britain on 115 gsm
Fineblade coated cartridge, and bound, by The Garden
City Press, Letchworth, Herts. for the publishers, Patrick
Stephens Limited, Denington Estate, Wellingborough,
Northants, NN8 2QD, England.

Contents

Preface

This third volume, bringing the history of British locomotives from 1960 up to the present time, covers a period of very rapid evolution. Yet that evolution was not only technological; it was no less sociological, and there were many times when the second factor tended to inhibit the first to an alarmingly serious extent. No engineers, particularly railway locomotive engineers, enjoy the luxury of a completely free hand to develop their ideas. In the period covered by the first volume of this work the constraints were various, some arising from parsimony in management, elsewhere from short-sightedness — if not plain ignorance — from some of their colleagues in other railway departments. In the period of the second volume, and certainly in the time between the two World Wars, most of the trouble was simply lack of cash. One can nevertheless feel that those who have had to carry on since the launching of the great Modernisation Plan of 1955 must many times have looked back rather wistfully to earlier days when the constraints, tiresome though they could be, were infinitely more straightforward, and neither so deviously entwined and encompassed with political, as well as practical considerations, nor haunted by the spectre of glaring and inexpert exposure in the media on every occasion when something went wrong! This was inevitable, of course, when finance for improvement and development was voted not by a tightly knitted body of private shareholders, but by the House of Commons.

Engineers henceforth had an uneviable task. At the very outset of the Modernisation Plan their carefully formulated plan for a three-year period of trial for a limited number of new diesel locomotives, of various types, was soon overridden, and orders placed for large quantities of relatively untried designs, before works and maintenance facilities were ready to deal with them. That the 'diesel revolution', as it has been called, was carried through with so little disruption to ordinary traffic, was due in very large measure to the devotion of the large body of steam locomotive men of all ranks who adapted themselves so readily to the new power. Before the Modernisation Plan had been under way for many years, also, it was evident that the traffic patterns were changing, particularly in freight. In passenger business too we were only just passing beyond the era of petrol rationing, and the rapid increase in private motoring was already making serious inroads into what had been staple traffics. In an age of increasing financial stringency, locomotive engineers not only had to assess and appraise the various new designs of motive power purchased, but rapidly to evaluate how it could best be deployed and developed to meet the competition for traffic that was arising in so many different ways, and which made some of the new power redundant within a very few years of its first introduction.

It was against this often traumatic background that British Railways climbed to the very forefront of world high speed passenger train service; for while the 'Electric Scots' and the HSTs in their start-to-stop average speeds do not quite attain the maximum heights of the Japanese Shinkansen, or the new French TGV, the frequency of service offered throughout the day, over routes used by a plethora of other trains of great diversity, is unparalleled the world over. The speed achievements of the two rivals of British Railways are made over routes reserved exclusively for super high speed

passenger trains. Nor has the development in freight service been any less striking, having regard to the working of nominated company trains, freight liners, and the merry-go-round coal trains, all of which require motive power of the highest class. The new '58' Class freight diesels are now taking their place alongside the '86/2' and '87' Class electrics, and the mixed traffic '37' and '47' Class diesel-electrics, as milestones in the history of the British locomotive.

Nor must the relatively brief careers of certain other locomotive designs be forgotten, the lifespan of which began and ended within the period covered by this one book. apart from notable experimental prototypes such as the *Lion,* the *Falcon,* the GT3, the *Kestrel* and 'DP2', there was the extensive venture into diesel-hydraulic transmission carried out on the Western Region. The last mentioned project got off to a bad start, due to certain extenuating circumstances that led to 'under-design' of certain vital components; but the dedicated experimental analysis that diagnosed the troubles and led to their elimination was characteristic of British locomotive men, all down the years, and typified the way in which the good features of many designs that were not wholly successful in themselves have been skilfully extracted, and embodied satisfactorily elsewhere.

At the time when this book must go to press the experimental work on the epoch-marking Advanced Passenger Train project is still uncompleted; and although confidence in its ultimate success has been more than once expressed quite emphatically by the most senior engineers of the British Railways Board, there are still some 'creases' to be ironed out in its final design. One thing is, however, quite clear. The tilt feature of the passenger coaches, which has been the victim of so much ill-informed criticism, remains fundamental to the APT. To experience it at maximum speed on the sinuous northern sections of the West Coast Main Line, as I was privileged to do on a routine Glasgow-Euston round trip, was to be left with nothing but fervent admiration for the magnificent engineering built into this train: a fitting milestone in development at which to conclude this book.

Before doing so I must express my warmest thanks to the British Railways Board and its officers, both at headquarters and in the Regions, for their help. The nigh-thirty years which this book covers have seen very many changes, both in policy and personnel; and its is indicative of the rapid and fluctuating phases of evolution through which British locomotive engineering has passed that these changes, within an ostensibly unified organisation, have been as many and varied as witnessed in the total history of the four grouped railways in the inter-war years. It would be invidious to mention any individuals by name, when all have been so generous in their help, save perhaps for one, no longer with us, who, when others had quit the field, assumed the tremendous responsibilities of Chief Mechanical Engineer of the British Railways at the time of the launching of the Modernisation Plan, my great friend and co-author in the Institution of Mechanical Engineers, the late Roland C. Bond. A lifelong steam man up till then, he threw himself with the utmost energy, enthusiasm and dedication into the task of modernisation. In so doing, however, he was no more than typical of countless others, in varying degrees of responsibility, who did the same.

O.S. Nock,
Bath, November 1984

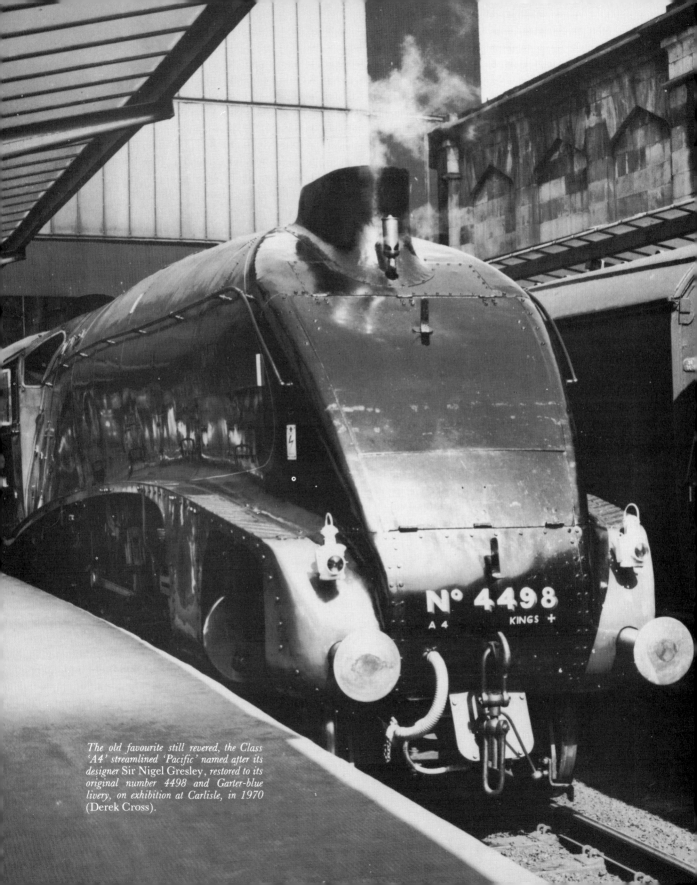

The old favourite still revered, the Class 'A4' streamlined 'Pacific' named after its designer Sir Nigel Gresley, restored to its original number 4498 and Garter-blue livery, on exhibition at Carlisle, in 1970 (Derek Cross).

1. The Great Modernisation Plan of 1955

In commenting upon the cataclysm in British railway operation set in motion by the great scheme of modernisation of 1955 it is dangerously easy to be wise after the event. Nevertheless, it is not as though the main streams of change and their numerous cross-currents are things that are over and done with. Repercussions from the euphoria of the gigantic spending spree launched in 1955 are still disturbingly frequent. Most of the trouble stems from the underlying fact that, from the moment the result of the General Election of 1945 became known, the railways of this country became the cat's paw of party politics. Long before the Nationalisation Bill reached the statute-book a campaign of denigration of the railways had been waged from the Government benches in the House of Commons, with scathingly deprecating remarks about their quality made by some of the most senior Cabinet Ministers, doubtless with the aim of reducing the amount of compensation to tbe paid to the railway shareholders for taking over their property. The spectacular success of the Labour party at the polls, and the virtual dismissal of Winston Churchill, came as such a shock to world opinion that sympathy and financial support so waned as to plunge the nation into an era of the deepest austerity.

Ten years later, after a change in Government, funds were made available for large scale modernisation, to an extent, on the first estimates, of £1,200 million; but it was not long before a reassessment of the costs increased the figures to £1,600 million. So far as this book is concerned the principal feature of the Modernisation Plan was the progressive replacement of steam locomotives by electric and diesel traction, with all this involved in new facilities and equipment at the Main Works, new motive power and rolling-stock maintenance depots, and massive programmes of staff training. By many the replacement of steam was regarded not only as regrettable on sentimental grounds but as unsound economically, since it necessitated the use of imported fuel instead of the indigenous kind of which it was believed there were still ample supplies. But the coal situation had changed dramatically from that existing before the Second World War. Then there were ample supplies of steam coal in a form that was ideal for use in the traditional designs of British locomotive; but, with the introduction of mechanised coal cutting and modern methods of handling the coal which was delivered to the railways, though of high calorific value, was often broken small and contained a considerable propor-tion of dust. This was far from ideal for use in locomotive fireboxes.

There were other factors beyond the mere quality of coal. The old traditions of work on the footplate were rapidly disappearing. In a time of full employment, which in many areas was then causing a serious shortage of labour, there were many alternative occupations in which young men could find jobs with regular hours that were more congenial than cleaning and firing steam locomotives; and while there remained a solid, if rather diminishing core of those who had steam in the blood, their numbers and their influence was on the wane. Furthermore, the anti-steam propaganda was unceasing. Even in the precincts of railway drawing offices, establishments with magnificent traditions of service, one could hear remarks that steam was 'antiquated', and should be scrapped and forgotten. Nevertheless, when the British Transport Commission's plan for modernisation was published, in 1955, with a great deal of publicity, the comprehensive package that it represented, to be completed in a very short time, could have led many people to imagine that modernisation was a once-in-a-lifetime exercise. Railway engineers, who would, after all, have the job of carrying out the motive power transition, felt that little credit had been given in the attendant publicity to the continuous modernisation that was ceaselessly in progress on British railways, and which, since the end of the Second World War had restored the overworked systems to their traditionally high standards, if not necessarily in passenger train speed. And so, with scant regard for all they had done in 15 years of unparalleled difficulties, they were faced with the colossal task of effecting a complete revolution in the form of motive power, in just another 15 years!

In its original form the plan envisaged electrification of the West Coast main lines as far north as Manchester and Liverpool, including, of course, the alternative route from Rugby to Stafford, via Birmingham and Wolverhampton, and the North Staffordshire line from Colwich, via Stoke-on-Trent. The East Coast was marked down for electrification from Kings Cross to Leeds, and possibly also from Doncaster to York, while from Liverpool Street, the former Great Eastern line, already in process of electrification from Southend, was suggested for extension to Clacton and to Ipswich. All Southern lines east of a diagonal line from London to Portsmouth were to be electrified. Everywhere else, apart from local electrification in Scotland, north and south of the Firth of Clyde, was

*The short lived 'BR9' 2-10-0 mixed traffic steam locomotive.
Although construction continued for some years after the modernisation plan was launched, except for a few preserved units all were
withdrawn by 1968. Engine No 92000 is here seen working the
'Pines Express' on the Somerset and Dorset line.*

to be changed over to diesel traction, using multiple-unit railcar sets for the branch lines. It is noteworthy that in its original form the Modern-isation Plan made no reference to any form of route rationalisation, or curtailment of service. The network was taken just as it existed, and no provision was made for any immediate variation from the existing train service. The expected higher utilisation to be obtained from electric and diesel locomotives was, however, reflected in the proposed reduction in the number of main line locomotives. The initial plan provided for four broad categories of main line diesel locomotives, with Type '1' covering units of 800 up to 1,000 horsepower; Type '2' from 1,000 up to 1,,250; Type '3' from 1,500 to 1,750, and Type '4' of 2,000 horsepower and upwards.

Intense interest had naturally been created among the manufacturing firms by the announce-ments of the Modernisation Plan. It was just what they had been waiting for ever since nationalisation. As Chief Mechanical Engineer, R.C. Bond had the task of getting the specifications for the new power drawn up, and the 'Plan' envisaged the building of about 2,500 locomotives in Types '2', '3' and'4' by the end of 1970. Invitations to tender were sent out to all the British locomotive manufacturers, to three in the USA to one in Canada and to one in Australia. The response was almost overwhelming, because more than 200 separate proposals were received, and, while Bond's staff were well-nigh

submerged by the volume of paperwork that was entailed in the classifying and appraisal of all these different designs, there was a debate in the House of Commons on the subject of the Modernisation Plan. Industrialists, and indeed all who had the welfare of British Railways at heart, were horrified to hear an influential speaker from the Government side of the house state that he would have no objection to large numbers of the diesel-electric-locomotives required being ordered from the USA. At this stage may I interject a personal memory of this crucial period.

At that time a great friend of mine, editor of one of the foremost journals then dealing with railway business, immediately took steps to contact some of his closest personal associates in the railway hierarchy, and discovered that the comment tossed across the floor of the House of Commons was not merely the view of an influential private member, but was in fact the policy that a majority of the British Transport Commission were preparing to impose upon their engineers, whatever recom-mendations Bond and his staff were likely to make.

One of the first of the new 2,000 hp diesel-electric main line locomotives, as originally numbered D210, later BR Class '40' (British Railways).

Something had to be done about it, and urgently. A small and highly confidential meeting was hastily convened. To the four of us who attended, the repercussions from the line of action on which the BTC was intent seemed to be threefold: a 'slap in the face' to British industry; untold difficulties on the railways themselves from the sudden implanting of large numbers of foreign-built locomotives, before any maintenance or back-up facilities were available; and a great disservice to British prestige, so far as export business was concerned. My own editorial connections with *The Engineer* newspaper, and my then fairly frequent leading articles were considered as a good impartial platform from which to deliver a 'broadside', and between us we decided the salient points of a strongly worded 'leader' which was published soon afterwards under the title *Railways and Industry*. How near to the brink of ordering diesels from the USA the BTC had progressed we are not to know, nor the extent to which that leader of mine helped to tip the scales. But the scales were tipped, and Bond and his men were able to proceed in an orderly manner with their recommendations for the pilot scheme of diesel introduction.

While appreciating that so far as diesel traction was concerned there was everything to be gained from standardisation, decisions on what to standardise among the many alternative designs available required a wide range of experience and, what was more important, time to acquire that experience. Orders were placed initially for no more than 174 locomotives, and these included seven different makes of engine, eight variants of transmission, and mechanical parts from seven different locomotive builders. These, it will be appreciated, were a mere drop in the ocean compared to the tremendous variety of designs that had been submitted. Even so, a notable breadth of experience was assured from the working of the types chosen, and it was hoped to have adequate time to amass that experience. Bond and his men strongly recommended that no further orders for new locomotives should be placed for a period of three years, while experience was gained with those included in the pilot scheme. This was not an unduly generous interval, seeing that men with a lifetime of work in steam had to familiarise themselves with something quite different, apart from making assessments of variations in the new power itself. The BTC accepted the recommendation from the engineers and at first all was well. Without any initial reference to the power classifications it was announced in 1956 that the allocation of the 174 locomotives in the pilot scheme would be Eastern Region 80; LM Region 65; Southern Region 15; and Western Region 14.

Before a single new diesel locomotive had been delivered the Commission had thrown overboard the wise recommendation of a three-year trial period made by their technical advisers. Less than two years after the Modernisation Plan was launched the promise of dieselisation had done nothing to halt their declining financial fortunes, and in the naive assumption that all would be well once they had got rid of steam, they instructed their engineers to press on regardless, with two over-riding requirements: first that the number of designs of locomotive should be kept to the absolute minimum; and second, that the end products should be thoroughly reliable and capable of doing the work for which they were intended. The second directive would, in retrospect, appear to be somewhat fatuous, because one could hardly imagine the experienced band of engineers on Bond's staff embarking on designs that they believed were otherwise! But by casting aside the three-year period, which would have given time to gain experience on which to achieve the two principal requirements laid down by the Commission, much of the technical ground had been cut from beneath the feet of the engineers; and they were pitchforked into a replacement of steam by diesel at a breakneck speed. Although no more than 140 units of the original 'pilot batch' of 174 had been delivered by the end of 1958, by the spring of 1959 orders for more than 900 additional main line locomotives had been placed, gratifyingly all with British builders.

All except ten of the new diesel-electric loco-motives put into service before the end of 1958 were of no more than medium power, 800 up to 1,250 horsepower. The power characteristics of diesel locomotives, and the way in which they differ from those of steam need some attention at this stage, for a clear appreciation of the new motive-power to be obtained. The horsepower figures quoted are those of the engine and do not represent the power that is available for hauling a train. Tests carried out with the 2,000 horsepower diesel-electric locomotive of the Southern Railway, No 10203, showed that the maximum drawbar horsepower was about 1,400; and, while there could be variations with individual types, a value of about 75 per cent of the nominal engine horsepower could be taken as a rough guide to the maximum drawbar horsepower that could be expected in service. When the LMS introduced the prototype 1,600 horsepower main line diesels Nos 10000 and 10001 in 1947, with a maximum draw-bar horsepower of 1,200, it was arranged for the two of them to work in tandem on duties that would require maximum output from a single LMS steam 'Pacific' engine of the 'Duchess' class.

At the same time it has to be borne in mind that, unlike a steam locomotive, a diesel attains its maximum thermal efficiency when working at full power. While the capacity of the new locomotives in the Type '2' power range, of 1,000 up to 1,250 nominal horsepower, with an expectancy of 750 to 950 maximum drawbar horsepower, might have seemed low compared to the capacity of some of the steam locomotives they were intended to replace, the latter would very rarely be expected to work 'all-out', whereas the diesels were designed to be driven in just that way. One region, having regard to the standardisation of its future motive power, suggested to headquarters that there was no need to have any units larger than Type '2', and that all requirements for higher power could be met by coupling two units in multiple. This, Bond and his staff did not favour, as a mode of regular usage. He pointed out that one Type '4' locomotive of 2,300 horsepower would, at 1955 prices, cost about £100,000, and weigh about 135 tons, whereas two Type '2' locomotives to produce the same horse-power would cost about £150,000, and weigh any-thing up to 200 tons. The case for a limited number of larger locomotives seemed unassailable. The 'pilot' scheme, called for no more than ten Type '4' of English Electric build and of 2,000 horsepower to be developed directly from the prototype 10000-1 of 1947.

While from the outset it had been determined that principal reliance would be placed upon electrical transmission, which had been so widely and apparently successfully adopted in North America, considerable interest had been aroused a few years earlier by the development, by the North British Locomotive Company, of a system of turbo-hydraulic transmission. Before the launching of the Modernisation Plan it had been used in some small diesel shunting locomotives, and already the company had produced designs for both 1,000 and 2,000 horsepower main line locomotives which

Opposite page, top to bottom
Introduction of diesels on the West Coast main line: one of the 'D200' Class, No 317 on a Manchester to Glasgow express climbing the Beattock bank at Greskine siding, where a freight train hauled by one of the Crosti-boilered '9F' 2-10-0s, No 92024 has been berthed to give preference to the express (Derek Cross).

The new look at Stratford, Eastern Region: at the diesel maintenance depot, from left to right a Brush Type '2' 1,250 hp, an English Electric Type '4' 2,000 hp No D205, and a Type '1', North British 800 hp (British Railways).

A diesel on 'The Royal Scot': early days in modernisation, with semaphore signals remaining at Shap Summit in 1963 (Derek Cross).

Left *One of the new 2,000 hp English Electric diesels hauling the up 'Royal Scot', passing a typical ex-Caledonian country station in Upper Clydesdale, Lamington. The station was subsequently closed and all traces of it removed* (Derek Cross).

Below *Further new-look on the Caledonian line: two of the short-lived '17' Class Clayton diesels working a southbound freight train conveying permanent way materials near Abington* (Derek Cross).

Left *One of the Birmingham Railway Carriage & Wagon Co's 1,250 hp diesel-electric locomotives, introduced in 1958, now Class '27' on an express from Glasgow arriving in Edinburgh and passing through the Princes Street Gardens* (Brian Morrison).

would meet the BR specifications. It was however the production in 1953, by the firm, of two 0-6-0 locomotives of 625 hp for the Mauritius Railway that largely inspired a major BR development. These locomotives ran on the British standard gauge, and before they were shipped abroad a series of tests was carried out with both freight and passenger trains on Scottish Region, the latter, indeed, over the former Caledonian route between Glasgow Central and Edinburgh Princes Street. Bond himself accompanied some of the trial runs, and he was sufficiently impressed with the performance to initiate a critical examination of the transmission design, and to follow it to Germany—the country of its origin.

The Great Western Railway, from its first espousal of the broad gauge, had, over its long history, established a reputation for doing things

differently from everyone else, and when the Modernisation Plan was launched the Western Region was chosen for a full-scale application of the turbo-hydraulic system of transmission for its diesel locomotives. The first six units, of 2,000 horsepower, and having the A1A-A1A wheel arrangement, were built by the North British Locomotive Company; they were included in the original pilot scheme drawn up by Bond, and took the road late in 1957 at about the same time as the first 2,000 hp diesel-electrics were delivered from English Electric. Details of the diesel-hydraulic locomotives, and of their development and track record, is given in a later chapter of this book. It was agreed at first that their use should be confined to the Western Region, with appropriate steps for their maintenance to be established at Swindon. With the highly sophisticated facilities for locomotive testing on the Western Region, the economics and general standard of their performance could be accurately established.

While the change from steam to diesel traction would produce by far the greatest numerical part of the revolution in British Railways motive power included in the 1955 Modernisation Plan, no less important were the provisions for full-scale electrification. In fact, in the longer term view they could be regarded as the most important sections of all, in that they represented the ultimate foreseeable form of traction, regarding the diesels as no more than an intermediate stage on certain routes. At the time when the modernisation scheme was launched, the way ahead on main line electrification could well have seemed the most clear cut of any, except of course that the high capital cost imposed a limit on the number of schemes that might immediately be put in hand. Unlike the case with diesel traction, the systems available were established, and well proved technically. In the Southern Region, for example, there was no thought of departing from the 750-volt, third-rail, dc system, with the use of multiple-unit trains for all passenger services. Elsewhere, the recommendations of the Weir Committee of 1931, for use of the 1,500-volt dc system with overhead wire current collection, had been followed in the Trans-Pennine electrification of the former Great

Central line, with success in the handling of very heavy mineral traffic, and an admixture of fast passenger trains. It was also in course of installation on the Great Eastern suburban network from Liverpool Street.

The 1,500-volt dc system had been installed with conspicuous success in the Paris-Orléans electrification before the war, and it had unhesitatingly been adopted when, as part of the massive post-war reconstruction of the French railways, the electrification of the South-East Region main line between Paris and Lyons had been authorised. British Railways seemed on a very safe course when the first decision to continue with the 1,500 volt dc system was taken. But then in the zone of Western Germany which was occupied by French forces after the war there was a short electric line connecting the Rhine valley with a tourist region in the Black Forest that was equipped at 20,000 volts alternating current, at the commercial frequency of 50 cycles per second. It had been made experimentally because the normal German system of railway electrification used 15,000 volts ac at a frequency of $16\frac{2}{3}$ cycles per second. French engineers became intensely interested in this experimental system, because it gave promise of very considerable reductions in the capital cost of the fixed equipment. The locomotives would probably be a little more expensive than those for 1,500 volts dc, but the investigations proved so promising that authorisation was obtained to install it on a 48-mile stretch of main line between Geneva and Chamonix. Detailed estimates showed that the cost of installation would be no more than two thirds of that of the 1,500 volts dc system.

Then in 1954 there had come the 16th International Railway Congress, the first to be held in England since 1925. 'Question 3', to be considered by the delegates was . . . 'To Investigate the technical and economic aspects of the basic characteristics of electric traction now in use with a view to deciding whether and to what extent there are relevant reasons for preferring one system to another. In particular are there any reasons in regard to—(a) power supply (b) overhead line and fixed track installations (c) motive power units (d) working and maintenance costs?' Mr S.B. Warder, then Chief Officer (Electrical Engineering) of the British Transport Commission and later Chief Electrical Engineer, together with a distinguished Italian engineer, was asked to report on this question. I attended the session at which Mr Warder's report was submitted, and was interested to learn that, on what proved to be almost the eve of the launching of the Modernisation Plan, British Railways was still firmly in favour of the 1,500-volt dc system. He expressed the view that while the high-voltage ac system might be cheaper in fixed equipment the savings would be outweighed by the higher cost of locomotives, and that on a heavily worked line there would be little to choose between the two systems financially. His other point was that there would be a considerable advantage in using the high-voltage system on long main lines carrying *a light traffic.*

The Italian reporter Professor Guzzanti generally concurred with Stanley Warder's views, but was

Double-headed electrically-hauled coal train on the Manchester-Sheffield Wath 1,500v dc line, in mountain country near Woodhead (Brian Morrison).

clearly looking over his shoulder towards the latest French development. Strengthened by the success already achieved with the short line equipped on the 25,000-volt ac 50-cycle system, it had already been announced that they were to electrify 200 miles of the mainly freight route between Valenciennes and Thionville, on the north-to-south line running near to the north-eastern frontier. Passenger trains were relatively few, but at busy times there were sometimes more than 80 freight trains a day, with an average load of around 1,000 tons each. Details of four different types of locomotive on order were published in June 1954, and it was clear that all of them were intended for freight service—none having a maximum speed of more than 60 mph. But from informal conversations during that Congress one formed the impression that, despite the statements of Mr Warder, British Railways was having very serious second thoughts about the traction system to be adopted as a future standard. Although the first of the new locomotives for the Valenciennes—Thionville line had not yet been delivered, the French were enthusiastic and confident about the outcome, and these sentiments undoubtedly began to influence some of the British engineers, not that the many-sided implications of so high a voltage as 25,000 were minimised.

One of these issues was clearance between the

overhead wire and earthed structures such as overhead steelwork, bridges and tunnel roofs, which would have to be much greater with 25,000 volts ac than with 1,500 volts dc. But in any case no fewer than 478 overbridges between Euston, Liverpool and Manchester would have to be raised to give the four inches clearance that would be required for 1,500 volts dc. Another 223 would need raising to provide the 11 inches clearance necessary for 25,000 volts ac. At first it was also thought that the long tunnels on the London Midland line would present a major problem in clearance, but further investigation revealed that there was adequate clearance for 25,000 volts in all the double-line tunnels; it was only the single-line bores, such as that of the down fast line at Leighton Buzzard, which might present problems. But it was the experience of the French Railways on the Valenciennes—Thionville line with its electric locomotives which finally tipped the scales; because after no more than a year's experience it had been found that the high-voltage ac locomotives were proving not only cheaper in first cost and in maintenance, but were more powerful and thermally efficient. Although this experience had been acquired in relatively slow, heavy freight haulage it had been such as to convince French Railways that the 25,000-volt ac system at 50 cycles should be the future standard for all new electrified lines, and early in 1956 the British Transport Commission decided to follow suit.

In the early stages of modernisation there was a strong body of opinion, not entirely confined to non-technical members of the Commission, that appreciable acceleration of service beyond the best that had been achieved with steam was unnecessary, and that the panacea for eliminating all financial

Below *25 kv electrification in Scotland: an electric mutliple-unit train from Motherwell arriving at Glasgow Central station.* (Derek Cross).

Below Right *New-look in the Newcastle area. One of the so-called 'super-trams' on the 1,500v dc electrified Tyne and Wear network over former BR lines* (GEC).

troubles was to get rid of all steam traction as soon as possible. For the Euston–Liverpool–Manchester electrification a single class of locomotive was envisaged, so that maximum utilisation could be obtained by working out-of-service diagrams including the haulage of both passenger and freight trains. Two requirements were initially laid down:

a) 'The locomotive to be capable of hauling a 475-ton express passenger trailing load from Manchester to London (Euston) with a balancing speed of 90 mph on level tangent track and a maximum speed of 100 mph. The average speed is 67 mph with one stop of one minute, and four miles at 15 mph additional speed restrictions for track maintenance.'

b) 'The locomotive to be capable of hauling a 950-ton freight train between Manchester (Longsight) and London (Willesden) at an average speed of 42 mph with a maximum speed of 55 mph. The locomotive will also have to work 500-ton express freight trains (fully fitted) at a maximum speed of 60 mph over this section. The locomotive to be capable of making three consecutive starts with the 950-ton train up to 20 mph on a 1 in 100 gradient, and to be capable of working without damage to the equipment with this train for ten miles at 10 mph on any part of the route.'

There is no doubt that in recommending the 25,000-volt ac system Warder was taking a plunge, if not exactly into the unknown, then certainly into a sphere of electric traction in which there was little

previous experience, either on British Railways or with the various manufacturers of traction equipment. Neither did the Valenciennes–Thionville installation in France help, because on that line four different types of electric locomotive had been introduced, all of them to a large extent experimental. I shall never forget my surprise at first seeing one of these locomotives. Their extraordinarily utilitarian aspect had not entirely impressed itself upon me from the photographs I had seen when the line was first put into commission. But in continuing electrification from Dijon to the Swiss frontier at Vallorbe the 25,000-volt system was used for the last 60 miles from Dole, and there I had the privilege of riding in the cab of one of them, working an engineers' inspection special. It had a strangely antique appearance, with a high central cab and what looked like immensely long motor-car 'bonnets' extending fore and aft of the cab. This latter was surmounted by a double set of pantograph gear, an incredible amount of ironmongery carried on the top of the cab. Knowing how British Railways had been influenced by the reports of working on this system I could not help wondering if locomotives looking something like this would soon be hauling the expresses out of Euston!

In one respect the French had the advantage over British Railways and British industry, in that there was already some experience of building ac traction motors. The Valenciennes–Thionville line had four different traction systems, including direct ac

Left *Variety in the new top-line power: the first of the Derby-built Type '4' diesels, with 2,300 hp Sulzer engines, 1-Co-Co-1 Type, No D1* Scafell Pike, *and known as the 'Peak' class* (British Railways).

Right *Later diesel development on the West Coast main line: one of the Brush 2,750 hp diesel-electrics on the Caledonian line near Lamington, still mechanically signalled, with an Anglo-Scottish express.* (Derek Cross).

single-phase traction motors, and a mixed system in which the single-phase line voltage was transformed into 3-phase for the traction motors, of which type there was ample experience on the Continent. But for BR Warder decided to play safe and use the well-tried direct current traction motors, converting from the single-phase ac line voltage by rectifiers. Although there had then been massive progress in the development of the semi-conductor type of rectifier for high power outputs it was not felt there had been sufficient experience to warrant their use on the new locomotives, and the mercury-arc type was specified. In other respects British Railways were venturing into the unknown with the first ac electric locomotives, and in no way more so than in the wheel arrangement, and in the purely mechanical design. Again practice was influenced by Continental experience.

While hitherto it had been thought desirable to include some carrying wheels in the design of a non-steam locomotive intended for the fastest express running, to ensure good riding and the first diesel-electric Type '4' locomotives having the 1-Co + Co-1 wheel arrangement were excellent in this respect, both in Switzerland and France highly sucessful electric locomotives, of the Bo + Bo type, with no carrying wheels had been introduced. From the tractive effort point of view they had the advantage that the entire weight of the locomotive was available for adhesion, and in view of the intention to use the new BR units in freight as well as in passenger service this was a major point. While the engineers of British Railways were attracted towards the Bo + Bo type, in view of its spectacular success on the Paris-Lyons route, albeit working on 1,500 volts dc, the civil engineers were equally mindful of the disturbance that can be caused to the track by such locomotives running at speeds up to a maximum of 100 mph; and while the maximum axle-load for steam locomotives had been fixed at 22½ tons, a maximum of 20 tons was laid down for the new electrics, with a minimum wheel diameter of 48 inches. Thus the maximum weight of a Bo + Bo electric locomotive could not exceed 80 tons, against which it must be recalled that the adhesion weight of one of the Duchess class steam 'Pacific' locomotives was 67 tons.

While liaison between British and Continental railwaymen was close and cordial it was thought to be undesirable to take the Swiss or French bogie design and attempt to adapt it to British conditions—fortunately so, in view of experience in another connection—and the question of bogie design was approached afresh. Four manufacturers were invited to submit designs for consideration. Each was given a free hand within the overall parameter of a locomotive not exceeding 80 tons in weight. It was hoped by this invitation to establish a synthesis of the best proven features that could be incorporated in a future national standard. As a result of this invitation, the trial batches of locomotives, as accepted by British Railways, included five different

A present-day stronghold of steam: the shed at Bridgnorth, Severn Valley Railway, with locomotives, left to right, ex-LMS three-cylinder 4-6-0 No 5690 Leander, ex-GWR 4-6-0 No 7819 and ex-LMS 2-6-0 No 43106 (Severn Valley Railway).

designs of underframes and four different designs of bogie. It will be appreciated at this stage how vastly different the process of design was from that which had characterised British locomotive development up to this stage in history. Hitherto the major drawing offices at long-established centres like Crewe, Doncaster and Swindon had been able to draw on very many years of hard, solid experience and produce new locomotive designs on which the fundamental features were well known. There had been no need to invite outsiders to submit their ideas. The process that had to be adopted in the case of the new electric locomotives was enough to indicate something of the profound changes that the Modernisation Plan was imposing upon British Railways.

And then, when the pilot scheme for electrification of the line between Manchester and Crewe was barely under way there came the very real possibility that the entire project of main line electrification might be cancelled. The finances of British Railways were dipping still deeper into the red. The promise of complete elimination of steam had done nothing to stop the decline, and at that stage the effect of electrification—what came later to be

described as 'the sparks effect'—had made no impression. Faced with the high capital cost of full electrification the Commission took fright, and for several traumatic months work was stopped. Furthermore, the companion scheme for electrification of the East Coast main line from Kings Cross to Leeds was not authorised at all, and only today more than 25 years later has it received the go-ahead. Fortunately the Euston–Liverpool–Manchester project was not held up for too long, though the insistence upon economy in capital expenditure led to a severe watering down of the signalling modernisation. Between Liverpool and Nuneaton, instead of having modern panel signal boxes, the existing mechanical plants were retained in most places, though converted to operate long-range colour light signals, as elsewhere on the modernised lines. Details of the new electric locomotives and their work is contained in Chapters 7 and 8 of this book.

2. Modernisation—the diesel-electrics

It would be difficult for the most factual and dispassionate of observers to write of what has been called 'the diesel revolution' without some personal sentiments obtruding. In my own case, deeply involved in various aspects of the modernisation work as a professional engineer, a frequent contributor to some of the leading technical journals of the day, not infrequently in an editorial capacity, I would ordinarily have had little room for concern with anything but hard facts had I not also been a lifelong railway enthusiast and, like many professional railwaymen, had a deep affection for the steam locomotive. So, keenly as I looked forward to the new age and judged its potential for the future as much as its immediate impact, it was inevitable that I found myself making comparisons of present with past. Perhaps I did so more critically than some of

my contemporaries in the literary world, who seemed ready enough to write off the steam era as a regrettable episode best forgotten. At the opposite extreme may be set the vapourings of those die-hard steam supporters who were always ready to delight in any failure of the new diesels. My own earliest and most extensive travelling experiences with diesels were with those having hydraulic transmission, and working on the Western Region. A special study of their design and performance is contained in Chapter 4 of this book.

As representing the first of the new power to take the road, in 1957, the group of medium-powered designs in the 'Type 2' power class may first be considered. The first 20 of the A1A—A1A Brush locomotives of the 'D5500' Class had engines of 1,250 bhp. In later ones the engines were uprated to 1,365 bhp but all were subsequently de-rated to the original 1,250 of the first 20. In view of the way in which British Railways and their contractors were stepping so much into the unknown it is remarkable that three out of the six designs proved so successful

Brush 1,250 hp A1A-A1A diesel-electric locomotive, originally D5500 series, now Class '31': side elevation and plan view (Locomotive Magazine).

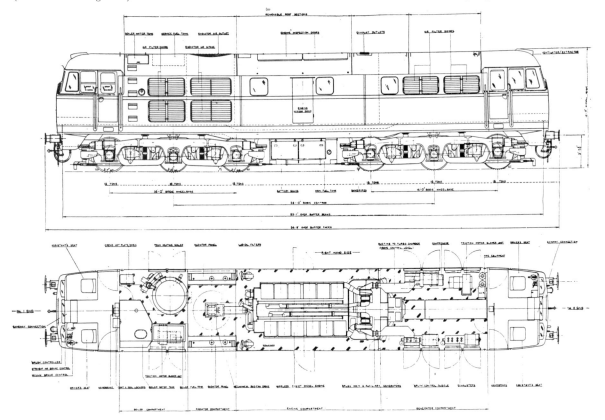

Left *Birmingham RCW/Sulzer Type '2' 1,160 hp diesel electric locomotive No D5304 (later Class '27') the Carlisle-Edinburgh stopping train on the now closed Waverley route at Steele Road* (Derek Cross).

Below *Derby-built 1,160 hp Bo-Bo diesel-electric locomotive, originally D5000 series, later developed to Class '25' side elevation* (Locomotive Magazine).

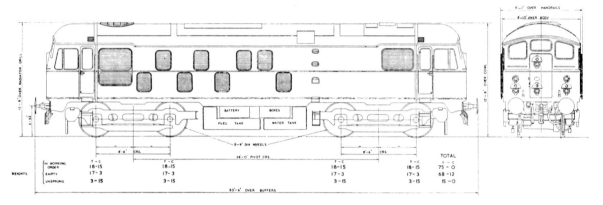

as to become standard types, and to be built in quantity later. Naturally, in the light of early experience both in running and maintenance, some changes were made in both detail design and major components; but taken all round the Type '2' group proved a sound investment. Early opportunity was taken to subject both the Brush A1A—A1A, and the BR Derby Bo—Bo to full dress trials under the auspices of the Locomotive Testing Committee of British Railways, and from these tests some typical examples of the speeds that could be expected in different conditions of loading and gradient may be quoted (see the table below right).

All these speeds are the expectations of performance when the locomotives are worked at full power, which is the ideal and most efficient condition with a diesel-electric locomotive. I had the privilege of making many runs in the driving cabs of the new locomotives, on routes extending from Dover to Inverness, and I was able to see how closely the predicted design performance was realised in actual practice. So far as usage was concerned, the Brush A1A—A1A series was concentrated on the Great Eastern line. The Metropolitan Vickers Co—Bo Class, with Crossley engines, was allocated to the

former Midland line, on which I had some interesting footplate journeys between Derby and Manchester, while some of the Derby-built Bo—Bo, with Sulzer engines, were used on the Kent Coast trains of the Southern Region, before those lines were electrified. These locomotives, and also the Birmingham, and North British-built Bo—Bo types were used in Scotland. Details of some personal experiences with all of them are included later in this chapter.

Gradient	Load (tons)	Sustained speed (mph) BR—Bo-Bo	Brush A1A-A1A
Level	200	74	76
	300	67	69
	400	62	64
Rising 1 in 200	200	57	58
	300	46	49½
	400	39	43
Rising 1 in 100	200	41	43
	300	31	34½
	400	25	27½

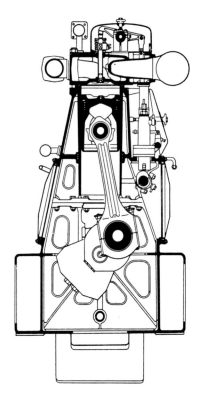

Above *One of the Met-Vickers/Crossley Type '2' 1,200 hp locomotives with the unusual Bo-Co wheel arrangement, No D5712, used in pairs on the 'Condor' fast freight service (British Railways).*

Right *Cross-section of the Sulzer six-cylinder '6LDA28' diesel engine installed in the Derby 1,160 hp locomotives (British Railways).*

Below *Birmingham RC&W 1,160 hp Bo-Bo diesel electric locomotive, with Sulzer '6LDA28' engine later developed to Class '27': side elevation and plan (Locomotive Magazine).*

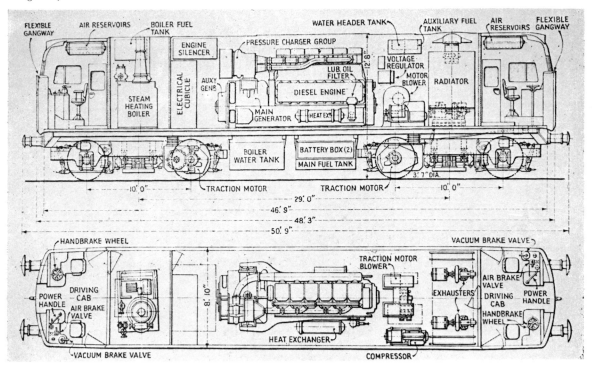

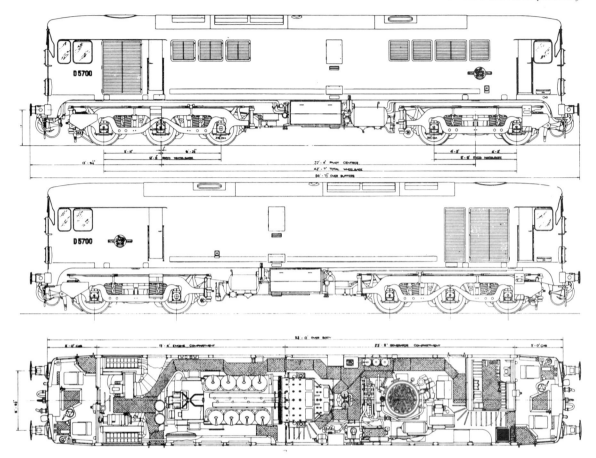

It must not be imagined, however, that with all the accurate predicting of performance which was possible with the new power, (such a contrast to the vagaries so often experienced with steam traction) that the diesel revolution was effected without a good deal of trial and tribulation, particularly in the running sheds. In the previous chapter I have mentioned how the top management of the British Transport Commission overrode the strong representations of their most senior technical advisers, who had recommended a three-year period in which to try out the new power before bulk orders were placed. As things eventuated however it was not design, or constructional details that provided the major headaches in the early stages of modernisation. The Commission was in such a hurry to obtain its new power that delivery was taken of large numbers of new locomotives before the running sheds and other back-up facilities were ready to receive them, with the result that in many areas the new diesels had at first to be accommodated alongside steam. Even in the most efficiently run steam

Above *The Metropolitan-Vickers Co-Bo 1,200 hp diesel electric locomotive, with Crossley engine, D5700 series* (Locomotive Magazine).

Right *One of the Bo-Co Type '2' diesels, No 5707 on a coke train for Workington, at Kingmoor Yard, Carlisle* (Derek Cross).

shed, conditions were hardly ideal for the maintenance of any form of internal combustion engine, and the results in some less organised centres, which had been mainly concerned with steam freight locomotives, became near catastrophic.

It was at this time also that some very disturbing news began to come in from the USA. There is little doubt that the eagerness of the British Transport Commission to invest in large numbers of diesel locomotives at a speed considered far from wise by their most experienced engineers had been influenced by the apparent success of the dieselisation programme in America, carried out with phenomenal rapidity since the end of the Second World

War. At the end of November 1960 a paper was presented in London to the Institution of Mechanical Engineers, by H.F. Brown, dealing with the operating economics of diesel locomotives, based on statistics quoted yearly in the USA by the Interstate Commerce Commission, which showed that the repair costs of steam locomotives were far less than those of diesel-electrics as the age of both types increased. At the same time account must be taken of the differing circumstances in which the new locomotives were purchased in Great Britain and America. Here, with one small but notable exception, the diesels were bought outright by the BTC in the same way as steam power obtained from contractors had been purchased in the past. In the USA, on the other hand, practically all the new power had been obtained from one or other of the manufacturers on advantageous hire-purchase terms. Coming at such a time in British railway history, when the entire motive-power situation was in upheaval, Mr Brown's paper, his evidently most thorough analysis and his concluding words could not come as other than a shock: 'The diesel locomotive has not "revolutionised" American railway economics. In road service, diesel motive power has added to the financial burden of the railways'.

Although the presentation of this paper and the disturbing statistics it contained gave added weight to some of those of high professional status who deplored the precipitate replacement of steam, the mechanical troubles experienced on British Railways proved fortunately to be no more than a very tiresome passing phase; and while the diesels did not make the overall financial position look much better, they certainly settled down to provide reliable, and in some areas accelerated service.

With the aid of driver's cab passes I had a number of interesting journeys, which between them showed off the potentialities of the new power.

Most of my trips were made on passenger trains, because in the early days of the modernisation scheme, when I had high responsibilities in my ordinary daily work, time was not exactly on my side! But the new diesels had been designed, and were being used as mixed-traffic units, and one of my earliest experiences was with the Metrovick Co-Bo 1,200 hp locomotives allocated to the Midland line. I rode on them between Derby and Manchester, but one of their most interesting duties was the overnight container train known as the 'Condor' which ran five nights a week between Hendon and Gushetfaulds goods station, Glasgow, taking about ten hours for the 400-mile run. The train consisted of 27 wagons each conveying one large and one small container, making up a gross load of 550 tons. To haul this train, which was fully braked throughout, a pair of the new diesel-electric locomotives was required.

British Railways commissioned the celebrated artist Terence Cuneo to produce a poster, advertising this train, but he was not very enthusiastic. He described it afterwards as: 'My fight to romanticise a Diesel! The turbulence of the "Black Five" on the left, the coaling plant on the right, together with the "movement" in the sky and the exaggerated super-elevation of the track were all carefully thought out ingredients to give "Condor" a majesty which I feel she barely warrants'. Be that as it may, the result was terrific!

Recalling that 'Condor' had to be hauled up to Aisgill in the course of its run over the Midland line to Carlisle, it was not surprising that two 1,200 hp diesels were needed for a 550-ton load, even though it represented a total of 194 tons of locomotive power; but when I had a cab pass to join the 12.25 pm express from St Pancras to Manchester, at Derby, I was surprised to have a similar pair of diesels for a load of no more than 198 tons. That

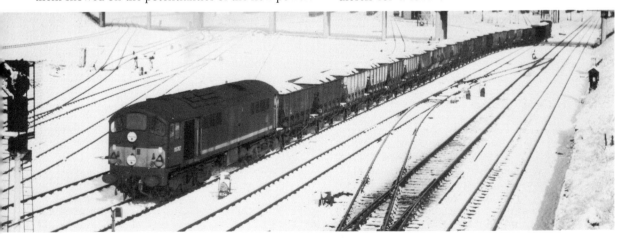

train however was subject to the 'XL' limit of loading, namely 140 tons for a Type '2' diesel, yet 275 tons for a Stanier 'Jubilee' Class steam 4-6-0, and 300 tons for a Class '7' steam, either a 'Scot' or a 'Britannia' 4-6-2. The route, now alas closed, was subject to many speed restrictions on account of curves, and the only chance the driver had for showing off the capacity of his two locomotives was up the long stretches of 1 in 100 ascent from Rowsley. There full power was used, and a speed of 55 to 56 mph sustained on the gradient. But with 194 tons of locomotive for 198 tons of train this was not particularly impressive.

I had an interesting run with one of the Derby-built Bo-Bo diesels with the Sulzer engine on the Folkestone service just before the Kent electrification was completed. These trains will always remain vividly in mind for me because of the admirable performances put up by the Southern Railway 'Schools' Class three-cylinder 4-4-0s in the 1930s, and on the diesel-hauled 4.10 pm from Charing Cross we had about the minimum load that used to be hauled in steam days; nine coaches, 305 tons. It was interesting to see how the working of the locomotive, No D5007, compared with the predicted performance from the official tests, because except for observance of speed restrictions the locomotive was being driven at full power for the entire journey. We did well, slightly bettering the predicted speeds both in the climbing to Knockholt tunnel and in the level running after Tonbridge. In the latter case against a predicted 67 mph we slightly exceeded 70 mph and on the 1 in 120 gradients, whereas the official tests quoted 31 mph on 1 in 100, our minimum speeds were around 37 mph on 1 in 120.

The Bo-Bo locomotives built by the Birmingham Railway Carriage and Wagon Company have the same Sulzer engine as the Derby 'D5000' Class but, with 3 foot 7 inch wheels against 3 feet 9 inches, have a slightly higher tractive effort. I had some interesting runs in Scotland on the Birmingham type, 'D5300' Class, which again showed a performance closely corresponding to predictions. In Highland conditions the anticipated speeds of the Derby series were as follows:

BR-Sulzer Type '2' D5000 Class
Sustained speed at full power

Gradient	Gross trailing load (tons)			
	150	200	250	300
1 in 50	29	24	20	17
1 in 60	33½	27½	23½	21
1 in 70	38	32	27	23
1 in 80	42	35	30	26
1 in 100	47½	40½	35	31½
1 in 150	58	50	45	40
1 in 200	62½	57	51	46

Left *A Birmingham RCW Type '2' diesel on Glasgow-Edinburgh push-pull service in 1976, then re-numbered 27201, leaving Falkirk High for Edinburgh (Brian Morrison).*

Top left *One of the Class '27' diesels, No 27003 on Glasgow to Fort William train on the West Highland line at Glen Douglas (O.S. Nock).*

Top right *Two BR built 1,250 hp diesels (Sulzer engines) Class '25' on southbound stock train on the former G & SW line Nith Valley section near Drumlanrig Tunnel (Morrison Bryce).*

Above right *Birmingham RCE/Sulzer diesel (later Class '27') No D5316 on Edinburgh-Carlisle stopping train, near Harker, in the Border Marches (Derek Cross).*

Right *Brush A1A-A1A Type '2' diesel-electric locomotive No D5535 introduced in 1957 with train of 40 insulated containers on Eastern Region (British Railways).*

On the Highland main line between Perth and Inverness the Type '2' locomotives were used in pairs and sometimes, with no more than moderate loads, there was an abundance of power. It was certainly so one morning in November 1961 when I rode the leading unit of the 6.47 am Mail, and we had a load of no more than 251 tons tare behind the second locomotive. The gross trailing load was 270 tons. This would have been taken by a single 'Black Five' 4-6-0 in steam days, but following a late start from Perth there was time to be made up, and the driver chose to do this on the long ascent from Blair Atholl to Dalnaspidal. On the 1 in 70 gradient speed gradually fell to a sustained minimum of 46 mph, again rather better than might have been expected on such a gradient with each locomotive hauling about 135 tons.

The Brush A1A-A1A with the Mirrlees engine also did some very reliable work, though with carrying wheels on each bogie in addition to the powered wheels it is a considerably heavier locomotive, turning the scale at 104 tons. On a run with the 7.24 pm from Liverpool Street to Ely, with a ten-coach train making a gross trailing load of 350 tons, I found once again that the predicted performance was surpassed, and that on the final level stretch across the Fens north of Cambridge the speed rose to a maximum of 71 mph. This original design of 1957 was developed in 1959–62 substituting an English Electric engine of 1,470 hp for the Mirrlees type, and the 237 examples of the class now in service all have the later engine. The ten Bo-Bo type, D5900 Class, sometimes referred to as the 'Baby Deltics', are referred to in more detail in a later chapter.

Turning now to the lowest power class, the Type'1', all Bo-Bo, and of 800 to 1,000 horsepower; of the four designs introduced between 1957 and 1962 only one, that of the English Electric Co, remains in service today. The 800 hp built by BTH

and North British were not numerous, but when the Clayton type of 1962 was introduced it was announced as a BTC standard for use in Scotland. It was distinctive in having a central cab, of full width, raised above and set between low bonnets of equal length which housed the engines and equipment. The first order was for no less than 88 locomotives all except two of which had the Paxman type of engine. Those two had the Rolls Royce eight-cylinder Type D. A further 29 locomotives were subsequently added, but had Crompton Parkinson, instead of GEC traction motors. These Clayton 900 hp Type '1' Bo-Bos must have had the shortest life of any British locomotive class, diesel or otherwise, especially for one introduced as a 'standard' and built in such relatively large quantities from the outset; because in July 1968, only five years after its first introduction, one of them was withdrawn for scrapping, and from November of that year there began a steady procession to the graveyards. One may well question why this should have been so, but in 1969

what was euphemistically described as the National Traction Plan was formulated, and then apparently it was discovered that many of the diesels ordered in such haste under the 1955 'plan' were not wanted!

It is perhaps not generally realised that in 1968, in the final scramble to be rid of steam, British Railways were also scrapping main line diesels that were less than ten years old. By the end of that year more than half of the 58 North British Type '2' Bo-Bos of the 'D6100' series had been withdrawn, and the Crossley Co-Bo Class on the Midland was also on the condemned list. Under the National Traction Plan some statistical genius evolved what was described as a uniform method of calculating the number of locomotives required. It was first necessary to calculate the future train mileage, and then to divide this by the target average speed multiplied by the target average hours occupied in train haulage. This gave the total number of loco-motives required. What a hope! This book is, of course, concerned primarily with locomotives, their design and performance; but the history of the early

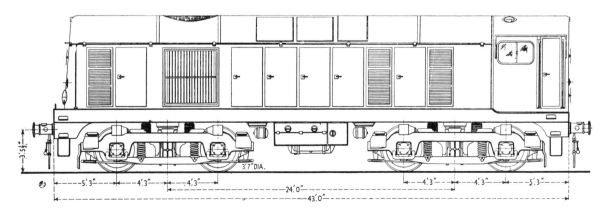

stages of the diesel does not make sense unless it is related to the politico-industrial upheavals that rocked 'the corridors of power' at 222 Marylebone Road in those early days. And the first general indications from studies under the National Traction Plan seemed to show that already the Commission had too many Type '2' and '3' diesels, and not enough Type '4's. This cut across the view of at least one Region, which had in the first place asked for nothing larger than Type '2', intending to use pairs of them in multiple when greater power was needed.

Despite first reactions to the findings of the National Traction Plan, the two varieties of Type '3' diesel-electrics introduced in 1960-1 proved successful and all except two of the Birmingham-built Bo-Bo series of the present Class '33', and the entire strength of the English Electric Co-Co, Class '37', 308 of them, are still in service today, more than 20 years later, and in striking contrast to the ill-fated Clayton Type '1'. The Birmingham Type '3' had the well-tried Sulzer engine, eight cylinders of 1,550 hp with Crompton Parkinson traction motors. With a rated maximum speed of 85 mph they proved an excellent investment. At the time of their introduction, currently with the corresponding Birmingham Type '2' of the 'D5300' series, and the British Railways built Type '2' of the 'D5000' Class, there was some concern that diesel engines of Swiss origin should be incorporated, after the threat of mass purchases from the USA had been averted. But arrangements were concluded for the manu-

Above left *One of the unusual looking Clayton Type '1' diesels of 900 hp D8548 (introduced 1962) working an Elvanfoot-Carstairs pick-up goods train* (Derek Cross).

Above *Two Clayton Type '1' diesels, D8578 and D8570 working a southbound goods on the Waverley route, near Fountainhall, in 1966* (Derek Cross).

Left *English Electric Type '1' 1,000 hp Bo-Bo locomotive* (GEC).

Right *A Birmingham RCW Type '3' diesel No D6535 on the Southern Region working a Margate to Charing Cross express via Dover, approaching Hildenborough* (British Railways).

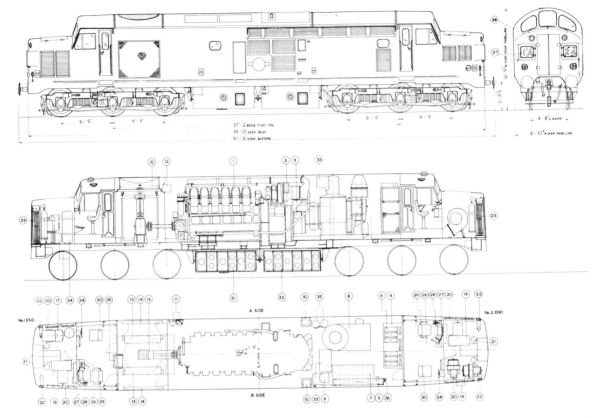

facture, under licence, of the Sulzer type of engine at the Barrow-in-Furness works of Vickers, and a large number of 6, 8, and 12-cylinder engines of the LDA 28 type were eventually built at Barrow.

The English Electric Type '3' Class, later Class '37', followed on the prototype model introduced by the LMS in 1947, when H.G. Ivatt was Chief Mechanical Engineer, in having a bonnet-fronted cab. This styling was also followed on the Type '4' 1-Co-Co-1 Class built at Derby from 1960 onwards. In the majority of new diesel-electric locomotives put on the road in this era the manufacturers' designs had to be accepted; but my great friend R.C. Bond, who was then Chief Mechanical Engineer, told me how he had insisted on having the bonnet-fronted cab on all the larger types built in British Railways workshops. It followed on the English Electric designs of 1947, which was repeated in the Type '3' and Type '4' units later. Bond felt it was necessary to put something in front of the driver as a protection in the event of a collision. In later designs both of diesels and straight electric locomotives this philosophy was not followed. If it had been, one wonders if the lives of the men involved in the terrible level-crossing

accident at Hixon, in 1968, might have been saved.

The Type '3' English Electric diesels, with engines of 1,750 hp proved another excellent investment. One of the most impressive assignments to which these locomotives were allocated was the working of the 2,700-ton iron ore trains in South Wales from Port Talbot to the Llanwern steel works of the British Steel Corporation. These great trains were fully braked throughout, and hauled by three Class '37' locomotives in multiple unit. They were timed to cover the 40 miles from Margam Moors to Newport, pass-to-pass, in 61 minutes, and this involved running at around 60 mph on the favourable gradients between Llanharan summit and the approaches to Cardiff, and between 55 and 60 mph on the level between Cardiff and Newport. It was an impressive run to experience in the cab of the leading locomotive. But Class '37' were essentially mixed-traffic locomotives, and had a rated maximum speed of 90 mph.

In 1963 Dr Richard Beeching, having become Chairman of the Railways Board, put that fireball of an operator, Gerard Fiennes, in as Chairman and General Manager of the Western Region, and he wanted substantial acceleration of the passenger train services. On June 3 1965 a high-speed round trip from Paddington to Plymouth and back was made with a ten-car train, representing a total trailing load of 355 tons. To haul it there was used, not one of the usual diesel-hydraulic locomotives exclusive to the Western Region, but a pair of Class '37's.

It was a business exercise carrying only those with specific duties on the train. No dynamometer car or other recording equipment was carried, but Mr Fiennes invited me to go to do the official timing, and a breathlessly exciting day it proved to be. The normal speed limit for the class was specially raised to 100 mph just for this one day. On the down journey, made by the normal Cornish Riviera route via Castle Cary the numerous minor speed restrictions, on account of curves, were most carefully observed, yet we ran the 173½ miles from Paddington to Exeter in 132¼ minutes, an average speed of 78.8 mph from start to stop. The maximum speed of 98 mph was attained on level track, but the high average speed was made possible by the fast climbing of the steep gradients, notably between Taunton and Whiteball summit, where the lowest speed was 64 mph. Nevertheless a total motive power weight of 200 tons, for an engine horsepower of 3,500 would not be regarded as an economic proposition as a regular thing. It was to provide a demonstration of the speed that could be made on the West of England route. On the return journey,

made via Bristol, a very fast concluding run was made from Temple Meads to Paddington, via Bath, covering the 118.4 miles in 86½ minutes start to stop, an average of 82.3 mph. A maximum of 100 mph was attained on the very slight descending gradient just to the west of Didcot station. Quite apart from spectacular runs such as this, the English Electric Type '3', now Class '37', has proved a very successful locomotive, and 308 of them are in service today.

The English Electric Type '4', now Class '40', was the first locomotive of 2,000 engine horsepower to be introduced under the 1955 Modernisation Plan. From the viewpoint of machinery it was a larger and considerably heavier version of the Class '37', and because of its total weight of 133 tons it was necessary to use the 1-Co-Co-1 wheel arrangement to avoid having any axle load greater than 20 tons. Between the production of Class '40', in 1958, and Class '37' in 1960 some considerable refinements in design were effected, in that the horsepower per ton of weight was increased from 15, on Class '40' to 17.3 on Class '37', and on the latter the Co-Co wheel arrangement could be used. Quite apart from its weight, and the carrying wheels fore and aft, which made it a very steady and comfortable locomotive to ride, the Class '40' gave excellent all-round service. I had many runs as privileged observer in the cab over all the routes on which they regularly worked and found them

Left *English Electric Type '2' 1,750 hp Co-Co locomotive later Class '37'.*

Right *An English Electric, Type '3', working a westbound oil-tank train through Newport High Street station, Western Region* (O.S. Nock).

Inauguration of Type '4' diesel electric service on Eastern Region in April 1958. The first London-Norwich express leaving Liverpool Street, hauled by locomotive D200. (British Railways).

consistently reliable, while I had innumerable runs behind them when I was travelling passenger, with equally satisfactory results. But, in recalling these journeys and the fast times frequently made, it is important to appreciate that on many occasions the locomotives were being worked at full power for long periods, as indeed they needed to be to maintain schedule time. The maximum power they could sustain at the drawbar was considerably less than that of the largest and most powerful steam locomotives, although the latter were not often required to develop such power.

Where the diesels showed up to such advantage was that full power was available for a mere 'turning on of the taps', as it were. On a steam locomotive, even one in perfect condition, maximum performance was obtained from a skilful partnership of brains and brawn, between driver and fireman, and in the early 1960s these skills were frequently lacking. Still more frequently engines were not in the best condition, neither was the fuel of the ideal quality that had made British locomotive performance the admiration of all in years gone by. Even in the 1960s the maximum efforts of old favourites like the Gresley 'A3' and 'A4' 'Pacifics', and Sir William Stanier's 'Princesses' and 'Duchesses' could far outshine the Class '40's, which of course was perfectly natural seeing that the latter could not produce more than about 1,500 horsepower at the drawbar; but there was consistency about their work, which could not be said about steam at that time. Furthermore, in my own travelling experience the Class '40's seemed to be less affected by the haste with which the diesels were introduced. On the Great Eastern line, on the East Coast route, and on the Western Division of the London Midland they came to be regarded as the new 'flagships', and were nurtured accordingly.

My first experience with one of the Class '40' on the Euston-Liverpool run gave some interesting comparisons with steam between Willesden and Stafford, as tabulated below.

This table illustrates so many of the varying factors that have to be taken into account when making such comparisons. For example, in the famous 'Claughton' trials of 1913, referred to in some detail in Volume 1 of this work, the average

Date of Engine	Engine class	Load tons gross behind tender	Net average speed (mph)	Calculated drawbar horsepower	Weight of loco	DHP per ton of loco	DHP per ton of tractive effort
1913	'Claughton'	435	61.7	680	116*	5.85	68†
1927	'Royal Scot'	505	61.2	775	139½ *	5.55	52.5†
1935	'Princess'	535	65.3	980	160*	6.12	54.5†
1958	Diesel '40'	535	68.8	1100	133	8.28	47.2‡

*Including tender. †Based on nominal te. ‡Based on max te value of 52,000 lb.

The Type '4' English Electric diesels in Scotland: locomotive No D219 hauling a Manchester to Glasgow express on the upper reaches of the Beattock bank (Derek Cross).

drawbar horsepower between Willesden and Stafford was nearly 1,000, approximating much more to a maximum performance than the ordinary service run in the above table. Similarly, I have instances of the 'Princess Royal' Class 4-6-2s providing outputs of more than 1,800 drawbar horsepower. In the foregoing comparison it is evident that the Class '40' diesel was being driven much nearer to all-out conditions than any of the steam examples, and of course with little or no physical exertion on the part of the crew. The last column of the table raises some pertinent questions as to why, for example, if the nominal tractive effort of the diesel is quoted at 52,000 lb, should it have so markedly less a maximum haulage capacity than a 'Princess' Class steam 4-6-2 with a nominal tractive effort of 40,300 lb?

The characteristic curve of drawbar horsepower for a diesel rises to its maximum before speed has attained 10 mph and it remains at a fairly constant value until about 50 mph after which it begins to fall. That of a steam locomotive increases more gradually, and reaches a maximum at about 40 or 45 mph. The performance characteristics of the Class '40' diesel are roughly equivalent, at passenger train running speeds, to those of an LMS 'Duchess' Class 4-6-2 when the latter was being steamed at about 25,000 lb per hour. The maximum that the latter engines were expected to produce continuously, with a single fireman, was 30,000 lb of steam per hour, but on test, with two firemen, the 'Duchesses' have been steamed up to

40,000 lb per hour, which would of course produce a performance vastly greater than the maximum one could expect from a Class '40' diesel. While to sustain such an output from a 'Duchess' for any length of time would certainly need the efforts of two firemen, these engines were frequently steamed up to such heights for short periods, producing values of 'equivalent' drawbar horsepower up to 2,500, as compared to the absolute maximum of about 1,450 that could be expected from a Class '40' diesel.

While the 2,000 hp English Electric diesels, later to become Class '40', did very satisfactory work from their first introduction, a more powerful class, also of the 1Co-Co1 wheel arrangement, and having the well-tried Sulzer 12 LDA 28 engine, was designed and built at Derby works. The first ten of what became known as the 'Peak' Class had a 12-cylinder twin-bank pressure-charged engine of 2,300 hp, while later locomotives had similar engines but of 2,500 hp. The six traction motors were of Crompton Parkinson type axle-hung, nose-suspended of 305 hp each. The first ten were named after famous English and Welsh mountains, thus giving the class as a whole the designation of 'Peaks' though many of the later locomotives of the class took regimental names formerly borne by steam locomotives of the 'Royal Scot' and 'Patriot' classes. There were three varieties of the 'Peak' Class, as tabulated overleaf.

These locomotives, some of the later batches of which were built at Crewe, were generally based on the Midland line. In addition to the usual duties performed previously by steam locomotives, including the strenuous 'double-home' turns between Leeds and Glasgow St Enoch, some very lengthy through workings were introduced on the

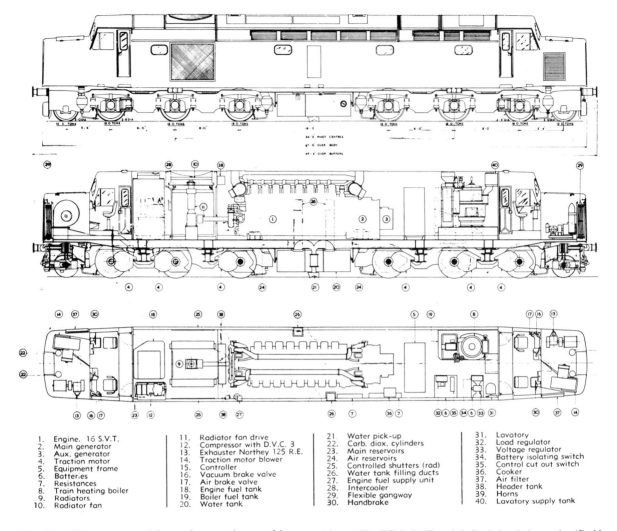

1.	Engine. 16 S.V.T.	11.	Radiator fan drive	21.	Water pick-up	31.	Lavatory
2.	Main generator	12.	Compressor with D.V.C. 3	22.	Carb. diox. cylinders	32.	Load regulator
3.	Aux. generator	13.	Exhauster Northey 125 R.E.	23.	Main reservoirs	33.	Voltage regulator
4.	Traction motor	14.	Traction motor blower	24.	Air reservoirs	34.	Battery isolating switch
5.	Equipment frame	15.	Controller	25.	Controlled shutters (rad)	35.	Control cut out switch
6.	Batteries	16.	Vacuum brake valve	26.	Water tank filling ducts	36.	Cooker
7.	Resistances	17.	Air brake valve	27.	Engine fuel supply unit	37.	Air filter
8.	Train heating boiler	18.	Engine fuel tank	28.	Intercooler	38.	Header tank
9.	Radiators	19.	Boiler fuel tank	29.	Flexible gangway	39.	Horns
10.	Radiator fan	20.	Water tank	30.	Handbrake	40.	Lavatory supply tank

North to West route, with one locomotive working between Newcastle and Bristol. These duties involved a great diversity in performance requirements, ranging from the lengthy uphill 'grinds' of the Settle and Carlisle line to the uninhibited high speed on the East Coast main line between Darlington and York, and such obstacles as the Lickey Incline.

When the 'Peak' Class was first introduced, stops were made at Bromsgrove on the northbound run for a bank engine, as with steam; indeed, on my

Above *The BR built Type '4' diesel-electric locomotive 'Peak' Class, originally of 2,300 hp with the Sulzer, double-bank in-line '12 LDA 28A' engine* (British Railways).

own first trip with a diesel we stopped for assistance even though the gross trailing load was no more than 325 tons. But, having taken the measure of the new power, the unassisted load for a 'Peak' was fixed at no less than 465 tons, and this virtually eliminated bank engine working with passenger

Original numbers	Nominal horsepower	Engine Sulzer	Traction motors	Later class
D1-10	2300	12 LDA 28A	Crompton Parkinson	44
D11-137	2500	12 LDA 28B	Crompton Parkinson	45
D138-193	2500	12 LDA 28B	Brush	46

Right *On the East Coast route: a Type '4' EE Co diesel on northbound express parcels train, York to Edinburgh, near Cockburnspath* (British Railways).

Right *A 'Peak' Class Type '4' diesel on Saturdays only Sheffield to Glasgow express: locomotive No D44 (original numbering)* (Morrison Bryce).

Below *On the Settle and Carlisle line: a mineral wagon 'empties', Carlisle to Sheffield, near Cotehill hauled by Type '4' EE Co diesel (Class '40') No 40182* (Morrison Bryce).

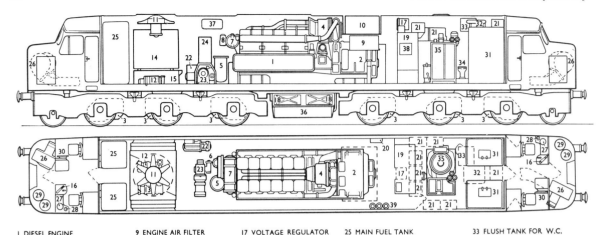

1 DIESEL ENGINE	9 ENGINE AIR FILTER	17 VOLTAGE REGULATOR	25 MAIN FUEL TANK	33 FLUSH TANK FOR W.C.
2 MAIN & AUX. GENERATORS	10 EXHAUST SILENCER	18 BATTERY BOXES	26 TRACTION-MOTOR BLOWER	34 W.C.
3 TRACTION MOTOR	11 RADIATOR FAN	19 MAIN CONTROL CUBICLE	27 VACUUM BRAKE VALVE	35 STEAM GENERATOR
4 PRESSURE CHARGER	12 COMBINED PUMP SET	20 INSTRUMENT CUBICLE	28 INDEPENDENT AIR BRAKE VALVE	36 BOILER-WATER FEED TANK
5 LUBRICATING OIL FILTER	13 CONVERTER SET	21 RESISTANCE FRAMES	29 AIR RESERVOIRS	37 FUEL & WATER HEADER TANK
6 LUBRICATING OIL STRAINER	14 RADIATOR PANELS	22 AIR COMPRESSOR	30 HANDBRAKE WHEEL	38 FUSE BOX
7 HEAT EXCHANGER	15 RADIATOR DRAIN TANK	23 EXHAUSTER	31 BOILER-WATER FEED TANK	39 FIRE-EXTINGUISHER CYLINDERS
8 ENGINE INSTRUMENT PANEL	16 MASTER CONTROLLER	24 BRAKE-GEAR CUBICLE	32 BOILER-WATER TREATMENT TANK	

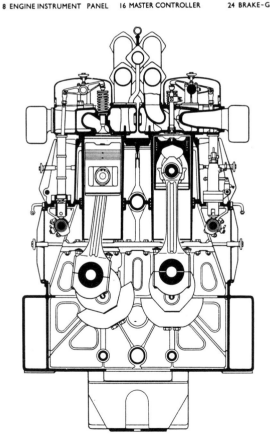

Above *The BR-built Type '4' diesel locomotive 'Peak' Class, originally of 2,300 hp with the Sulzer double-bank in-line '12 LDA 28A' engine* (British Railways).

Left *Cross section of the Sulzer '12 LDA 28A' double-bank engine used on the BR Type '4' 'Peak' Class* (British Railways).

trains. The running I noted in the summer of 1962 revealed the 'Peaks' as very competent locomotives, though like their English Electric counterparts of Class '4' they were heavy in relation to their tractive power.

The generous allocation of practically the entire stud of Class '45' and '46' diesels to the Midland lines was fortunate in one respect, because it was at the major running sheds involved that the managerial folly of flooding the railways with new power before maintenance facilities were ready to cope with it was most seriously experienced. The situation was further exacerbated by the fearful wintry weather encountered in the first months of 1963. At times, not by any means entirely due to the weather, no more than half of the 'Peak' Class diesels allocated to the Midland lines were available for traffic. Had not the orders placed for these locomotives greatly exceed the numbers actually required for running the trains, the situation could have become desperate, for by that time the scrapping of steam locomotives was proceeding with breathless haste. Fortunately, by dint of unremitting attention by the staff concerned, this storm was successfully weathered; but only those who were actually involved, or who were in close touch in other respects, as I was then, appreciated what a mighty close-run thing it was. It was no fault of a fine locomotive.

Much of the running out on the line was exhilarating to record, especially to one having long familiarity with characteristic steam performance. On the Settle and Carlisle line in particular, the long stretches of 1 in 100 gradient were climbed at *double* the previous speeds. With nine-coach trains of about 320 tons behind the tender, the sustained speeds on those inclines would rarely have been more than about 30 to 35 mph with Class '5' 4-6-0s, or 'Jubilees', yet on my first diesel run with the 'Thames-Clyde Express' we sustained 60 mph for many miles above Settle. I was in the cab, and saw that full power was being used and the equivalent drawbar horsepower of 2,070 was just about what one would expect from a locomotive with a nominal engine horsepower of 2,500. It was interesting that on my first unassisted run up the Lickey Incline with one of these locomotives the equivalent drawbar horsepower also worked out at exactly the same figure, 2,070, though at a much lower speed. Then also we had a nine-coach train of 325 tons and, after slowing to the restricted speed then imposed through Bromsgrove stations (about 40 mph) we settled down to a steady 26 mph on the 1 in 37 gradient. With the maximum rostered load of 465 tons I estimated that they ought to be able to climb the bank at about 19 to 20 mph. On this first unassisted diesel run of mine we covered the 22 miles from Abbots Wood Junction to Kings Norton, including the ascent of the Lickey Incline, in 22¾ minutes—a striking example of the revolution in train working made possible by the diesels. On one of my best runs in steam days, when I was on the footplate of a 'Black Five' 4-6-0 and the driver was going hard to make up some lost time, we took 30¾ minutes for the same stretch, including the assistance of two 0-6-0 tank engines up the Lickey Incline.

The later diesel-electric locomotives are dealt with in a subsequent chapter.

Left *A 'Peak' Class on the 'Thames-Clyde' express just after topping Aisgill summit, Settle and Carlisle line: locomotive No 45002 (Morrison Bryce).*

Right *The Southbound 'Thames-Clyde' express near Garrochburn on the Nith Valley line hauled by 'Peak' Class Type '4' diesel No D176 (original numbering) (Derek Cross).*

3. Diesels: railcars and set trains

The first phase of British Railways modernisation initiated by the so-called 'Plan', of 1955, was not really modernisation in its truest and most far-reaching sense at all. It was little more than the replacement of steam by diesel traction, in a shipwreck hurry; and in the initial stages little thought was given to the re-shaping of the timetables, or the general pattern of service to meet the changing needs of the times. In the early stages of what has been termed the 'diesel revolution', there did indeed seem to be little or no appreciation in high places of how profoundly the overall traffic pattern of the whole country had begun to change, or of the fact that it was a change from which there was little possibility of reversal. In this respect however the bitter harvest had yet to be reaped. In the late 1950s the drive to eliminate steam was pursued as inexorably on the secondary routes and the branch lines as on the longer-distance and 'star' express passenger services. The pattern had already been set. In the 1930s the Great Western had shown how smartly styled, lively diesel railcars could immeasurably improve the attractiveness of local services, while the Brighton, Eastbourne and Portsmouth electrification on the Southern demonstrated very clearly that the multiple-unit type of train was capable of ready development to medium-distance express passenger service which required corridor coaches, restaurant, buffet and Pullman cars, and speeds of at least up to 70 mph.

With the pattern there for the copying, the Railway Executive of the mid-1950s set out on a colossal programme of steam locomotive replacement, on the secondary services. The initial plan of 1955 included the introduction of diesel-multiple-unit trains amounting to a total of no less than 4,600 vehicles and envisaged the momentous step of turning the entire local services of the country over to diesel railcars. As in the case of the main line locomotives, speed was the very essence of the changeover programme. Even before the main programme was launched, plans for railcar development had been initiated by the Railway Executive, but in the early 1950s Great Western practice was not in favour at 'The Kremlin', and the successful working of the handsome semi-streamlined cars with AEC-type engines was laid on one side. It is true that the latter had mechanical gear-change in their transmission, and that more sophisticated methods of control were undoubtedly desirable. In the £2 million plan for developing lightweight railcar services initiated by the British Transport Commission, in advance of the major

Modernisation Plan, the control in the first cars, using the Leyland 125 hp bus engine, was electro-pneumatic. In view of the very widespread introduction of the new cars that was proposed any difficulties with gear changing were to be avoided, if possible.

The car bodies were designed and built at Derby Works and very great care was taken to reduce weight wherever possible. The body frame, underframe structure and panelling was of light aluminium alloy, and was designed as an integral unit. It was a beautiful piece of engineering design, in which all the framing members were of extruded sections, and even the rivets used were of light alloy. The effect of such intense efforts in design was that a two-car set, each vehicle having two 125 hp engines, their transmission equipment, controls and tanks containing 232 gallons of fuel oil, weighed no more than 54 tons. The philosophy underlying this advanced example of vehicle design was that by reducing weight the size of the engine, and consequently the fuel consumption, could be minimised. It was intended that the trial runs of diesel service modernisation should be made in West Cumberland, north of the former Cockermouth, Keswick and Penrith line and in a first rationalisation of local services in the West Riding of Yorkshire, based upon the local services radiating from Leeds and Bradford. Actually it was only in the last-mentioned area that the cars with Leyland 125 hp engines went into service. The West Cumberland scheme was powered by cars with larger engines.

The onset of the major Modernisation Plan pushed the earlier £2 million scheme into the background. But it was not just a case of replacing steam with diesel. The railcars and the multiple-unit trains gave promise of considerable economies in manning. It had long been established on the Southern that such trains required only one man in the cab; but while this was important regarding the wage bill it was a relief in that a real shortage of footplate men had developed since the war. In an era of full employment, which proved to be no more than transitory, there were occupations with regular hours and free weekends that provided more attractive jobs than shift work as cleaners and firemen, especially on the less glamorous local train, and trip goods duties. And while there were many who stayed, having steam in their blood as it were, there were many who left. The possibility of having diesel railcars, and multiple-unit trains in large numbers seemed so attractive that a survey was

Right *BR Modernisation: A Metropolitan Cammell two-car railcar set, in the Norwich area, in 1957* (British Railways).

Below *Diesel train—mechanical transmission general layout* (British Railways).

taken of the design and constructional capacity of the locomotive and carriage industry throughout the country in order to obtain the largest number of railcars and coaching stock as quickly as possible. As with main line locomotives and with other major features of the Modernisation Plan, thoughts of immediate standardisation of types had to be set on one side for economic reasons.

Where the branch lines and the shorter distance services were concerned, the engineers were not to be granted the three-year period at first agreed in which to run, test, and properly assess a few chosen types. It was decreed that the replacement of steam on these secondary and local services should be carried out at maximum speed. So, the necessary supply of cars and power units could be achieved only by parcelling out the work between every car and wagon-building contractor who was prepared to take it on. There was not enough time for the preparation of any standard designs. A broad specification was issued, and individual manufacturers were asked to submit designs and tenders for railcars which they themselves were prepared to build at top speed. At the outset it was agreed that the lightweight bodies included in the Derby-built prototype cars were not worth the additional cost, though Derby Works, tooled up for their production, continued to build to this design. Other cars were built by Metropolitan-Cammell, the Gloucester Railway Carriage and Wagon Company, Cravens, the Birmingham Railway Carriage and Wagon Company, and the BR Works at

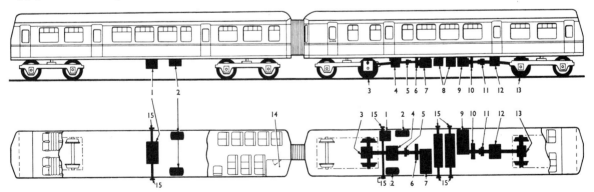

1 HEATER FUEL TANK	5 No. 2 FREEWHEEL	9 No. 1 ENGINE	13 No. 1 FINAL DRIVE
2 HEATERS	6 No. 2 FLUID FLYWHEEL	10 No. 1 FLUID FLYWHEEL	14 LAVATORY
3 No. 2 FINAL DRIVE	7 No. 2 ENGINE	11 No. 1 FREEWHEEL	15 TANK FILLERS
4 No. 2 GEARBOX	8 FUEL TANKS	12 No. 1 GEARBOX	

Swindon. The great majority had six-cylinder 150 hp horizontal type engines, either of AEC or Leyland build, though a few cars had Rolls-Royce engines of 180 hp. In all cases the power equipment was under the floor, leaving the rest, except for the driving cabs, available for passengers, luggage racks, toilets and so on.

In view of the speed with which such quantities of cars were put into traffic, they were remarkably successful, and the majority of this large fleet are still in service today. So far as the initial urgency was concerned it is interesting to recall that no fewer than 97 power cars, together with their associated driving trailers, were in service by mid-March 1956. Most numerous eventually was the Metropolitan-Cammell Class '101', with AEC-built engines, more than 300 of which are in service today. After them come the Derby Works-built Class '116', with more than 200. These latter have the Leyland-built engine. The transmission was in all cases mechanical with the arrangement of apparatus as shown in the accompanying diagram. The fluid flywheel acts as an automatic clutch

between the engine and the rest of the equipment, while the cardan shaft, with a universal joint at each end, provides the link between the members that are fixed to the chassis of the car and the final drive and reversing mechanism, which is carried on the axle and subject to the movement of the axle on its springs. Two units in the transmission system need particular reference, because they were novel in the world of British railway locomotive practice, namely the fluid flywheel and the epicyclic gearbox.

The fluid flywheel, or coupling, is shown in the accompanying drawing. It shows how the outer casing, incorporating the flywheel driving blade, is coupled to the engine crankshaft, while the driven blade is secured to the output shaft. The casing is filled with oil up to the level of the filler plug, shown on the drawing. When the engine is started and the driving member rotates, oil is thrown from the centre of the coupling towards the outer edge, and it is accelerated from a low speed at the centre to a high speed when it leaves the driving member. When the engine is just idling nothing further happens, but when the engine speed is increased, preparatory to starting away with the train, oil is forced from the pockets in the driving member into the pockets of the driven member, which then begins to rotate. It continues faster and faster until both the driving and the driven members are rotating at almost the same speed. It should be emphasised that in this design there is no positive mechanical connection between the engine crankshaft and the output shaft. The link between the two is the working fluid in the coupling, that is the oil, as it is thrown from the driving member into the pockets of the driven member.

The Wilson epicyclic gearbox, used on the majority of British multiple-unit power cars may, from the accompanying drawing, look a rather fearsome 'box of tricks'; but it is an appliance into which a vast amount of brains have been packed, with the result that it has proved simple to handle, and reliable in service. It has the following main features:

Above left *Railcar working in South Wales: a Rhymney to Penarth three-car Met-Cammell set entering Cefn On station* (British Railways).

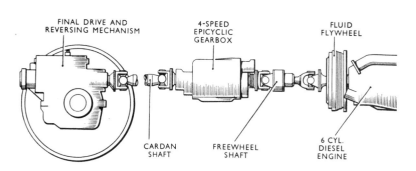

FINAL DRIVE AND REVERSING MECHANISM

4-SPEED EPICYCLIC GEARBOX

FLUID FLYWHEEL

CARDAN SHAFT

FREEWHEEL SHAFT

6 CYL. DIESEL ENGINE

Left *Arrangement of Railcar transmission* (British Railways).

Above *One of the Derby-built two-car sets (Class '108') introduced in 1960 working in the Wirral area* (British Railways).

Above right *A Derby two-car set on the picturesque run from Llandudno to Blaneau Ffestiniog, here seen leaving Bettws-y-coed* (Derek Cross).

Below *The Wilson epicyclic gearbox, used on the majority of railcar trains* (British Railways).

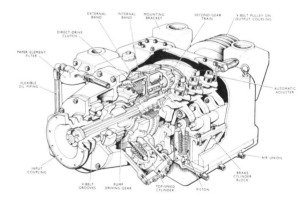

1) It is simple to control because of: a) its constant-mesh epicyclic-gearing; b) its power operated gear change.

2) As the gearbox is used in conjunction with a fluid flywheel there is no need for an external clutch.

3) The controls are electro-pneumatic, which ensures that a number of gearboxes, on power units in the same train, make the same gear change at the same time.

In running, the appropriate gear is selected by the driver, using the gear-selector in his cab. Then an electrically operated air valve admits compressed air into the operating cylinder controlling the band brake of the gear selected. This causes the band brake to grip and stop the brake drum revolving until it is released again. Drivers are instructed that it is most important to have the fourth gear engaged when coasting, as this permits the whole gear-train mechanism to be locked and revolve as a whole. This ensures that the lubricating pump, vacuum exhauster and generator continue to be driven via the road wheels. When first introduced, all diesel multiple-unit trains were vacuum-braked. In 1960 the first of the Swindon-built cross-country multiple-unit trains were built, with the larger Leyland 230 hp engines; but before looking at these in any detail reference must be made to some actual running experiences with the 150 hp units, which show their versatility in widely differing traffic requirements.

The first of these runs was in purely local branch line service in Norfolk, with some Met Cammell two-car sets over lines most of which are now closed. This excursion took me from Thetford via Watton to Swaffham, thence eastwards to Dereham, and then northwards via Fakenham to Wells-next-the-Sea. Then I retraced my steps down this branch but continued to join the main line at Wymondham, and so into Norwich. The branch cutting through hilly country had some quite stiff gradients, including a bank of 1¾ miles at 1 in 87-77, between Walsingham and Fakenham. A summary of the return trip from Wells through to Norwich (overleaf) gives a good impression of the smartness of the performance.

Length of trip	43½ miles
Total time	83½ minutes
Time excluding 12 stops	67 minutes
Average speed (on running time)	39 mph
Maximum speed	69 mph

With the privilege of a driver's cab pass I was able to study the technique of driving these little trains. Care has been taken in their equipment to give the drivers every assistance in their efficient manipulation. There is an indicator on the dashboard showing the engine speed, in revolutions per minute, and a red sector on this dial marks the upper and lower limit to be used. When accelerating in one gear, the time to change up into the next is indicated by the needle reaching the upper limit of the red section. Generally speaking I found that first gear was used up to about 15 mph, second up to 25 mph, third up to 40 mph, and top gear above 40. As previously mentioned, the actual gear changing is effected by electro-pneumatic control. These Eastern Region cars were relatively new when I travelled in them, and the riding was generally good, but some two years later I had occasion to travel passenger by the 9.30 pm express from Manchester to Liverpool along the Cheshire Lines route. It was at the time when trains by the Euston route to Liverpool had been much decelerated because of extensive work on the line in preparation for electrification, and it was actually quicker to travel by the Midland route from St Pancras and change in Manchester. But although the four-car diesel set ran fast enough, with speeds sustained between 63 and 72 mph, it gave us a terribly rough ride. With intermediate stops at Warrington and Widnes we covered the 34 miles from Manchester to Liverpool in 43¾ minutes.

I had some interesting runs with the Swindon-built three-car inter-city sets that were working in Scotland between Inverness and Aberdeen. There were two motored cars each with AEC-type 150 hp engines and a trailer between them. Some of the route was single-tracked and had been equipped for token exchanging at speed, using the Manson type of apparatus. But with a railcar, and only one man in the cab, the exchange could not be made from the front end, and these three-car trains were specially equipped so that the exchanging could be done by the guard. The 2.30 pm up from Inverness stopped only at Nairn, Forres, Elgin and Keith, and apart from the long final downhill stretch from Kennethmont it was fairly sharply timed. But with 600 hp 'under the floor' there was plenty of power in hand, even in climbing the 1 in 60 bank from the crossing of the River Spey beyond Orton. Here speed was sustained at 39 mph. The downhill 32.8 miles from Kennethmont to Aberdeen took as much as 43¾ minutes, yet still we were running to time. On a northbound run with the 1.50 pm out of Aberdeen another of these three-car sets passed Kennethmont summit in 37 minutes from the start at Aberdeen, and covered the 28.7 continuously ascending miles from Bucksburn in a few seconds under the even half-hour; an average speed of 57.4 mph.

In January 1961 the inter-city 'Trans-Pennine' diesel express service was introduced between

One of the Birmingham RCW diesel set trains (Class '110') used on the Trans-Pennine service from York to Liverpool among others (British Railways).

Liverpool and Hull, serving Earlstown Junction, Manchester, Huddersfield, Leeds, Selby and Brough. The distance is 127.7 miles, and these new cross-country trains had a total running time of 163 minutes, an average speed of 47 mph. Except between Manchester and Leeds the gradients are not difficult, and the six-car express sets with a total engine horsepower of 1,840 normally had plenty in reserve. On these trains the larger Leyland engine of 230 hp was fitted on four cars out of the six. These trains, like many of the principal London and North Western cross-country expresses in earlier days, took the severely graded Heckmondwike Loop Line between Huddersfield and Leeds, thus bypassing that portion of the former LYR main line through Mirfield. The westbound Trans-Pennine trains had thus to climb the 3½-mile bank at 1 in 70 through Gildersome Tunnel. Just a year after the first introduction of the service I had a driver's cab pass for the westbound run leaving Hull at 9.10 am, and it included the kind of troubles that seemed to affect the new motive power in so many areas of British Railways in the relatively early years of modernisation.

When I joined the train at Hull, the inspector who was to accompany me through to Liverpool said that one of the eight engines had been cut out, so that we had a total of 1,610 instead of 1,840 engine horsepower available. A further hindrance was a very strong adverse wind throughout. We were fortunate however in experiencing few

A three-car diesel set eastbound from Morecambe to Leeds passing Settle Junction (C.J. Marsden).

incidental delays, otherwise with the deficiency in engine power there might have been some considerable loss of time. On the open and level sections of line east of Selby, despite the adverse winds, the train ran at 68 to 70 mph, and we were keeping sectional time. After Leeds also we did reasonably well to sustain 38 mph up the 1 in 70 of the Gildersome Tunnel bank. But there was a marked deterioration after Huddersfield, on the seven-mile ascent at 1 in 105 to Standedge Tunnel. My friends in the cab said that with 'a good train' the speed here would rise to nearly 60 mph. However, the best we could do was 42 mph, and we lost 1¾ minutes on the scheduled allowance of ten minutes for the 7.1 miles from Huddersfield to passing Marsden, near the entrance to the long tunnel. There was also a defect in the air system and, when the engines were running at idling speed for long periods, as when coasting downhill, the compressors were not able to keep air due to slight leaks, and we were losing pressure. Downhill from Standedge Tunnel to Stalybridge pressure had dropped to the extent that it was insufficient to ensure proper engagement of the change-speed and reverse gears. The driver had to stop the train and 'rev' up the engines to restore pressure. With this stop, and with a permanent way check to 5 mph near Miles Plating we were four minutes late into Manchester—42 minutes for the 26 miles from Huddersfield.

It showed me the extent to which the new diesel trains could vary in their performance, when one might have imagined that the elimination of steam would have resulted in uniformity. It was thought on this occasion that a leaking, or blown gasket was causing the leakage in the air system, though why

one of the eight diesel engines was out of action was not known. Once we were away from Manchester, and the engines were running at full power, the air compressors were able to cope with the leakage and there was no more trouble on that account; but after a long experience of steam locomotive working, and the occasional stop for a 'blow-up' to restore steam pressure in the boiler, it seemed strange to have to stop to blow up air pressure for working the auxiliaries on a *falling* gradient! Small amounts of 'recovery time' in the running schedule helped to restore the balance in places, but in all the circumstances I felt that we were lucky to be no more than seven minutes late on arrival in Liverpool.

In this book I am naturally concerned with the motive power side of the new equipment rather than with the passenger facilities provided; but a much more ambitious attempt at a luxury diesel multiple-unit train was made in 1960, with the introduction of the so-called 'Blue Pullmans'. I am tempted to write that I wish I could be more enthusiastic about these trains, into which an immense amount of care was lavished in the design stage. But their early demise tells its own story. First of all, the traffic potential of the new trains was sadly misjudged. The initial and only order was for five sets. Two, of six cars each, were all first-class, for the Midland line. The other three, of eight cars, had seating for both first- and second-class passengers, and were allocated to the Paddington–Bristol and Paddington–Wolverhampton routes. As first introduced, the duty rosters clearly aimed for maximum utilisation of the stock. For example, the up Midland Pullman, which at first left Manchester at 8.50 am and ran non-stop fom Cheadle Heath to St Pancras, at a booked average speed of 60.8 mph, then made an afternoon trip to Leicester and back, before returning non-stop to

Top left *A Swindon-built Class '124' Trans-Pennine four-car set working the 09.33 Leeds to Morecambe, just beyond Settle Junction* (Brian Morrison).

Above left *A Trans-Pennine unit, Class '124' leaving Doncaster for Hull, in December 1979* (C.J. Marsden).

Left *The prestige train that did not succeed: a 'portrait' of the six--car all-first class Midland Pullman, introduced in 1960 between St Pancras and Manchester* (C.J. Marsden).

Above right *Another view of the Midland Pullman, showing the elaborate Pullman insignia on the nose* (C.J. Marsden).

Right *Diesel-electric multiple-unit stock: diagram of power car* (British Railways).

Cheadle Heath at 6.10 pm. Similarly, the Bristol Pullman running up non-stop via Badminton at 7.45 am returned via Bath at 10.05 am to provide a midday service back to London, before its final non-stop return run to Bristol via Badminton. The Wolverhampton train had a midday return trip to Birmingham and back intermediately. The daily mileages on the three routes were 576.8 Midland, 471.8 Bristol, 467.2 Wolverhampton. Detailed reference to these trains is made in Chapter 9.

It will be appreciated that the Blue Pullmans, unlike the great majority of diesel trains on British Railways at that time, had electric rather than mechanical transmission. The other exception was on the Southern and their introduction, in 1957, came in an indirect way. In the Modernisation Plan of 1955 the Kent Coast, Folkestone and Dover services were to have priority for electrification, but services on the Hastings line of the former SE & CR had been subject to frequent criticism, particularly from those who used these trains commuting to London from Tunbridge Wells. The difficulties confronting improvements with steam were manifold. Gradients were severe; difficult junction layouts and severe curvature imposed many permanent speed restrictions; while in the tunnels between Tunbridge Wells and Wadhurst the structural clearances were sub-standard, making neces-

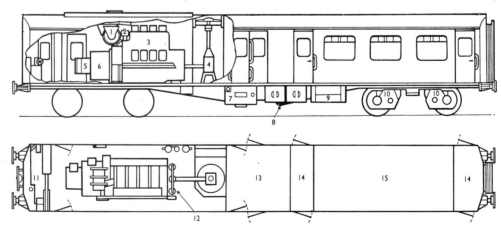

1 Turbo-charger	5 Auxiliary generator	9 Starting battery	13 Guard's compartment
2 Engine speed governor	6 Main generator	10 Traction motor	14 Vestibule
3 Diesel engine	7 Main fuel tank	11 Driving cab	15 Passenger compartment
4 Engine cooling fan	8 Main control frame	12 Lubricating oil filters and strainers	

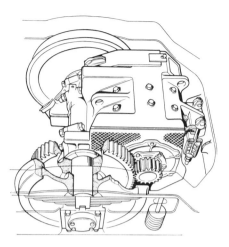

sary the use of special coaches with a narrower cross-sectional profile. Furthermore, the platforms used by these trains in the London terminal stations were restricted in length, and to accommodate an 11-coach train with a 4-4-0 steam locomotive of the 'Schools' Class between the buffer stops and the clearance point at the outer end limited the length of coach to 56 foot 11 inch underframes, instead of the standard Southern 63 feet 5 inches. By way of appeasement to public pressure for improvement, 32 new coaches for steam locomotive haulage were put in hand in 1955.

What with the programme of electrification elsewhere in Southern Region, the earliest stage at which attention to the Hastings line could be given seemed to be about 1963, and improvements were urgently needed before then. It was in this situation that Mr W.J.A. Sykes, Chief Mechanical and Electrical Engineer of the Southern, recommended what he termed 'diesel electrification', and that the 32 new cars then being built should be converted into five six-car diesel-electric multiple-unit sets.

They would have traction motors identical in all respects to those used on the latest Southern express and multiple-unit suburban electric stock and therefore already well known and appreciated by all concerned with maintenance. Power for the traction motors was to be furnished by 500 hp diesel-engined generator sets of a standard English Electric design that was already well tried and had been exported in considerable numbers to the complete satisfaction of overseas railways, on which conditions of service were severe. The results were extremely successful, not only in demonstrating to the hard-tried commuters that something was being done to modernise their service and speed it up, but by eliminating the locomotive there was space along the platforms at Cannon Street for an extra coach. On the busiest services two six-car sets were coupled in multiple unit.

This was not all. At the time that the decision was taken to go diesel-electric on the Hastings line the 56 foot 11 inch underframes for the locomotive-hauled coaches were in hand, and no change could economically be made; but when the scheme was extended to provided for complete dieselisation of the Hastings services via Tunbridge Wells, it was found possible to use the standard Southern 63 foot 5 inch underframes, and provide additional pas-

Above left *Pictorial drawing of traction motor mounted on axle* (British Railways).

Below left *Southern Region: one of the Class '201' diesel-electric six-car sets with narrow coach bodies, built at Eastleigh works from 1957 for the Hastings line here seen just after leaving Polhill Tunnel* (C.J. Marsden).

Below *A striking view, looking towards Sevenoaks Tunnel of one of the later Hastings diesel-electric six-car sets, with coach bodies 65 ft 6 in, instead of the 58 ft of the original Class '201'* (C.J. Marsden).

senger accommodation. The tare weight of a six-car train with longer standard underframes was 227 tons, and the calculated performance on different gradients was as follows:

Gradient	Balancing speed (mph)
Level	69
1 in 250 rising	58
1 in 100 rising	40
1 in 50 rising	23

The 'balancing speed' is that which would be attained and sustained, under full power conditions, on a continuous length of such a gradient. The Hastings line, particularly that part of it south of Tonbridge Junction, has practically no lengths of even gradients where speed can settle down to a steady figure; but before going into public service one of the new diesel-electric sets was tested between Waterloo and Southampton and gave figures closely agreeing with the calculated values, at any rate for level running and on a rising 1 in 250 gradient. The official maximum speed for these Hastings line diesel-electric sets is 75 mph.

Below *The narrow body and straight sides of the Hastings diesel-electric stock are very apparent in this photograph of the 11.45 Charing Cross to Hastings train approaching Tonbridge* (C.J. Marsden).

Bottom *Diesel-electric express train, Hastings to Charing Cross passing Bopeep Junction, West St Leonards in August 1982* (C.J. Marsden)

4. Type '4' diesel development

However much British engineers sought to establish an independent view of motive power modernisation, the evident success of the diesel-electric type in North America could not be without its influence. Nevertheless, those who were not overawed by the 'scrap steam at any price' attitude of some of the non-technical hierarchy at headquarters, and who looked to the continent of Europe as well as to the USA for portents for the future, felt that the hydraulic system of transmission was worth a trial. That this was eventually made *in extenso* on the Western Region was sometimes attributed to a continuance, in the days of the nationalised railways, of the historic Great Western determination to do things differently from everyone else; and with the experiment with gas-turbine propulsion having produced negative results they must next go diesel-hydraulic. This was not so. In the first phase of modernisation, in which a limited amount of new power was envisaged, R.C. Bond, as Chief Mechanical Engineer of the central staff, was anxious that diesel-hydraulic traction should be given a trial, and, as it would have been undesirable to mix the forms of traction in any one region, the Western was chosen, just as the Midland lines of the LM Region were chosen for the introduction of the 'Peak' type of diesel-electric, as referred to earlier, in Chapter 2 of this book.

The diesel-hydraulic type of locomotive had already made considerable headway in West Germany, and as early as 1954 the North British Locomotive Company had entered into an agreement with the firm of Maschinenfabrik Augsburg Nuremberg AG, the designers and builders of the MAN diesel engine, to enable NBL to manufacture that engine for service in Great Britain and on Commonwealth railways. Just at the time the British Railways Modernisation Plan was launched the company obtained orders for 0-8-0 shunting locomotives for the East African Railways. The British Railways order was for five 2,000 hp locomotives for express passenger service. They had the standard German L12V 18/21 engines of 1,000 hp each, of which the general appearance can be appreciated from the photograph on page 47. They were supercharged by a Napier exhaust-gas turbo-blower, and as will be seen the cylinders were arranged in V-form. The engine was flexibly mounted on the underframe of the locomotive, and connection from the engine shaft to the transmission was through a cardan shaft. The transmission itself

The Western Region 2,200 hp Bo-Bo diesel hydraulic locomotive 'Warship' Class (British Railways).

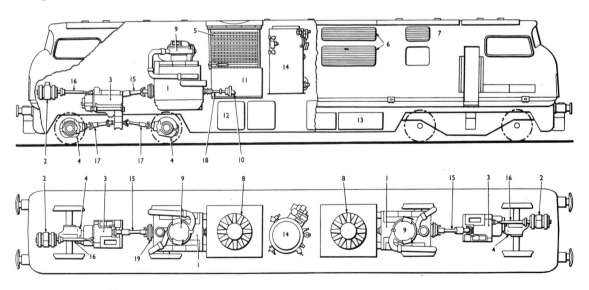

1 DIESEL ENGINE	6 RADIATOR AIR INTAKE	11 TRAIN-HEATING BOILER TANK	16 CARDAN SHAFT DRIVING DYNASTARTER
2 DYNASTARTER	7 AIR INLET TO TURBO BLOWER	12 FUEL TANKS	17 CARDAN SHAFT TO FINAL DRIVE
3 TRANSMISSION	8 RADIATOR FAN	13 D.P. BATTERIES	18 DRIVE TO HYDROSTATIC FAN PUMP
4 FINAL DRIVE	9 PRESSURE CHARGER	14 SPANNER TRAIN-HEATING BOILER	19 VIBRATION DAMPER
5 RADIATOR	10 HYDROSTATIC FAN PUMP	15 PRIMARY CARDAN SHAFT	

'A1A-A1A' Type diesel-hydraulic locomotive No D602 Bulldog *on the up 'Mayflower' entering Sonning Cutting in July 1959* (the late M.W. Earley).

was of the Voith-North British type, as shown in the accompanying diagram.

It contained three torque-converters. Infinitely variable torque multiplication was inherent in the design of each hydraulic torque-converter, but one was designed to be the most efficient at starting and at low speed, the next for intermediate speeds and the third for high speeds. One converter was filled as another was emptied and the change was made without interruption to the transmission of torque to the wheel. Transmission oil was cooled in a heat exchanger in which the heat was transferred to the engine cooling water. Only the outer axles of the six-wheeled bogies were powered, and the drive from each hydraulic transmission to the axle-mounted gearboxes was through cardan shafts fitted with needle-bearing universal joints. The mechanical design of the bogies was such that traction, braking and transverse forces were taken by an inner and outer centering ring. The outer part of the ring was integral with the bogie bolster, the inner part being attached to the underframe. The total weight of the main frame was taken by four widely spaced bearing pads resting on a double swing-link bolster. This bolster, in turn, rested on

transverse laminated springs, supported from the bogie frames by spring link planks and swing links. The suspension is referred to here in some detail in view of the difference in design adopted in the later diesel-hydraulic locomotives of the Western Region.

The principal dimensions of the North British-built A1A-A1A locomotives were:

Diesel engines (2 per loco)
    Rated output   1,000 bhp at 1,445 rpm
       or   1,100 bhp at 1,500 rpm
    Cylinders (12)   180 mm (7.087 in) diameter
                    210 mm (8.268 in) stroke
2 inlet and 2 exhaust valves per cylinder
Transmission (Voith-NB type)
    Maximum rating 925 hp at 1,445 rpm
                    1,036 hp at 1,500 rpm
Weight of locomotive in working order, 117.4 tons
    Fuel capacity   800 gal
    Water capacity   1,000 gal

The five locomotives were named after ships of the Royal Navy, thus *Active, Ark Royal, Bulldog, Conquest* and *Cossack,* and became the first group of the 'Warship' Class. The title accorded to the first of them was something of a misnomer at the start, because on a demonstration run staged by British Railways in February 1958, from Paddington to Bristol and back, *Active* became a partial failure. On the return journey a stop was made at Hullaving-

ton, at which it was discovered that one of the engines had seized up. The rest of the trip was made with only one engine.

I rode the *Ark Royal* non-stop from Paddington to Plymouth on the down 'Cornish Riviera Express' one day in the late autumn of 1958. At the time the train was then running to the four-hour timing, 56.4 mph average speed, worked to in the last days of steam. The load of 375 gross trailing tons was not heavy by previous Great Western standards, and we passed Exeter, 173.5 miles, in 163¼ minutes, nearly two minutes early; but a delay at Exminster put us three minutes down when we passed Newton Abbot. Up to this point keeping time with this relatively moderate load had not involved any work that could not have been done by a 'King' Class steam 4-6-0 with ease; but to recover the lateness over the severe gradients and curvature of the South Devon line required an all-out effort from the diesel, with all seven notches of the controller between Aller Junction and Dainton Tunnel, and again between Ashburton Junction and Rattery signal box. It is interesting to compare the result with the performance of a 'King' Class engine, hauling a rather heavier load of 405 tons over this same stretch of line (see the table below).

Except that the diesel with the lighter load accelerated more rapidly from the Newton Abbot speed restriction, there was little in it between the two locomotives.

In retrospect however, and significantly in view of later diesel-hydraulic history on the Western Region, one of the most interesting features about the performance of the *Ark Royal*, as experienced in the driver's cab, was the very smooth and comfortable riding. My notes include a favourable comment on this when we were traversing the curves of the Westbury bypass line, at just over 70 mph; but it was after we passed Castle Cary, and the locomotive was opened out for a 12-minute spell of full-power running over the Somerton cut-off line that the riding was most impressive. Here a stretch of 10.8 miles from Keinton Mandeville to Curry Rivel Junction was run at an average speed of 82 mph with a maximum, on a descending gradient, of 90 mph. In the course of ordinary business

Engine		*King Edward V*			*Ark Royal*		
Load, tons gross		405			375		
Distance		Time		Speed	Times		Speed
(miles)		m	s	mph	m	s	mph
0.0	Newton Abbot (pass)	0	00	33	0	00	35
1.1	Aller Junction	1	54	48	1	36	53
3.8	Dainton Box	7	09	21½	6	21	22
8.6	Totnes	12	59	56	13	12	51
11.4	Tigley Box	17	35	23¼	17	58	22½
13.2	Rattery Box	21	29	31	21	51	32
15.5	Brent (pass)	24	54	51	25	08	50

travelling between Bath and Paddington I had a number of runs behind these locomotives, but with one exception none with a load heavy enough to provide a real test of capacity. One evening however, on the 6.30 pm from Paddington, booked to cover the 94 miles to Chippenham in 94 minutes start to stop, we had a gross trailing load of 510 tons, behind the first of the NBL diesels, No 600 *Active*, and the performance was excellent. Sustained speeds of 68 mph up the gradual 1 in 1,320 rise between Maidenhead and Twyford, and 65½ mph on the 1 in 754 rise towards Shrivenham, indicated an all-out performance from the locomotive with equivalent drawbar horsepower figures of about 1,150 in each case. Nevertheless, for a locomotive with a nominal engine horsepower of 2,000 this did not seem very high. On my own footplate run with the *Ark Royal*, use of the sixth notch (out of seven) and a speed of 72½ mph between Maidenhead and Twyford showed an equivalent drawbar horsepower of a little over 900.

Interest in contemporary German locomotive practice had not been confined to the procurement by the North British Locomotive Company of manufacturing rights in the MAN engine. The firm of Krauss-Maffei of Munich was also developing the diesel-hydraulic system and, following the exhibition of a 2,000 hp locomotive with the Bo-Bo wheel arrangement at the German Railways Traffic Exposition, in 1953, the Class 'V200' 2,200 hp design, with the Co-Co wheel arrangement was developed, and 50 were acquired by the German Federal Railways. The first of these were in service in 1957 and British Railways' interest was such that arrangements were made for locomotives of similar design to be built at Swindon.

The first point that strikes one on reviewing this design is the remarkable saving in weight that had been achieved, largely by following German practice. Existing Type '4' diesel locomotives already running on British Railways turned the scale at 133 tons for the English Electric design, 138 tons for the 'Peaks', and 117½ tons for the NBL 'Warships'. The new Swindon-built diesel-hydraulics weighed no more than 78 tons. I must confess to viewing that last figure with a certain amount of suspicion—not for one moment doubting its veracity, but I am little doubtful about some of the design features by which it was achieved. Instinctively one looks at the purely mechanical part of the design, and its function as a vehicle, rather than at the motive power; for these locomotives were going to have to travel fast, and that very lightweight construction would be subjected to severe running conditions.

The very high power-to-weight ratio was achieved largely by use of the stressed-skin form of construction, whereby the superstructure bears much of the weight of the locomotive. Although the frame could be considered in two main parts—the underframe and the superstructure—they were welded together to form one load-carrying unit. Two tubular members with a 6½ inch outside diameter running the whole length of the locomotive from one buffer beam to the other formed the basis of the underframe. Their centres coincided approximately with the buffer centre lines, and therefore transmitted the buffing forces directly. Deep longitudinal plate members provided strength to resist bending and the tractive forces. The superstructure was a beautifully designed fabricated steel assembly, entirely welded. The steel 'skin', forming the outer casing, was welded to the superstructure framing, and formed a box-like construction. It was a very novel design so far as British

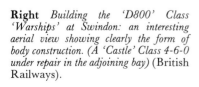

Above left *The second of the NBL diesel-hydraulic locomotives of the 'A1A-A1A' Type No D601* Ark Royal *on the Cornish Riviera Express near Reading West in September 1958* (the late M.W. Earley).

Right *Building the 'D800' Class 'Warships' at Swindon: an interesting aerial view showing clearly the form of body construction. (A 'Castle' Class 4-6-0 under repair in the adjoining bay)* (British Railways).

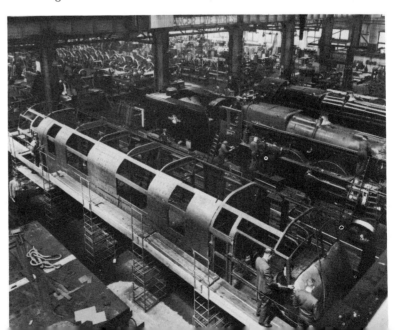

practice was concerned, and that it was so success-fully produced was a resounding tribute to the craftsmanship of Swindon Works. In these loco-motives, and also in the NBL 'Warships', Bond had to be content with a somewhat truncated version of the 'nose' cab, to which he was so partial.

It was, however, in the bogies and the associated suspension gear that the greatest novelties were incorporated. Whether these were a direct adapta-tion of German practice I cannot say; but one thing is fairly certain: the 'V200' diesel-hydraulics of the German Federal Railways that were based on Frankfurt, Hamburg, Essen and Karlsruhe did not have to work any trains that involved such high speeds as that of the 'Bristolian', which on its accelerated diesel timings required running up to the full 90 mph officially quoted as the maximum for these locomotives. Now, as to the bogie, its centre was a hollow rectangle into which there pro-jected a part of the underframe and the lower part of the transmission containing the output shaft and flanges. The traction and braking forces were transmitted between bogie and underframe by means of curved manganese steel rubbing plates. Transverse forces were transmitted by a linkage system connecting bogie to underframe, which allowed the former to turn relative to the latter about a geometrical centre. The ends of the links were originally provided with flexible rubber bearings which were expected to need no lubrica-tion. The body weight was transmitted to each bogie by brackets, connected by pin joints to the buckles of two large laminated springs. From these springs the weight was transferred through coil springs to the top of the roller-bearing casings and finally to the axle. No axle boxes and horns of the conventional type were used, but each bearing was contained in a casing forming an arm which was connected to the bogie frame by means of large pins with flexible rubber bearings.

The diesel engines were of the Maybach type with 12 cylinders in V-form, while the hydraulic trans-mission was of the Maybach Mekydro type, the principal dimensions were:

Diesel engines (2 per loco)
 Rated output per engine
 1,056 hp at 1,400 rpm (first 3 locos)
 1,152 hp at 1,530 rpm (subsequent locos)
 Cylinders (12) 185 mm (7.283 in) diameter
                     200 mm (7.874 in) stroke
Transmissions (2 per loco) Mekydro Type K104
 Maximum rating of each:
  966 hp at 1,400 rpm
  1,035 at 1,530 rpm
Weight of locomotive in working order, 78 tons
 Fuel capacity 800 gal
 Water capacity 1,000 gal

The first of the new locomotives, No D800, was named *Sir Brian Robertson* after the then Chairman of

Below left to right

A 'Warship' No D807 Caradoc *entering St David's station Exeter, with a Sunday only Truro to Bradford express in July 1961 (J.N. Faulkner).*

A 'Warship' No D860 Victorious *approaching Hereford with the 06:10 Penzance-Liverpool express in July 1962, before the transfer of these trains to the Midland route north of Bristol (J.N. Faulkner).*

After transfer of some of the 'Warships' to the Southern Region, No D822 Hercules *on a Weymouth to Waterloo express near Wimbledon (J.N. Faulkner).*

Among last duties for the 'Warships', a return empties stone train Gatwick to Westbury, in August 1972 (J.N. Faulkner).

the Railway Executive, but the remainder were also named after warships; the second and third units, which had the reduced power rating, were Nos D801 *Vanguard*, and D802 *Formidable*.

The new locomotives came into general service towards the end of 1958. The 6.30 pm from Paddington to Bristol, with its 60 mph run to Chippenham, became a regular diesel turn, and in the course of my ordinary business travelling I saw a lot of their work. In the nine months after their introduction on the service I had 16 runs behind one or another of the first ten. With an average gross trailing load of 399 tons the average net start-to-stop time was 91½ minutes. The best was with engine D802 and a 435-ton load, in 88 minutes net. As always, individual drivers varied in enterprise and in making up time when delays supervened. On one evening when I had a driver's cab pass and rode down on D808 *Centaur* I saw that no more than the fifth notch out of seven was needed to sustain 70 mph on level track with a load of 420 tons, about 800 drawbar horsepower, and I have a note: 'Didn't sound at all nice in "6"'! Four notches produced a maximum of 86 mph down Dauntsey bank, at which station power was shut off and we coasted over the remaining 6.3 miles in 6½ minutes, to arrive in Chippenham in 92 minutes from Paddington. I had also a run with No D802 on the up 'Cornish Riviera Express' when it was quite new, in January 1959, but, with a load of no more than 335 tons, it was not a severe test. With this light load no more than three notches were needed to sustain 72 mph on level track, about 700 drawbar horsepower.

For the summer service of 1959 five minutes were cut from the 'Bristolian' schedule, requiring in future a start-to-stop average speed of all but 71 mph. Until this time, despite the availability of the diesels, 'Castle' Class steam 4-6-0s had been retained on this prestige service, and in those final months net times of 100 minutes or slightly less were common enough. My own last four runs, with engines 5054, 5056 twice, and 5067 all gave excellent results. The D800 Class diesels were put on to the accelerated train, and in that first summer I had three runs with engine D805 *Benbow*. On the first I was a passenger, and hindered by two permanent way checks we did not quite keep time, and the second, when I had a cab pass, we had to stop at West Drayton with both engines failed. We eventually struggled into Paddington 18 minutes late. The third time, again with a cab pass, I noted a punctual run despite delays costing about five minutes. There was plenty of use of the seventh notch on this occasion, chiefly when accelerating from speed restrictions, though the sixth gave us speeds of 87 to 88 mph on level track. Continuous use of notch 7 on the 1 in 300 rise to Badminton gave speeds of 74 to 75 mph uphill, about 1,040 drawbar horsepower. Down the Vale of the White Horse, on gradients falling at 1 in 754, notch 4 gave us a sustained 90 mph. Care was taken, when I was in the cab, to limit this to the 'official' maximum, though in that first year of running I noted speeds of up to 95 mph from the train.

I cannot say that I was impressed with the 'D800' Class. Their nominal capacity of 2,200 horsepower was a travesty of what they could actually do, even when driven continuously at full power, but what was more serious was their appallingly bad riding at high speed. The runs I had with D805 on the up 'Bristolian' were the only times I have been really scared on the footplate; and that was not from lack of experience in my case. I was relieved to hear subsequently that the train itself had been decelerated, and the 'D800' Class limited to a maximum speed of 80 mph. Nevertheless, in view

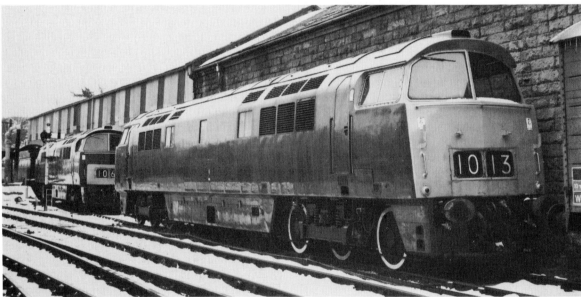

of the relentless haste with which the 'scrap steam' programme was being propagated, construction continued at Swindon until there were 33 in service, and in the meantime an order for a further 33 had been passed to the North British Locomotive Company. These latter differed from the original Swindon-built units in having the NBL/MAN engines and Voith transmission as in the 'D600' Class. Externally they were virtually indistinguishable from those built at Swindon, but were slightly heavier, turning the scale at 79.5 tons. Construction of the 'D800' Class ceased for a while after delivery of D865 from North British Locomotive Company, in 1962; but a further five were added later, built at Swindon, and having the Bristol Siddeley-Maybach engine and the Mekydro K104 transmission.

Then, at the end of 1961, came the larger diesel-hydraulics of the 'Western' series, having the nominal total horsepower of 2,700, some built at Swindon, and others at Crewe. They were of the Co-Co wheel arrangement, and had the Maybach MD655 type of engine, and Voith-North British hydraulic transmission. Outwardly they were of highly distinctive and to many eyes anything but pleasing, appearance. It was understood that at about this time British Railways had set up a 'design panel', in an attempt to establish styles in appearance of equipment that came prominently into the eye of the public, and that the new 'Western' Class was one of the subjects chosen for their attention. One of the cherished features of diesel-electric locomotives to disappear as a result was the nose-cab; but another quaint idea was to deck the pioneer locomotive of the new series,

Left *One of the Co-Co diesel-hydraulic locomotives No 1067* Western Druid, *on an up West of England express in Sonning Cutting, April 1974* (Brian Morrison).

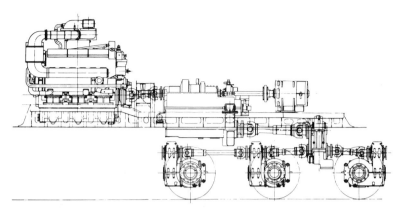

Below left *Two withdrawn 'Western' Class Co-Co diesel-hydraulics, without numbers or names, at Bridgnorth, Severn Valley Railway, in February 1979. They were actually D1013* Western Ranger *and D1062* Western Courier (Brian Morrison).

Above right *Engine and transmission layout on the 'Western' Class diesel-hydraulic locomotives* (Institution of Mechanical Engineers).

Right *The Birmingham RCW 2,750 hp prototype diesel-electric locomotive* Lion *on trial on the Western Region, beside steam locomotive No 7013* Totnes Castle (BRCW Ltd).

'D1000', in an experimental livery of 'desert sand'. Whether this was to anticipate any extraneous matter getting into the bearings, and causing overheating, or to match the insufferably hot atmosphere which developed in their cabs I do not know; but I must admit that in view of first reports of running conditions I was in no hurry to ask for cab passes! They had the same method of suspension as the 'D800' series, and were at first reported to be just as lively and uncomfortable in their riding. A total of 35 was built at Swindon and a further 39 at Crewe.

There was apparently no question of prototype building so far as the diesel-hydraulic locomotives of the Western Region were concerned. This was in some contrast to what was happening elsewhere in the British locomotive field, where a number of privately sponsored prototypes were built and tried in varying grades of passenger and mixed-traffic service. The outstanding English Electric 'Deltic', representing the most powerful express passenger diesel locomotive type ever to run regularly on British Railways, was in a class apart, and is dealt with in a later chapter. I am now concerned with the diesel-electric prototypes *Lion* and *Falcon*, and the comparison they afford to the 'Western' Class diesel-hydraulics, of which they had approximately the same nominal engine power, 2,700–2,800. *Lion* was built by a consortium of three firms, Sulzer Brothers, AEI, and the Birmingham Railway Carriage and Wagon Company. *Falcon* was built by the then Brush Electrical Engineering Co Ltd, now part of the Hawker Siddeley group. The difference was that while *Falcon* was built as a privately

Locomotive	'Western'	*Lion*	*Falcon*
Type	Co-Co	Co-Co	Co-Co
Total weight in working order (tons)	103	114	115
Diesel engines, make	Maybach	Sulzer	Maybach
Diesel engines, horsepower	2,800	2,750	2,800
Transmission	Voith-North British	Electric AEI type '235'	Electric Brush

financed venture it was done in consultation with British Railways, whereas *Lion* was apparently quite independently designed and produced. Basic details, in comparison with the 'Western' type were as shown in the above table.

It is interesting that the *Falcon* had the same diesel engines as those used on the 'Western' hydraulic type. Bearing in mind the innate and historic conservatism of the Great Western Railway, and that apart from the wartime economies of plain green the passenger engine livery remained unchanged from broad gauge days until the onset of nationalisation, the setting up of competition for styles of painting on the 'Western' type diesel seemed rather pathetic. One could hardly imagine the strong managements of earlier days allowing its publicity department to pander to transient popular taste. I always recall the story of Sir Felix Pole's reaction when he was told that BR was going to paint the 'Kings' blue. He is said to have

commented: 'Well thank God I'm now blind, and cannot see them!' Then there was the gifted optimist who decreed that the prototype *Lion* should be painted white!! Anyway, the public competition saw an end of the 'desert sand' style for the 'Westerns', and gave us maroon, which in due course was also applied to the 'Warships'. What the Design Panel thought about this I do not know; but they devised an entirely different style, in two-tone green, for the new Type '4' diesel electrics that came from Brush later.

The *Lion*, despite its optimistic and impractical painting style, was a handsome locomotive, but its short career seems to have been wrapped in mystery, not least in its exclusion from all reference in the usually admirable indexes in *The Railway Magazine*. In the text itself the first reference was in a frontispiece plate in July 1962 showing the locomotive at Paddington, ready to leave on the 7.10 pm express for Wolverhampton. In the

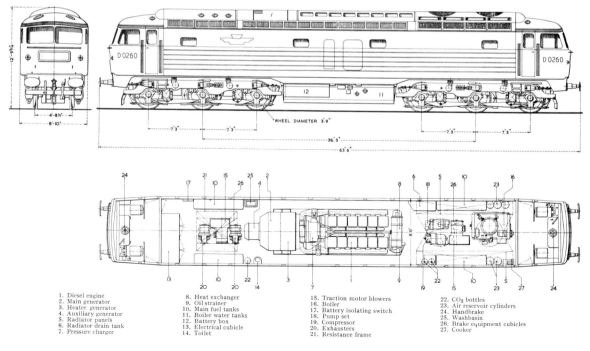

1. Diesel engine	8. Heat exchanger	15. Traction motor blowers	22. CO₂ bottles
2. Main generator	9. Oil strainer	16. Boiler	23. Air reservoir cylinders
3. Heater generator	10. Main fuel tanks	17. Battery isolating switch	24. Handbrake
4. Auxiliary generator	11. Boiler water tanks	18. Pump set	25. Washbasin
5. Radiator panels	12. Battery box	19. Compressor	26. Brake equipment cubicles
6. Radiator drain tank	13. Electrical cubicle	20. Exhausters	27. Cooker
7. Pressure charger	14. Toilet	21. Resistance frame	

Below left *The prototype* Lion *2,750 hp diesel-electric locomotive ex-Birmingham RC & W Co.* (Railway Magazine).

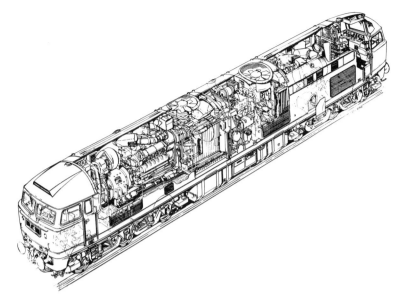

Right *The Brush* Falcon—*diesel-electric 2,800 hp prototype locomotive, cut-away drawing* (Institution of Locomotive Engineers).

Below right *Tractive effort—speed curve for the prototype* Falcon *locomotive* (Institution of Locomotive Engineers).

locomotive news in the same issue it was reported as having taken up regular work on that route on May 14, making two return trips from Wolverhampton to Paddington daily; but then, on May 17 it failed at Leamington, and that was literally the last that was ever heard of its activities. In August of that same year a five-page article describing the design of the locomotive in detail was published, and even this escaped the usually perspicacious sub-editor of *The Railway Magazine* who compiled the index. It needed a page-by-page thumbing through of several volumes to find it. The accompanying drawings show the layout of the machinery of this locomotive. It was stated that on test a train of 638 tons was accelerated smoothly from a standing start on the 1 in 37 gradient of the Lickey Incline, and that a maximum speed of 100 mph was attained with a 16-coach passenger train.

The full story behind the competing prototypes *Lion* and *Falcon*, and why one was accepted, to some extent, and the other dropped like a red hot coal, will probably never be known. The Birmingham Railway Carriage and Wagon Company had built a number of the smaller diesels, but in 1961-2 was known to be in financial difficulties. British Railways needed large numbers of diesels in the Type '4' Class, but more powerful than either the English Electric design, or the 'Peaks'. BRCW was in desperate need of more work and, having got together with Sulzer's and the Associated Electrical Industries, produced the *Lion* entirely on their own. *Falcon*, on the other hand, produced by Brush, though with British Railways' advice, had every appearance of being the favourite from the outset,

and when the *Lion* failed in traffic no one seemed to take any further interest in it. It was taken back to the BRCW works, dismantled and the parts sold off to pay creditors. AEI took back the electrical equipment, and the diesel engine went back to Sulzer's. The odd thing about it all is that when the new standard 2750 hp Type '4' was designed, to

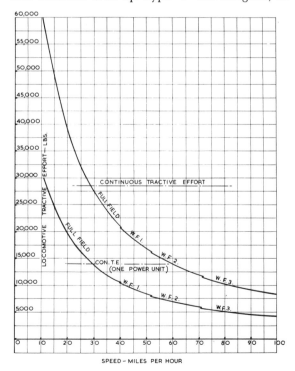

SPEED – MILES PER HOUR

Above *The Brush* Falcon *prototype, immediately after construction, with the* Falcon *motif painted on.* (Brush Elec M/Cs Ltd, G. Toms collection).

Left *The* Falcon, *at Loughborough in 1962, with the 'Master Cutter' headboard* (Brush Elec M/Cs Ltd, G. Toms collection).

Below Falcon *on dynamometer car test runs in 1962, climbing the Lickey bank, with the later WR dynamometer car* (Brush Elec M/Cs Ltd, G. Toms Collection).

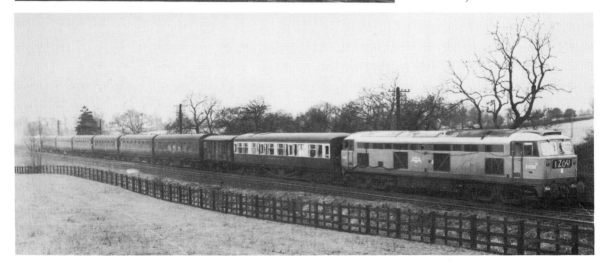

Above Falcon *hauling a dynamometer car test train approaching Teignmouth* (Brush Elec M/Cs Ltd, G. Toms collection).

Below *One of the first Brush Type '4' diesel-electric locomotives of 2750 hp (later Class '47') in the original two-tone green livery* (Hawker-Siddeley-Brush).

become the very numerous Class '47', it was the Sulzer engine that was adopted, and not the Maybach used in the *Falcon*. In fact *Lion* had the very first example on British Railways of the 12 LDA 28C engine, which was standardised on Class '47'.

The prototype Brush *Falcon* locomotive made its bow in the technical press at about the same time as the *Lion*, but it had actually been making some experimental runs on the Great Eastern line of the Eastern Region at the end of 1961. It then went to the Western for some comprehensive trials, through which it passed successfully. It returned, still on loan from the manufacturers, to enter regular express passenger service between Kings Cross and Sheffield. The new standard Type '4's were based closely on the *Falcon*, and the first production batch came from Brush at the end of 1962. BR were going for them in a big way. Many more were to be built for general service on all regions except the Southern, some at railway workshops. It was soon evident that they were fast and powerful machines with an authorised maximum speed of 95 mph, and my first run behind one of them was an exhilarating experience. Despite the introduction of the diesel-hydraulic 'Westerns' at about the same time as *Falcon* and the *Lion*, these larger hydraulics did not seem to come into regular service at all readily; and, although I was travelling as frequently as ever between Bath and Paddington, it was not until 1965 that I had my first run behind one of them. The regular work was done by the 'Warships', still officially limited to a maximum speed of 80 mph.

Brush Type '4's were allocated to the Western Region and I had indeed travelled several times behind them before I had my first run with a 'Western'. Apart from the trouble with the riding and the insufferably hot cabs, there was trouble with fatigue failure of the axles, including at least one derailment. Every one of the axles had to be replaced. Although when these troubles were cured the 'Westerns' took their rightful place as fast and powerful locomotives, it became evident from the many runs I logged with them, and from reports on even more sent to me by correspondents in connection with my 'Locomotive Practice and Performance' articles in *The Railway Magazine*, that they were showing the same deficiency in actual power put forth at the drawbar as the 'Warships' had done, even before the limitation in maximum speed had been placed upon them. The highest output with a 'Western' that came to my notice was an attained and sustained maximum speed of 85 mph near Maidenhead going east, with a gross trailing load of 560 tons, on a slight gradient descending of 1 in 1,320. The equivalent drawbar horsepower would have been around 1,500. At the same time it is important to appreciate that, with these locomotives, schedules which would have been impracticable with steam were maintained in the heaviest loading conditions. With the 'Cornish Riviera Express', at one time booked to cover the 142.7 miles from Paddington to Taunton in 123 minutes, start to stop, I have seen an arrival just over two minutes early with a gross load of 525 tons; an average speed of 71.1 mph. Running such as this, that involved full power working for much of the way, could be readily achieved with a diesel, requiring no physical work from the crew.

It was soon evident however, from no more than my own observations in regular travelling between

Above *A Glasgow-Manchester express, diverted to the Settle and Carlisle line, passing Kirkby Stephen, hauled by Class '47' diesel No 1948 (original numbering) still in the two-tone green livery, in June 1967* (Derek Cross).

Below *Euston-Perth express in the Lune Gorge, July 1967, before the M4 mtoroway was built. The locomotive is D1949 (Class '47') in original livery and numbering* (Derek Cross).

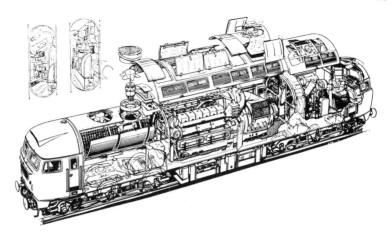

Paddington–Chippenham and Bath that the Brush Type '4' diesel-electrics 'had the edge' on the 'Westerns'. My very first run with one of them in June 1963 gave me an actual time of 73 minutes start-to-stop for the 94 miles from Paddington to Chippenham, with a gross trailing load of 380 tons, and a maximum of 94 mph on dead-level track, near Goring. About two months later I was on the footplate of another locomotive of the class on the Anglo-Scottish express from Kings Cross and with a trailing load of 405 tons noted a sustained 77 mph up the 1 in 200 gradient from Huntingdon towards Abbots Ripton. This showed an equivalent drawbar horsepower of around 2,000, which was more in keeping with the engine horsepower of 2,700 than the 1,500 maximum which seemed to be the best the 'Westerns' could do. In July 1964 I also noted some very fast running and some slight 'bending of the rules' on the 12.45 pm from Paddington to Chippenham, on which we passed Milepost 75, from Paddington, in just under 75 minutes inclusive of a three-minute station stop at Reading and a signal stop for 45 seconds at Moreton Cutting box, near Didcot. A sustained speed of 88 mph near Shrivenham indicated an equivalent drawbar horsepower of about 1,700, while after Swindon we attained 98 mph at the foot of the Dauntsey Incline, and sustained 97 mph for four miles thereafter on no steeper gradient than 1 in 660. The Brush Type '4's were officially limited to a maximum speed of 95 mph and there is much more to be written of these fine locomotives later in this book.

Quite apart from the disparity between the nominal and the actual power available for traction, which was far greater in the diesel hydraulics than in their diesel-electric counterparts, the hydraulics suffered from problems with the transmission, vibration, wear of parts, and torsional oscillation and it was left to a paper presented to the Institution

of Locomotive Engineers by S.O. Ell, to pin-point the cause of the very bad riding of the 'Warships', of which I had some hair-raising personal experiences. It has been mentioned in this chapter that the 'Warships' were the British equivalent of the German Krauss-Maffei design, and that the 'Westerns' had the same form of suspension; it has also been mentioned that the thrust from the pillars of the body to the ends of the inverted laminated springs was taken through rubber blocks, to absorb the twist. In this paper Ell described, in technical language, the oscillations experienced at high speed, which at times felt as though the body of the locomotive was shaking like a jelly! But it was far more serious than that, and the Western Region was fortunate not to have a derailment in the early days when these locomotives were running up to the full 90 mph.

How the troubles were analysed and eradicated, one by one, makes a fascinating technical story. One stage involved the discarding of the Krauss-Maffei link and bell-crank gear, and reducing the centering arrangements to a diesel locomotive version of the old Dean carriage bogie of the Great Western Railway; while the substitution of steel pads for the rubber blocks of the original secondary suspension inspired Ell to a peroration to his paper that bid fair to eclipse that great historian, E.L. Ahrons, at his wittiest. 'Preceptors of old', Ell concluded 'advised us what happens to houses built on sand, and on rock, but because the material had not then been invented, they could not advise us what happens to a house which is built on rubber stilts. This momentous discovery was left to British Railways. Hence the replacement of the rubber with a metal block and the end of the trouble with Krauss-Maffei bogies due to "under design".'

In 1961 a third variety of diesel-hydraulic locomotive was introduced on the Western Region, of

Left *One of the smaller diesel-hydraulic locomotives 'D7000' Class with Hymek transmission, on the 06:40 Pembroke Dock to Paddington express in July 1963, near Pangbourne, locomotive No D7057* (J.D. Faulkner).

Below *Western Region 'D7000' Class diesel-hydraulic locomotive.* (Institution of Mechanical Engineers).

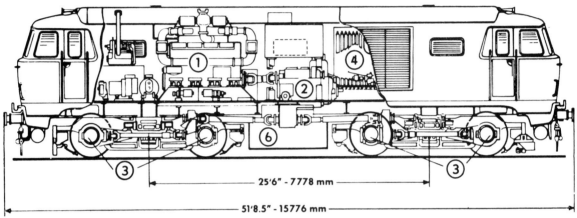

25'6" - 7778 mm

51'8.5" - 15776 mm

Type '3' capacity. An order for no fewer than 95 of this design was placed with Beyer Peacock (Hymek) Ltd, in which firm Bristol Siddeley Engines Ltd, and J. Stone & Co (Deptford) Ltd were partners with Beyer, Peacock & Co Ltd. The new locomotives were built at Gorton, where so many famous steam engines of the Beyer-Garratt articulated type were built. These Type '3' diesel-hydraulics, which became colloquially known as the 'Hymeks', had

the Bristol Siddeley- Maybach 'MD 870' engine and the Stone-Maybach hydraulic transmission. The rated engine horsepower was 1,700. The accompanying outline diagram shows the general proportions of the locomotive, and it was notable that the bogies and suspension were of more conventional design than that used on the 'Warships' and 'Western'. The bogies were of the 'Commonwealth' cast steel design, with swing bolsters, and the suspension system comprised triple elliptical spring nests between the equaliser beams and the bogie frame, with laminated springs under the bolster. A cross-sectional drawing of the Mekydro transmission is also shown herewith. Intended for mixed traffic, rather than the heaviest of main line passenger duties, these locomotives were not often seen on the principal express trains; and I had no opportunity of riding them personally. Exceptionally, however, one of them, No D7009 was on the 7.32 am Bath to Paddington one morning when I

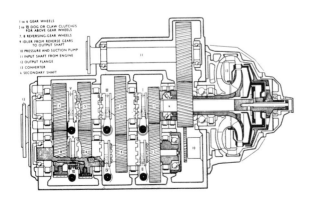

Left *The Mekydro transmission used on the 'D7000' locomotives.* (Institution of Mechanical Engineers).

Above *A 'Hymek' diesel-hydraulic locomotive No D7016 entering Salisbury, Southern Region, with a Cardiff to Portsmouth train in August 1964* (J.N. Faulkner).

Below *The Mekydro converter showing turbine blading engaged and disengaged* (Institution of Mechanical Engineers).

was a passenger, with a heavy load of 442 tons tare, 470–5 tons gross trailing. An excellent performance was put up, including an attained maximum speed of 75 mph on level track.

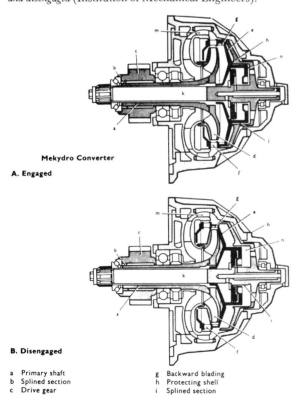

Mekydro Converter

A. Engaged

B. Disengaged

a	Primary shaft
b	Splined section
c	Drive gear
d	Impeller
e	Turbine
f	Forward blading

g	Backward blading
h	Protecting shell
i	Splined section
k	Secondary shaft
m	Guide vanes
n	Oil-pressure-operated cylinder

5. The 'Deltics'

In a work of this kind it is perhaps inevitable that the record of development at times gets out of true chronological sequence; and in dealing with what could be called 'mid-term' Type '4' history, including reference to the privately financed prototypes loaned to British Railways, I have so far bypassed by several years the most famous and successful prototype of them all, the English Electric 'Deltic', which took to the road in the autumn of 1955, less than a year after the launching of the great Modernisation Plan and well ahead of any top-line passenger locomotives authorised by that plan. The project followed the successful development and application by D. Napier & Son Ltd of a new form of lightweight diesel engine, which had already proved itself in naval and other applications where a lightweight form of construction was desirable. Recalling that the pioneer British main line diesel-electric locomotive No 10000, built by the LMS, with English Electric engines and traction motors had a nominal engine horsepower of 1,600, and weighed 127.6 tons, the prospect of a locomotive of 3,300 horsepower that would weigh little more than 100 tons was little short of sensational.

The 'Deltic' engine, so named because of the arrangement of its 18 cylinders in the form of the Greek letter Δ, is of the opposed piston type, water cooled, and operating on the two-stroke cycle. The cylinders are arranged in three banks of six, each bank containing a crankshaft, with the cylinders forming, in 'end view' an equilateral triangle. At the driving end of the engine a train of gears connects the three crankshafts to the main output shaft at the centre of the triangle. In the prototype locomotive, the general layout of which will be seen from the accompanying diagram, there were two entirely separate 'Deltic' engines, each with its main and auxiliary generator. For normal working in railway service it was intended that both power units would be run together. The engines were simultaneously controlled, with the torque automatically adjusted to the load and speed setting. Changeover switches were included in the equipment so that either engine unit could drive all six traction motors, though with only one power unit in operation the locomotive was expected to operate at approximately half speed.

The performance claims for the prototype locomotive made at the time of its introduction were modest enough, though far in advance of any diesel-electric locomotive then running. With a trailing load of 500 tons, the following speeds were predicted, on various gradients.

Gradient	Expected speed
1 in (rising)	(mph)
Level	90
200	69
100	52
66	40

With a trailing load of 400 tons, the speeds were expected to be 75 mph on 1 in 200, 59 on 1 in 100 and 47 mph on 1 in 66. The prototype had a nominal maximum speed of 90 mph, and with a 600-ton load the speed on level track was 85 mph. The locomotive was built at the Preston Works of English Electric, and at once began trial running on the London Midland Region. From local working it quickly graduated to express passenger service between Liverpool and Euston. Its handsome

Left *The prototype 'Deltic' after 450,000 miles of trial running en route for installation in the Science Museum, South Kensington* (GEC).

Top right *General layout of the 'Deltic' locomotive* (Locomotive Magazine).

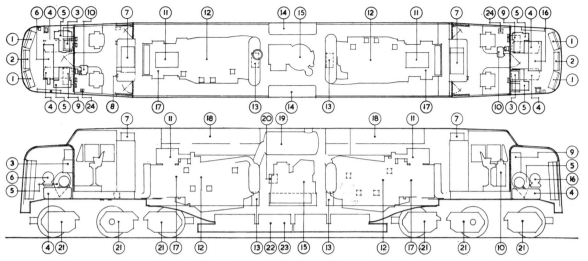

General layout of "Deltic" locomotive

1. Generator Field Resistances
2. Resistances, Main and Auxiliary Generator Fields, Exhauster Motor Divert etc.
3. Load Regulator (Main Generator)
4. Main Air Reservoirs (2 in each nose)
5. Traction Motors Blower and Motor
6. Exhauster
7. Traction Motors Field Divert Resistances

8. Wheel wear Compensator
9. Brake Equipment
10. Master Controller
11. Auxiliary Generator
12. Engine
13. Fuel Pump
14. Battery
15. Train Heating Boiler
16. Compressor

17. Main Generator
18. Coolers (Radiators)
19. Engine Silencer
20. Battery Isolating Switch
21. Traction Motors
22. Water Tanks
23. Fuel Tanks
24. Air Brake Valve

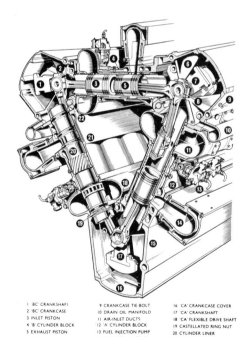

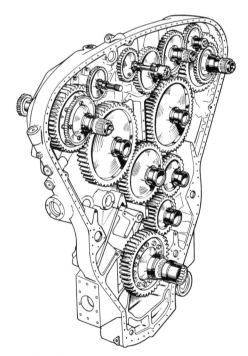

1 'BC' CRANKSHAFT
2 'BC' CRANKCASE
3 INLET PISTON
4 'B' CYLINDER BLOCK
5 EXHAUST PISTON
6 'AB' CRANKCASE
7 'AB' CRANKSHAFT
8 CONNECTING ROD
9 CRANKCASE TIE-BOLT
10 DRAIN OIL MANIFOLD
11 AIR-INLET DUCTS
12 'A' CYLINDER BLOCK
13 FUEL INJECTION PUMP
14 EXHAUST MANIFOLD
15 'CA' CRANKCASE
16 'CA' CRANKCASE COVER
17 'CA' CRANKSHAFT
18 'CA' FLEXIBLE DRIVE SHAFT
19 CASTELLATED RING NUT
20 CYLINDER LINER
21 'C' CYLINDER BLOCK
22 BLOWER DRIVE SHAFTS

Above *The 'Deltic' engine: perspective drawing* (British Railways).

Above *The 'Deltic' engine: gear phasing arrangement* (British Railways).

styling and gay livery of pale blue with yellow stripes, soon made it a familiar object to regular travellers. Although the machinery based on the quick-running aero-type engine was so different from the conventional slow-running type of marine diesel that was generally favoured by British Railways, the performance was so good as to induce the carrying out of full-dress dynamometer car trials on the Settle and Carlisle line. The heaviest and fastest trains on the LM main line did not call for a power output anything like the maximum output of the 'Deltic'.

When, in a commentary written for *The Engineer*, in July 1958, I came to compare the power output with that of existing non-steam locomotives already running on British Railways for which equally comprehensive test reports had been published, the truly astonishing attributes of the 'Deltic' design became apparent.
The characteristic curves of drawbar horsepower as shown in the accompanying diagram are revealing

Above *The prototype 'Deltic' locomotive hauling a Euston to Liverpool express past the site of the former Great Bridgeford station, north of Stafford* (GEC).

Above right *Down Anglo-Scottish express passing Tollerton, hauled by 'Deltic' No D9001 St Paddy* (C. Ord).

Above far right *'Deltic' locomotive: drawbar horsepower characteristics—both engines working* (Engineer).

enough and prove that the high tractive power claimed for the 'Deltic' was a reality. Moreover, it seemed that the prototype locomotive had remarkably little in the way of teething troubles and it rode very smoothly and comfortably. The performance characteristics were obtained by use of the mobile test plant developed just before nationalisation by the London Midland and Scottish Railway and with the new dynamometer car; the various values of engine speed ranging from 700 up to 1,500 revolutions per minute. In view of the criticism

Loco Number	Type	Maximum dhp at 70 mph	Maximum drawbar pull at 70 mph (tons)	Total weight (tons)	Pull weight ratio
18000	Gas turbine Brown-Boveri	1,300	2.9	119.2	0.0245
10201-2	Diesel-electric Southern	950	2.23	135.0	0.0165
10203	Diesel-electric Southern	1,200	3.0	132.8	0.0226
'Deltic'	EE Co diesel-electric	2,400	5.8	106	0.055

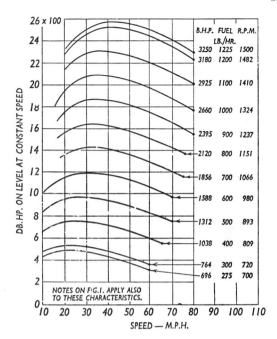

C.V. OF FUEL — 19,530 B.Th.U/LB.

made in the preceding chapter of the rather striking disparity between the engine horsepower and that available for traction in some of the Type '4' diesel locomotives, it is interesting to study the diagram which shows how the power of the 'Deltic' was distributed when working at maximum engine speed, over the entire range of train speeds from 20 up to 80 mph. From this it will be seen that the ratio of drawbar horsepower to output at the engine shaft reached its maximum of 80 per cent at 40 mph but was still as high as 73.8 per cent at 70 mph.

At the time these tests were conducted a trailing load of 500 tons was considered as about the normal for an express passenger train. The report included a composite diagram showing the performance and traction efficiency over the full range of working conditions, with both diesel engines in operation, ranging from an engine speed of 700 revolutions per minute up to the maximum of 1,500. The locomotive was not tested at a road speed of more than 80 mph though it was designed for a maximum of 105 mph. With the specified 500-ton trailing load the speed of 80 mph could be sustained with an engine speed of 1,237 rpm, against a maximum of 1,500, and the following features of performance are taken from the diagram.

Figures such as these were no doubt most impressive to locomotive engineers, but they needed a rather more vivid presentation to make the maximum impact upon operating men, and this was

500-ton express passenger train

Gradient	Engine (rpm)	Train speed (mph)	Available traction efforts (tons)
Level	1,237	80	3.3
1 in 300	1,237	63	4.28
	1,410	71	4.69
	1,500	76	4.91
1 in 200	1,237	55	4.91
	1,410	64	5.22
	1,500	69	5.50
1 in 100	1,237	39	7.02
	1,410	47	7.28
	1,500	51	7.46

done on dynamometer car test runs from Carlisle to Skipton and back over the 1,151 feet altitude of Aisgill summit with a 20-coach train making up a trailing load of 642 tons. In Volume 2 of this work, Chapter 17, details were given of a maximum load test run with one of the 'Britannia' Class of standard mixed-traffic 'Pacific' locomotives on which a remarkable engine performance was achieved, but only by the employment of two firemen, to maintain a coal rate of no less than 5,600 lb per hour. This, of course, was very far beyond the range of practical day-to-day working. A more comparable test was one on which the coal

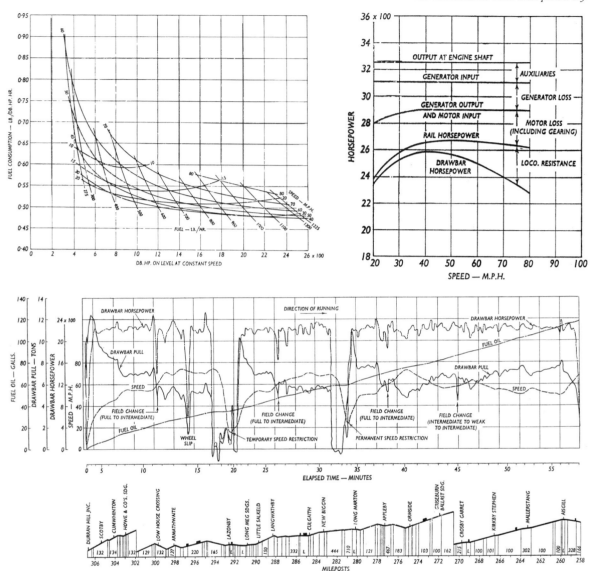

rate was 3,360 lb per hour, maintained for half an hour on the southbound ascent to Aisgill summit. Even this rate of fuel consumption was above the maximum of 3,000 lb which it had been agreed was the most that could be expected from a single fireman. This latter run makes an interesting comparison with the southbound test of the 'Deltic', which was not confined to one half-hour period but continued from the start at Durran Hill Junction, just outside Carlisle, till the train had surmounted Aisgill summit. In studying the times and speeds set out in the table it should be borne in mind that, whereas the steam 'Pacific' engine was passing

Top left *Diagram: fuel per drawbar horsepower hour (two engines)* (Engineer).

Top right *The 'Deltic' power distribution at 1500 rpm (two engines)* (Engineer).

Above *Chart of test run with 'Deltic' with 642 tons at maximum power on the Settle and Carlisle line* (Engineer).

Lazonby at well over 70 mph, the 'Deltic' was slowed to 15 mph near the station to observe a temporary speed restriction. Both locomotives were subjected to a permanent restriction between New

Dynamometer car test runs on Settle & Carlisle line

Locomotive			Steam '7MT'		'Deltic'	
Load (tons)			4-6-2			
trailing			540		642	
Distance		**Time**	Average		Average	**Time**
Miles		**m s**	speed mph		speed mph	**m s**
0.0	Lazonby	0 00	—		—	0 00
3.1	Little Salkeld	2 35	72.0		36.0	5 10
4.5	Langwathby	4 00	59.3		56.0	6 40
8.2	Culgaith	7 30	63.5		63.5	10 10
9.5	New Biggin	9 00	52.0		66.0	11 20
12.7	Long Marton	14 50	32.9		44.3	15 40
15.6	Appleby	19 00	41.8		49.8	19 10
18.0	Ormside	21 40	54.0		66.5	21 20
23.1	Crosby Garrett	28 10	55.6		61.2	26 20
Initial speed (mph)			71		15	
Final speed (mph)			40		59	

Biggin and Long Marton, though from this the 'Deltic' recovered much more rapidly.

The up 'Flying Scotsman' passing Monktonhall Junction in July 1962, hauled by No D9018 Ballymoss *(Derek Cross).*

The table above provides details of the whole of the 'Deltic' run, and it will be seen that in the final ten miles of the ascent to Aisgill, although the gradient is mostly 1 in 100 the time was only 11 minutes, and the minimum speed was 50 mph. An analysis of the two test journeys, with the 20-coach 642-ton load is as follows:

	Carlisle to Skipton	Skipton to Carlisle
Distance on test, actual (miles)	82.9	82.9
Distance under power (miles)	57.9	47.9
Time:		
actual running (min)	91	86
actual under power (min)	64	50
actual drifting and braking (min)	27	36
Average speed		
on running time (mph)	54.6	57.9
under power	54.3	57.5
Average actual drawbar horsepower	1,943	1,743
Average actual drawbar tractive effort tons	5.99	5.08
Fuel consumption:		
total used (pounds)	1,183	876
pounds per available dhp hour	0.571	0.602
pounds per mile	14.29	10.58
pounds per ton-mile	0.0222	0.0164

The difference between the time under power and the average drawbar horsepower on the two runs was due to Skipton lying some 250 feet higher above sea level than Carlisle. While most of the really hard work on the northbound journey was concentrated in the first 30 miles between Skipton itself and the entrance to Blea Moor Tunnel, the corresponding ascent to the famous 'Long Drag', up from Settle Junction, has its almost exact counterpart: from Ormside Viaduct to Aisgill it is preceded by more than 30 miles of almost continually adverse, if not such steep grading. On the southbound journey, the details of which are shown diagrammatically, had it

not been for the two severe speed restrictions at Lazonby and before Long Marton, the average speed from the start to topping Aisgill summit would have been little short of 60 mph.

While the results of the trials of this prototype locomotive, published in 1958, showed it to have a tractive ability far in advance of any locomotive then running on British Railways and notably better in operational economy than any of the diesel-electric units then running, it remained the property of the English Electric Company though continuing to do a remarkably increasing mileage of revenue-earning service on the London Midland Region. Although naturally suffering a number of teething troubles, it never once became subject to a failure that necessitated its removal from a train. Its last assignment, during 1958, involved a daily mileage of 704 miles:

7.45 am Euston to Liverpool	193¾ miles
2 pm Liverpool to Euston	193¾ miles
7.10 pm 'Royal Highlander', Euston to Crewe	158¼ miles
Up West Coast postal train, Crewe to Euston	158¼ miles

Though rendering such excellent service, and having clocked up a total of 259,000 miles in revenue-earning service in the short space of three years, the usefulness of the prototype locomotive was apparently ended. In the Modernisation Plan the London Midland West Coast main line was to be

The down 'Yorkshire Pullman' near Potters Bar hauled by an unidentified 'Deltic' in the original livery (English Electric).

Right *The up 'Flying Scotsman' passing the then-new panel signal box at Tweedmouth Junction, hauled by 'Deltic' No D9015, later named* Tulyar *(Westinghouse Signals Ltd).*

Below *Anglo-Scottish express crossing the Royal Border Bridge, Berwick-upon-Tweed, in August 1974 hauled by 'Deltic' No 55016 (new numbering)* Gordon Highlander *(Morrison Bryce).*

electrified, and it was found that at certain places there were structural restrictions that precluded its regular use over some parts of the East Coast route. In 1957 however that firebrand of an operator, Gerard F. Fiennes, had been appointed Line Traffic Manager of the Great Northern line of the Eastern Region. Plans were then being made for electrifying the main line, but costs had not yet been got out, and by the time they had, and been authorised—if that happened—it would be ten years before the electric service came into operation. Fiennes was not content to struggle through the intervening period with ageing steam 'Pacifics', and the diesels that were then being built were of no more than 2,000 horsepower. He wanted at least 3,000, and saw the answer in the 'Deltic'; but at first no one seemed to want it, and in certain quarters there were technical objections to features of its design.

In his celebrated autobiographical book *I Tried to Run a Railway* (Ian Allan Ltd), Fiennes wrote of that time: 'There was one small exception to the 2,000 hp mentality, the English Electric Company. Still,

now, ten years later, I never hear the high full throated hum of a 'Deltic' without returning thanks: thanks to the people in English Electric who thought of putting an engine off a motor gunboat into a locomotive; thanks to their Board who built at their cost a prototype; thanks to the London Midland who after extensive trials did not want it; thanks to our own people who over-rode the opinion of the experts that high revolution engines were out'.

Fiennes wanted 100 mph running, and there were men on the Eastern Region who remembered the difficulties there were when Sir Nigel Gresley introduced his first streamlined trains in 1935. Their brake power was inadequate to stop from maximum speed within the spacing of the existing signals, and the trains had to be 'double-blocked' throughout the mechanically signalled area between Kings Cross and York. Responsibility was placed on individual signalmen to obtain 'line clear' over two block sections ahead, instead of one, before they lowered their signals for the trains to proceed. In

Left *Kings Cross-Edinburgh express, near Reston Junction in June 1970, hauled by 'Deltic' No D9016 (old numbering)* Gordon Highlander *(Derek Cross).*

Right *The 07.45 Kings Cross-Newcastle express passing Selby in June 1974 hauled by 'Deltic' No 5017* The Durham Light Infantry *(Brian Morrison).*

March 1959 the unwanted prototype 'Deltic' was brought over from the London Midland Region, and used for a series of high-speed braking tests between Kings Cross and Grantham, certain stretches of which being specially cleared for 100 mph running. The actual braking distances recorded at speeds up to a maximum of 102 mph are of no particular interest today. The train was equipped with no more sophisticated apparatus than the ordinary standard vacuum brake, and therefore required 1,500 yd to effect a dead stop from 88 mph, and no less than 2,050 yd from 102 mph—both distances related to level track. But what did impress the Eastern Region management, and confirmed the confidence shown in the design by their Great Northern Line traffic manager, was the speed capacity of the locomotive, on the lengthy uphill stretch from Werrington Junction. Here the 20.6 miles were covered in 14 minutes 56 seconds an average of 82.7 mph, with speeds stepped up to between 86 and 92 mph on the most steeply graded section.

By the time these trials had been run it had already been announced that an order for 22 'Deltics' had been placed with English Electric to enable the complete replacement of steam; not only on the heaviest express train services of the Great Northern, but on the entire East Coast main line between Kings Cross and Edinburgh. The planned utilisation of the new locomotives was such that they were to do the work of around 60 steam 'Pacifics', and someone with a vision far in advance of anything that was usual in British Railways' management at that time realised that to obtain such utilisation it would need faultless maintenance. In the tremendous hurry in which the diesels of all types were being pitchforked into service, such

quality of maintenance was not to be expected in BR running sheds for some time to come, and so, at the same time as the contract was placed with English Electric for building the 22 new 'Deltic' locomotives, a second contract was negotiated for the routine maintenance of the fleet. In the original planning eight of the new locomotives were allocated to Kings Cross shed, six to Gateshead, and eight to Edinburgh, Haymarket. The first of them began trial running in March 1961, and from the official description published soon afterwards it was evident that no more than detailed changes had been made from the prototype, which had by then been withdrawn by the manufacturers, after amassing a service mileage of more than 400,000.

The new locomotives were finished in a handsome and refined livery of two-tone green; but the decision to continue the former East Coast practice of naming top-line locomotives after racehorses met with strong criticism from the distinguished technical journal *Diesel Railway Traction* towards the end of 1961, in a severely worded editorial under the heading: '*Is* Pinza *Good Enough?*'

'Apparently the naming policy', it began, 'is that applied to the well-known "Gresley A3 Pacific" steam locomotives, to which the names of celebrated racehorses were given. Celebrated racehorses are named before they become celebrated; the owner can choose anything he likes so long as it has not been used before and is not obscene. Yet often the name which gives pleasure, or "will do" as the foal is viewed is not that which will seem apposite as at a later stage the owner leads in his Derby winner. In the world of the Turf so many names have been used before that there is an admitted restriction on the present-day owner. No such restriction applies to the naming of locomotives. Names are not

entered in a stud book; names that have been used
before, and only recently, can be used again; and
indeed a name can be transferred from one locomotive to another—a practice by no means un-
common. Moreover a much more reasoned estimate can be made of future performance than in the
case of a foal. Perhaps it would not be wide of the
mark to say that the new "Deltics" form one of the
two aristocrats yet to be found among main line
diesel locomotive classes on British Railways. That
they should be named after something fleet of foot is
not unnatural; but even more natural and desirable,
is that they should be provided with names of dig-
nity and repute. *Hyperion* and *Persimmon*, yes—if
racehorse names *must* be used; but *Pinza*, no; that
could only be the prelude to *Pretty Polly* or *Spearmint*
or even to something like *Pronghorn* or *Puku* out of
the "blackbuck" series which still continue to
disgrace Edward Thompsons "B1" class steamers.
Surely there are 22 dignified and apposite names in
English history or English railway history, or words
in the English language, which are immediately
available, or which could be transferred from steam
locomotives shortly to be scrapped, and which
would eliminate all atmosphere of tote, turf, and
gamble from what should be the forefront of British
motive power.'

It seemed that serious note was taken of this
criticism because no more than eight of the 'Deltics'
received racehorse names. None of these, admittedly, would mean anything except to a racing man.
For the record the names were as follows:

D9001 *St Paddy*	D9012 *Crepello*
D9003 *Meld*	D9015 *Tulyar*
D9007 *Pinza*	D9018 *Ballymoss*
D9009 *Alycidon*	D9020 *Nimbus*

The fact that they were scattered about the
numerical range instead of consecutively, or
alphabetically suggests that the original intention
was to have all racehorse names; but early in 1962
the first locomotive of the class, D9000, was named
Royal Scots Grey, and thereafter the remaining units,
at varying intervals, all received regimental names.
Their performance was fully up to expectations
from the start, and thanks to the maintenance contract with English Electric there was no deterioration as time went on. This was all the more com-
mendable considering the planned utilisation of an
intensity quite without parallel at that time. I
became aware of it on the occasion of one of my
earliest footplate runs on one of these locomotives,
when I rode the 4 pm *Talisman* from Kings Cross to
Newcastle one evening, and then after a morning's
business on Tyneside I returned to the station to
catch the down *Flying Scotsman* to Edinburgh. To my
surprise it was hauled by the same 'Deltic' that I
had ridden down from London the previous evening. After arrival in Edinburgh it had taken the
11.50 pm 'sleeper' back to London, arriving at 6.40
am with comfortable time before starting north
again at 10 am with the 'Scotsman'.

It is worth recalling the mileages regularly
worked in the 22 diagrams allocated to the 'Deltic'
locomotives:

Shed	Diagram No	Weekly mileage
Kings Cross	1	4,060
Kings Cross	2	4,432
Kings Cross	3	4,182
Kings Cross	4	5,010
Kings Cross	5	4,968
Kings Cross	6	4,308
Kings Cross	7	4,472

Shed	Diagram No	Weekly mileage
Kings Cross	8	2,428
Gateshead	1	4,468
Gateshead	2	5,502
Gateshead	3	4,840
Gateshead	4	3,144
Gateshead	5	3,558
Gateshead	6	3,682
Haymarket	1	4,430
Haymarket	2	4,432
Haymarket	3	4,802
Haymarket	4	5,464
Haymarket	5	5,464
Haymarket	6	4,846
Haymarket	7	4,720
Haymarket	8	2,428

The above are remarkable figures, particularly those that involved mileages of more than 700 miles every 24 hours. The ingenuity with which they had been worked out, leaving approximate time for maintenance, and equally for periods of standing pilot is clearly apparent; and at the same time it must be emphasised that the programme was no pipe dream of a back-room planner, but a reality, continued month in, month out.

The details of one particular diagram were typical and are given below.

The following week a No 2 diagram was worked. It will be appreciated that such diagrams involved manning by many different crews, from different sheds, and it underlines the importance of the English Electric maintenance contract. I was accorded the privilege of many runs in the cabs of these splendid locomotives, and I found them uniformly good, and impressive in many ways other than that of sheer power output. When Charles Cock, General Manager of the traction department of English Electric read a paper before the Institution

Gateshead No 1 Diagram

Arrive		Depart	
	Newcastle	11.42 am	Sunday
5.38 pm	Kings Cross	8.20 pm	
2.05 am	Newcastle	2.17 am	Monday
4.40 am	Edinburgh	8.00 am	
10.01 am	Newcastle	10.04 am	
2.15 pm	Kings Cross	5.00 pm	
9.34 pm	Newcastle	light engine	
	Gateshead		
	MAINTENANCE		Tuesday
	Gateshead	light engine	
	Newcastle	10.15 am	
3.14 pm	Kings Cross	5.37 pm	
8.55 pm	Leeds	10.00 pm	
3.25 am	Kings Cross	8.00 am	Wednesday
12.16 pm	Newcastle	12.19 pm	
2.19 pm	Edinburgh	4.00 pm	
5.55 pm	Newcastle	5.58 pm	
10.00 pm	Kings Cross	1.00 am	Thursday
5.57 am	Newcaste		
	STAND PILOT		
	(8.0 am to 7.30 pm)		
	Newcastle	8.20 pm	
3.00 am	Kings Cross	9.05 am	Friday
1.47 pm	Newcastle	4.55 pm	
9.49 pm	Kings Cross		
	STAND PILOT		
	(1.00 pm Fri to 7.00 am Sat)		
	Kings Cross	7.45 am	Saturday
11.30 am	Leeds	2.10 pm	
6.12 pm	Kings Cross	11.35 pm	
4.17 am	Newcastle		Sunday
	STAND PILOT		
	(12.00 noon to 7.30 pm)		

The 'Deltic' No 55001 St Paddy, *emerging from Copenhagen Tunnel in June 1977, with the 09.00 express Kings Cross to Newcastle* (Brian Morrison).

of Electrical Engineers in December 1959 on experiences with the prototype 'Deltic', one of the troubles to which he referred was the vertical oscillation of the locomotive at speeds between 12 and 52 mph, particularly when accelerating rapidly. This was largely cured by the introduction of hydraulic shock absorbers between the equalised beams and the bogie frames. In the production batch of these locomotives the superstructure load was carried on four side bearers on each bolster and was transmitted through four nests of coil springs to two spring planks suspended by swing links from the bogie frame. Dampers were fitted between the bolster and the spring plank adjacent to each of the four nests of coil springs. From the bogie solebars the load was distributed through four pairs of coil springs to the equalising beams underslung from the axle boxes. The result, in the light of my own eventually extensive experience of riding on these locomotives, was an almost perfect ride at all speeds.

One of my first, and very impressive experiences was on the up *Heart of Midlothian* which I joined at York. When the accelerated service was first introduced an attempt was made to keep the loading of the fastest trains, particularly those with the six-hour schedule between Kings Cross and Edinburgh, down to a maximum of 11 coaches; but the locomotives soon displayed such a margin of power in hand that the traffic department began to add one or

two extras, at the time of heavy business, and on this trip of mine we had 13 on, totalling up to a gross trailing load of 530 tons. This, of course, would not have been regarded as anything out of the ordinary in the halcyon days of the 'Gresley A4 Pacifics', even on the schedule in operation when I made this particular trip. We were allowed 81½ minutes for the 82.7 miles to Grantham, and then 107½ minutes for the remaining 105.5 miles to Kings Cross. I have logged 'A4's to run from York to Grantham in 81 minutes, with loads as heavy as this, and to do the last stage in 102 minutes; but on this 'Deltic' occasion there were no fewer than four severe temporary speed restrictions in force, requiring reductions to 20 mph or less, not to mention one bad check for adverse signals and a late start of eight minutes.

At that time in the history of the East Coast route there remained not only all the permanent speed restrictions of steam days including 30 mph over Selby swingbridge, and 20 mph through Peterborough station, but there were lingerings of more recent track troubles, including a restriction to 60 mph, from over 80, at Muskham water troughs north of Newark, a restriction to 65 mph over the level fenland stretch south of Peterborough, and a general limit of 70 mph for some distance south of Knebworth. Yet despite all this hindrance we clocked into Kings Cross exactly on time. Allowing only for the six temporary checks, four for track repair work and two from adverse signals, the net running times were 74 minutes for the 82.7 miles from York to Grantham and 91½ minutes for the 105.5 miles to Kings Cross. This gave a net running average of 68 mph over the 188.2 miles from York. The maximum speed only briefly reached 90 mph twice on the journey, but the very rapid acceleration from speed restrictions was an impressive feature of the running. When the throttle was full open, and running at around 80 mph, the equivalent drawbar horsepower was about 2,750. It was an exhilarating trip not only in its display of complete mastery over a heavy load, but in the physical sense of power that it gave to its privileged visitor. I noted it first when we were no more than five miles out of York. Because of the need for moderate speed over Chaloners Whin Junction, and then over Naburn swing bridge, the locomotive was worked at first on no more than a moderate throttle opening, to restrain speed to a maximum of 60 mph; but once the tail of the train was over the bridge the throttle was opened to the full, and the surge forward could be felt in the cab. Never previously had I felt a positive thrust in my back, when in the second man's seat! In about three miles of roughly level track we were up to 84 mph. In years that followed we were to record numerous even more thrilling performances.

So far as maximum speeds were concerned, it was not often that one witnessed any excess over the official limit of 90 mph on the Great Northern Line in the early days of the 'Deltics'; but north of York, as early as December 1963 in *The Railway Magazine* I was able to set on record a run on which the 44.1 miles from Darlington to York scheduled in 37 minutes, start to stop, were actually run in 32 minutes 56 seconds, increasing the booked average speed of 71.5 mph to 80.5; and it was not until the train was past Northallerton, 14 miles on its way, that they *really* got going. That first 14 miles took 12¼ minutes; but then the ensuing 24.5 miles on to Beningbrough were covered at an average speed of 97.1 mph, with a maximum of 104 mph, and an average of exactly 100 mph for 16 miles south of Thirsk. In these early days of 'High Speed Trains', and continuous running at two miles a minute, the foregoing may not sound very wonderful; but in 1963 it was terrific, and the 'Deltics' were the first British locomotives to work up towards such standards.

Edinburgh Waverley, June 1977: the 16.00 to Kings Cross hauled by 'Deltic' No 55003 leaving with Class '47' diesel No 47432 standing on left (Brian Morrison).

Locomotive No 55005 The Prince of Wales Own Regiment of Yorkshire *at York prior to working a special train on November 1980* (L.P. Gates).

It is not generally known, however, that the English Electric Company also made a bid for entry to the 4,000 horsepower market, and that in 1966 a design was worked out for a 'Super-Deltic', of no less than 4,400 horsepower. It would have been slightly longer than *Kestrel*, with an overall length of 67 feet 6 inches over body, and the bogie pivot centres were to have been 42 feet 2 inches, against 37 feet 2 inches. But a notable feature was that the maximum axle-load was only 19 tons, against 21 tons in *Kestrel*, and that the total service weight was no more than 114 tons. It would have been essentially an express passenger, rather than a general service locomotive, and in view of the antipathy towards the 'Deltic' engine shown in some quarters on British Railways there is no doubt that the top management of the English Electric Company felt it was not worth going to the great expense of building a prototype which, unlike *Kestrel*, would not have had any interest for the export market. That it would have been an outstanding motive power unit there is no doubt.

6. The Indian summer of steam

While this third volume is essentially forward looking, and concerned primarily with a study and appraisal of the new power and assessments of its likely role in the future transportation network of this country, it would be graceless to let pass the opportunity to pay a final tribute to the system of traction that had served us so well for more than 130 years. This tribute, as it happens, does not by any means partake of pure nostalgia. Locomotives that originated from the major designs of the 'Big Four' of the Grouping Era were ending their working lives in a positive blaze of glory, while the work of S.O. Ell at Swindon, in postulating the principles of technical train timing, enabled comparisons of the maximum outputs of certain famous types to be made with far greater accuracy than was previously practicable. At the same time, as always when analysing steam locomotive performance, it was important to distinguish between transitory and sustained outputs. Ell supplemented the exhaustive series of tests he made on the one and only Class '8' 4-6-2 express locomotive in the British standard range, No 71000 *Duke of Gloucester*, by a comprehensive prediction of performance with various loads and various steaming rates over the entire distance between Euston and Carlisle; but while this was a highly ingenious and erudite exercise, from the practical viewpoint of running trains it had little value so far as engine No 71000 was concerned,

Below *The British Railways Class '8' 4-6-2 No 71000* Duke of Gloucester *trial running on the stationary test plant in Swindon Works* (British Railways).

because its road performance did not live up to theoretical predictions.

The engine which was hoped to be the climax of all British express passenger designs proved, unhappily, to be a great disappointment. To the surprise of the testing staff at Swindon, and to the sheer disbelief of the Derby drawing office, the boiler, which was based on that of the '7MT' 'Britannia', would not reach anything like the maximum steam rates attained by the latter; indeed its maximum was reached only at the expense of very heavy coal consumption. Swindon, with their wide experience in front-end design, felt that the draughting needed close examination; but the testing remit did not extend to this and, as the London Midland Region were anxious to have the engine back and put it into ordinary traffic, nothing further was done. It was put into the ordinary 'Pacific' link at Crewe North shed, and quickly gained a poor reputation as a heavy coal burner. It worked variously to London and to Carlisle, but not on the lengthy double-home turns to Glasgow and to Perth, involving through runs of 245 and 290 miles, which were regularly worked by the Stanier 'Princess Royal' and 'Duchess' Class engines. On one occasion, when I was privileged to ride in the dynamometer car on a test run from Swindon to Westbury, via Reading West, the performance of the engine was impressive to a degree, but in ordinary service my travelling experience was often of disappointing work and schedule time not maintained.

It was the pre-nationalisation designs that hit the

Opposite page top to bottom
The Duke of Gloucester *on a controlled road test with dynamometer car and load of 20 empty coaches from Swindon to Westbury via Reading West, here seen approaching Southcote Junction, in April 1955* (the late M.W. Earley).

The pioneer 'Castle' Class engine of the GWR, built 1923, No 4073 Caerphilly Castle *in her last days as a traffic department engine stationed at Bristol—she was the maker of many notable runs on the London expresses* (Kenneth H. Leech).

The GWR 'Kings', a memory of their pre-war zenith on the Cornish Riviera Express: the train in its post-nationalisation style with headboard and reporting number: engine No 6026 King John (the late M.W. Earley).

headlines in the last years of steam, albeit some of them, like the ex-Great Western 'King' Class 4-6-0s, incorporating certain modifications to design that had been made since 1948. In the very comprehensive series of tests undertaken at Swindon in 1953 with engine No 6001 *King Edward VII*, confirmed by dynamometer car trials on the road, both in that year and in 1955 between Paddington and Plymouth, Ell's exhaustive analysis of the results showed that, despite the magnificent performances obtained, the 'Kings' were nevertheless handicapped by excessive back pressure in the cylinders. The design dated back to 1927 and, although something had been done to improve the draughting experience with the testing of the BR 'Pacific', the *Duke of Gloucester* had suggested that use of a twin-orifice blastpipe and double chimney would greatly reduce the back pressure. Thus increasing the freedom to run at high speed while still maintaining a high rate of evaporation. The revised smokebox arrangement was fitted experimentally to engine No 6015 *King Richard III*, in the autumn of 1955, and proved extremely successful, so much so that rumours of extremely high speeds

Left *The 'Kings' modernised: engine No 6021* King Richard II *with twin-orifice blast pipe and double chimney in 1962* (Ivo Peters).

Below left *Dynamometer car test with double-chimneyed 'King' Class 4-6-0 No 6002* King William IV *on the 15.30 ex-Paddington, 'West of England' express approaching Reading* (the late M.W. Earley).

Right *The double-chimneyed 'King' that holds the official speed record of 108 mph, No 6015* King Richard III *climbing the Bruton bank with an up 'West of England' express* (Ivo Peters).

soon began to circulate. One ultra-ardent Great Western fan was talking of maximum rates up to 130 mph!

The origin of this story lay in an experimental trip on the 'Cornish Riviera Express' on which Ell's chief assistant, H. Tichener, and Chief Running Inspector W. Andress rode on the footplate of engine No 6015 and clocked, among other impressive figures, a maximum speed of 108 mph. What was more important was that the modified engine was showing a considerably reduced coal consumption. But it might have been even better. The entire front end of many engines of the class needed renewal and new cylinders with new front portions of the main frames were to be fitted. Ell went so far as to recommend to Alfred Smeddle, then Chief Mechanical Engineer, that instead of merely putting on cylinders that were a straight replacement of the old ones the cylinders should be redesigned according to the latest practice, with internally streamlined ports and passages, as had been done on the 'Gresley' and 'Stanier' 'Pacifics'. It would have involved making new patterns; but, although Smeddle himself was keenly in favour of it, authorisation for the expense involved was not forthcoming in view of the impending launching of the great Modernisation Plan, and the likelihood that steam traction would be eliminated in ten years at the most. Nevertheless, conversion of all the 'King' Class engines to the twin-orifice blastpipe arrangement and double chimney could be cheaply done, and in the event it proved well worth while.

In May 1956 Mr Smeddle invited me to accompany him in the dynamometer car on some test runs to be conducted upon engine No 6002 *King*

William IV, which had been fitted with the improved front end. The results on the West of England main line between Paddington and Plymouth made a very interesting comparison with those obtained from a 'Duchess' Class 'Pacific' from the London Midland Region which had been tested roughly a year earlier. Both engines were loaded equally, and kept good time. The following are the average results.

Region	Western	London Midland
Engine No	6,002	46,237
Trailing ton miles (per trip)	99,140	100,995
Coal per trailing ton miles	0.110	0.133
Coal per dhp	3.41	3.82

From this it would appear that the double-chimneyed 'King' had a very slight edge over the 'Duchess', though as it will be shown later when it came to maximum output the advantage was with the 'Pacific'. Some of the finest running that I noted personally with the 'King' during these dynamometer car trials was on the 3 pm express from Birmingham to Paddington, with a gross trailing load of 470 tons. The interest on this run was also to see the relatively low back pressure in the cylinders at high speed, notably no more than 2 lb per square inch, when we were doing 86 mph near Blackthorn.

An even finer run came to my notice in 1963, with engine No 6018 *King Henry VI* when that engine had already been withdrawn from ordinary service, but was brought out to work a special train for the Stephenson Locomotive Society, a round trip from Birmingham to Swindon and back, outward via Greenford, and return via Oxford. On the

Birmingham direct line, via Bicester, some very fast running was made between Banbury and a lengthy signal stop outside High Wycombe. After recovering from a speed restriction, the 30.9 miles of hilly road from Aynho Junction to the summit on the crest of the Chiltern Hills at Saunderton took no more than 27½ minutes, with a maximum speed of 88 mph at Blackthorn and a minimum, after seven miles of steep climbing, of 55 mph; all this with a gross trailing load of 440 tons. After the High Wycombe stop the downhill speed from Beaconsfield was even faster, reaching 91 mph at Denham. At the time of the 1953–5 tests on the single-chimneyed engines it was shown that the maximum drawbar horsepower that could be sustained at 70 mph when fired at a rate that needed two firemen, namely 4,000 lb of coal per hour, was 1,200; on the 1956 tests with a double-chimneyed engine, and again on this very fine run of 1963, the drawbar horsepower was more than 1,450. How much better still might it have been if Smeddle had been allowed to redesign the cylinders!

On the Southern it was the constant aim of the operating department to maintain the same regularity in passenger trains running with steam as with electric traction, and opportunities for display of any exceptional performance were consequently few. Reference was made in Volume 2 of this work to the insistence of the operating department on reducing the load of the 'Atlantic Coast Express' by one coach to compensate for the inclusion of the dynamometer car in the train when one of the rebuilt 'Merchant Navy' Class 4-6-2s was being tested. When I was writing the monthly articles on 'British Locomotive Practice and Performance', in *The Railway Magazine*, one of my most regular and valued correspondents spent a week of his annual

leave travelling every day by the up 'Atlantic Coast Express' from Exeter to Waterloo, and the outcome of this painstaking analysis was to reveal the uniformity of the running. The same engine worked through in every case, but while the same driver was on duty on every one of the six days from Salisbury to Waterloo, there was a different crew from Exmouth Junction shed every day of the week between Exeter and Salisbury. The uniformity of the running was all the more remarkable on that account, particularly so in that four different locomotives were involved.

The Bulleid 'Pacifics', both before and after their rebuilding, were very fast engines, and while Bulleid himself was still there I have often wondered if any thought was ever given to making an all-out speed record with one of them. The Southern had a magnificently straight and easily declining stretch of line between Litchfield tunnel and the outskirts of Eastleigh which would have been a good place to 'have a go'. No doubt the operating people, not to mention the civil engineer(!) would have vetoed it, if they had known in advance, as Gresley's historic exploit with *Mallard* would have been had it not been disguised behind the pretence of making brake tests. But officially inspired or not—almost certainly not!—the Southern did have one glorious fling on a day in 1961 when the 'Atlantic Coast Express' for some reason got a late start from Salisbury, and despite a severe permanent way check near Tisbury ran the 75.8 miles to Sidmouth Junction in 68¼ minutes, start to stop. Schedule time was then 75 minutes, and the net gain allowing for the check was no less than ten minutes. The scheduled average speed of 60.7 mph was thus stepped up to exactly 70, and such were some of the intermediate details that when I published the run in March 1962 it was

thought advisable to allow the actual engine to remain anonymous lest the considerable excesses over the limits of line maximum should land the driver in trouble. Although this line is very hilly the alignment was absolutely first class, and the friend who expertly logged the running details referred also to the very smooth riding of the coaches, even at the highest speeds.

It can now be revealed that the engine was No 35028 *Clan Line*, the member of the class that has been preserved and maintained in working order, and has done a considerable amount of running with charter trains in recent years. To appreciate the remarkable quality of this run on the 'Atlantic Coast Express' the gradients of the line must be mentioned. In profile they resemble a greatly enlarged saw-toothed effect, with the gradients getting longer and steeper the farther west one travels: 1 in 145 up to Semley; 1 in 100 to Milepost 107½; 1 in 100 from Templecombe to '113½'; 1 in 140 up Sutton Bingham bank; 1 in 80 from Crewkerne up to '133¼', and finally the tremendous Honiton Incline, at 1 in 80 continuously from Seaton Junction to the tunnel entrance at Milepost 152½. Were it not that absolutely full speed could be run on all the intervening descents, so working up impetus to charge these heavy gradients, it would not have been possible to schedule such an average speed as 60.7 mph from Salisbury to Sidmouth Junction. The accompanying log shows

Above *The 'Schools' Class three-cylinder 4-4-0s of the Southern were still doing some outstanding work in the Indian Summer of steam: here, engine No 30916* Whitgift, *near Betchworth, is working a through express from Ramsgate to Wolverhampton* (Derek Cross).

Left *Southern Region: rebuilt 'Merchant Navy' Class 4-6-2 No 35020* Bibby Line, *leaving Basingstoke, westbound on a dynamometer car test run using the Swindon car and testing staff* (the late M.W. Earley).

Right *Southern: an up West of England express leaving Buckhorn Weston Tunnel, near Gillingham, hauled by rebuilt 'Merchant Navy' Class 4-6-2 No 35016* Elders Fyffes (Ivo Peters).

Above *The down Atlantic Coast Express at Worting Junction, west of Basingstoke, hauled by the 4-6-2* Clan Line, *now preserved, which holds the speed record for the class, of 104 mph* (Derek Cross).

Left *One of the rebuilt 'Merchant Navy' Class 4-6-2s on the all-Pullman 'Golden Arrow' boat express from Victoria to Dover.*

Below *As befits their distinguished role in past years 14 of the Stanier 'Black Five' 4-6-0s have been preserved. In this photograph No 45171 is on a typical mixed traffic duty of the last years, hauling an express freight train up the Shap Incline* (E.D. Bruton).

how that scheduled speed was stepped up to 70 mph. (The official line maximum speed was, by the way, 85 mph.)

Southern Region: Atlantic Coast Express

Load: 12 coaches, 425 tons behind tender
Engine: rebuilt 'Merchant Navy' Class 4-6-2
No 35028 *Clan Line*

Distance (miles)		Time m s	Average speeds point to point (mph)
0.0	SALISBURY	0 00	
2.5	Wilton	6 13	24.1
8.2	Dinton	12 25	55.1
—		perm way slack	—
12.5	Tisbury	18 36	41.6
17.5	Semley	23 36	60.0
21.6	GILLINGHAM	26 51	75.7
28.4	TEMPLECOMBE	31 40	84.5
29.9	Milepost 113½	32 56	71.7
34.5	Sherborne	36 17	82.4
39.1	YEOVIL JUNCTION	39 17	92.0
41.3	Sutton Bingham	40 52	83.3
47.9	Crewkerne	45 37	83.3
49.7	Milepost 133¼	47 12	68.2
55.9	Chard Junction	51 43	82.5
61.0	AXMINSTER	54 52	97.2
62.9	Milepost 146¼	55 59	101.9
64.3	SEATON JUNCTION	56 55	90.0
67.0	Milepost 150½	59 02	73.8
69.0	Milepost 152½	61 03	60.0
—		eased tunnel	
70.0	Milepost 153½	62 17	48.6
71.2	Honiton	63 32	57.5
75.9	SIDMOUTH JUNCTION	68 18	—

It was after slowing down for the temporary speed restriction between Dinton and Tisbury, and losing about 3¼ minutes in consequence, that the driver and fireman of the *Clan Line* really began to pile it on. The gradients between Tisbury and the first summit point at Semley are steeply rising, yet here the average speed was 60 mph and then over that saw-tooth profile onwards to Honiton tunnel the average speeds tell their own tale. The maximum between Sherborne and Yeovil Junction was 95 mph, but it was after clearing the 1 in 80 bank from Crewkerne up to Milepost 133¼, at a minimum of 65 mph, that the most tremendous burst of high-speed running developed. Here it is downhill for 13 miles, and just below Axminster they reached 104 mph. The momentum from this took them up the bank to Honiton tunnel at a speed that so far as records go was quite unprecedented with a load of 425 tons. But approaching the tunnel, at Milepost 152½, and still on the 1 in 80 gradient, the driver eased the engine, to lessen the chance of incurring a heavy slip in the tunnel itself. In years before the

Second World War when the 'King Arthur' Class 4-6-0s were in their prime, and doing magnificent work over this route, I had four instances of what was then regarded as absolutely top-class work, and with similar loads to that hauled by the *Clan Line* the speeds at the entrance to Honiton tunnel were 19, 25, 23, and 26½ mph. On this outstanding run of 1961 the speed at the same location was 59 miles per hour—a phenomenal Southern contribution to the Indian summer of steam!

The West Coast main line, and particularly that part of it south of Crewe, became the most seriously affected by the forthcoming modernisation programme of all the principal main routes in Great Britain. In readiness for electrification and the accelerated service that was planned, the entire road bed had to be renewed, and the whole operation was more than once referred to as building a new railway above the track of the old one. Extensive permanent way works involved lengthy sections of restricted speed running, and express train schedules had to be decelerated. The year 1960 marked the end of old-time steam running south of Crewe, but an attempt was made nevertheless to avoid too appreciable a slowing down of the Anglo-Scottish services. To afford opportunity for recovery of time north of the areas most deeply involved with civil engineering works the drastic step was taken of limiting the loads of the principal day Anglo-Scottish expresses, the 'Royal and Midday Scots' and the 'Caledonian', to no more than eight vehicles, which, with the 'Duchess' Class locomotives, provided an ample margin of power for rapid climbing of the North Country banks. But, before the incidence of engineering works compelled deceleration, some remarkably fine work was being done on the Liverpool-London expresses, some of it, indeed, considerably better than average pre-war running on these same trains. It was interesting also in the frequent use of the 'Princess Royal' Class of 'Pacific' engine, turn and turn about with the later 'Duchess' Class.

On the evening express from Liverpool to Euston, which in post-war years was named 'The Red Rose', the pre-war record for the run was held by the pioneer 'Stanier Pacific' No 6200 *The Princess Royal*. At that time the train stopped at Willesden Junction with a time allowance of 142 minutes start to stop for the 152.7 miles from Crewe. On this occasion, with a load of 15 coaches, the run was made in 129½ minutes, an average speed of 70.7 mph. In 1959–60 the train ran non-stop from Crewe to Euston with a time allowance of 170 minutes for 158.1 miles; but just prior to that the timing was 155 minutes. When delays occurred and engines were still in reasonably good condition drivers were still

Engine No	Name	Load, gross trailing (tons)	Actual overall time	Net time (min)	Net av speed (mph)
			m s		
46250	*City of Lichfield*	460	149 21	146½	64.8
46239	*City of Chester*	490	152 15	147	64.5
46208	*Princess Helena Victoria*	490	145 36	139	68.2
46209	*Princess Beatrice*	490	153 09	140½	67.4
46203	*Princess Margaret Rose*	495	159 50	144	65.8
46253	*City of St Albans*	500	153 25	144¾	65.6
46237	*City of Bristol*	505	158 39	144	65.8
46237	*City of Bristol*	550	160 34	146¾	64.6

running up to their old standards of speed in recovering lost time. I have before me details of eight runs on the 'Red Rose' with gross trailing loads of between 460 and 550 tons, which gave the following results:

All the foregoing involved absolutely first-class running, but it is remarkable that the two with the fastest net times, and another with 'equal third' time, engines 46208, 46209 and 46203, were all of the 'Princess Royal' Class.

When it comes to comparing these results with the record run of No 6200 on June 27 1935, one could reckon that a stop could be made at Willesden Junction in about seven minutes less than at Euston, which would bring the equivalent time of the fastest post-war run to 132 minutes. But while those on No 6200, who had R.A. Riddles riding on the footplate with them, were out to break records from the start, it was only after Rugby that the drivers of Nos 46208 and 46209 went really all-out,

LMR: Rugby–Willesden Junction

Run No		**1**		**2**		**3**	
Engine No		6200		46208		46209	
Engine name		*The Princess Royal*		*Princess Helena Victoria*		*Princess Beatrice*	
Load, tons gross		475		490		490	
Distance		Actual	Av speed	Actual	Av speed	Actual	Av speed
(miles)		m s	mph	m s	mph	m s	mph
0.0	RUGBY (passing)	0 00	—	0 00	—	0 00	—
7.3	Welton	7 29	58.5	7 58	55.0	8 54	48.6
12.9	Weedon	11 38	81.0	12 31	74.0	13 31	72.5
19.8	BLISWORTH	16 53	78.8	17 47	78.7	18 52	77.3
22.7	Roade	19 18	72.0	20 11	72.5	21 19	71.0
30.2	Wolverton	25 01	78.8	25 56	78.2	26 48	82.0
35.9	BLETCHLEY	29 34	75.2	30 29	75.0	31 03	80.5
50.9	Tring	42 07	71.7	43 14	70.5	42 53	76.0
61.6	Kings Langley	50 16	78.7	51 25	78.5	50 43	82.0
65.1	WATFORD JUNCTION	52 46	84.0	54 07	78.1	53 03	90.0
69.3	Hatch End	55 54	80.3	57 15	80.5	55 56	87.5
74.5	Wembley	59 43	81.6	60 56	84.6	59 24	89.8
77.2	WILLESDEN	62 24	stop	62 51	pass	61 10	pass
82.6	EUSTON			70 04		68 50	
Average Blisworth–Wembley mph		80.4		79.7		84.6	

Maximum equivalent dhp: 'Duchess' Class

Ref No	Engine No & Name	Load, gross trailing tons	Locality	Gradient 1 in	Speed*	Estimated edhp
1	46221 *Queen Elizabeth*	280	Grayrigg	104	66½	2,150
2	46247 *City of Liverpool*	295	Shap Incline	75	60	2,600
3	46228 *Duchess of Rutland*	570	Shap Incline	75	40	2,360
4	46224 *Princess Alexandra*	465	Beattock bank	75	40	2,335
5	46232 *Duchess of Montrose*	510	Beattock bank	75	35	2,045
6	46234 *Duchess of Atholl*	510	Hatch End	335	67	1,700
7	46247 *City of Liverpool*	355	Ribblehead	100	56¾	2,200
8	46251 *City of Nottingham*	465	Southbound to Beattock	various	64-74	2,200

*Not necessarily sustained

---

and the times from Rugby to Wembley make an interesting comparison. The speed restriction through Rugby was then 40 mph, and apart from a rather slower recovery from it there was little between engines 6200 and 46208 between Weedon

Above left *One of the two preserved examples of the ex-LMS 'Princess Royal' Class 4-6-2s, No 46203* Princess Margaret Rose, *on the morning Birmingham to Glasgow and Edinburgh express, at Tebay water troughs, in 1952* (E.D. Bruton).

Left *'The Royal Scot' about the time of nationalisation with the 'Duchess' Class locomotive No 6245* City of London *in the lined-black livery of the last days of the LMS. The train is taking water at Bushey troughs* (British Railways).

and Wembley. There would have been even less had not the driver of the latter engine eased down markedly before Watford tunnel. The speed was 91 mph at Kings Langley and 90 again at Wembley. On the third run the train had been heavily checked by signal before Rugby, and entered upon the 'race' for Euston at little more than 20 mph; but from Blisworth onwards the running was the finest I have ever known, with three separate maxima of 90 mph or more, and the magnificent uphill average of 76 mph from Bletchley to Tring. The minimum speed here was 71 mph and it was followed by a terrific downhill dash with an average of 89.2 mph over the 19.1 miles from Hemel Hempstead to Willesden. The maximum speeds were 96 mph at Kings

Langley, and 93 mph at Wembley; all this with a load not far short of 500 tons! This would have involved a continuous output of about 1,400 equivalent drawbar horsepower for 40 minutes on end, a notably high figure at a speed of 85 mph.

This order of output was substantially exceeded in certain transitory efforts by the 'Duchess' Class engines, principally in making big uphill efforts in the North Country. Details of eight notable instances are tabulated herewith. Nos 1 and 2 occurred in the very last years of steam on the West Coast route when the loads were limited to eight coaches. That with the *City of Liverpool* was an absolutely sustained minimum speed of 60 mph up the Shap Incline, while No 3, with an exceptionally heavy load was the peak output of a high transitory effort lasting a little more than five minutes. No 6, the only one not in the North Country, was on the down 'Midday Scot', and was part of a spell of working sustained for nearly half an hour between Willesden and Tring. I was on the footplate, and saw that boiler pressure and water level were constantly maintained throughout. The second run with the *City of Liverpool*, No 7, was with a charter train over the Midland line, on which a very vigorous ascent was made from Settle Junction to Blea Moor. The last run of the group was on the southbound 'Midday Scot' when the train had been delayed in the early stages of the run and had passed Carstairs nearly eight minutes late. An outstanding effort was made uphill over the last eight miles to Beattock summit with the result shown in the table; not only this, but an exceptionally fast descent of the Beattock bank and a similar continuation resulted in the train being practically on time by Lockerbie. The average speed over the 19.6 miles from Greskine intermediate box to Lockerbie station was 90.5 mph, with a maximum of 105 mph.

These runs, involving such inspiring efforts,

when steam traction was being phased out, and many of the locomotives were not in the very best condition, provide remarkable examples of what the largest and most powerful express passenger classes could do when vigorously and expertly driven and fired. So far as the 'Duchess' Class locomotives were concerned, despite the criticism of their design so surprisingly made by E.S. Cox, and commented upon in Volume 2 of this work, their boilers were exceptionally free steaming, while the firemen were helped in two ways in meeting the needs for fuel. The tenders were equipped with steam operated coal pushers, so that the labour of getting coal forward from the back of the tender was eliminated; in addition the grates, though large, were relatively easy to fire. Heavy charges of coal, fed successively under the door, were spread evenly over the sloping grate by the riding action of the locomotive, thus obviating the need for precise placing of successive shovelfuls, which greatly increased the labour of firing on so many other large modern locomotives. A point that had to be carefully watched on the 'Duchess' Class engines was the water supply. They steamed so freely that a careless fireman could waste a great deal of steam (and water) through blowing off steam through safety valves; and in such cases I

have known additional stops needed to take on more water.

With the 'Duchess' Class locomotives one experience of my own, in the very sunset of the steam era, will always occupy an outstanding place in my memory. By the summer of 1963 the diesels had taken over all the principal express train workings between Euston and Glasgow, and in my regular travelling I was taking every opportunity to ride in the drivers' cabs, and generally get the 'feel' of the new power. The locomotive authorities were certainly generous enough in giving the necessary permissions. South of Crewe, by that time, the amount of permanent way working, with occasional diversions via Northampton, and occasional slow-line running on the quadruple tracked sections involved delay. But north of Crewe things were still fairly clear, and having some business in Glasgow I obtained an engine pass for the 'Midday Scot', hoping that if, as expected, delays would cause some loss of time to Crewe, there would be a chance of some fast running in recovery afterwards. What

neither I nor anyone else expected, however, was that on arrival at Crewe there was a slight defect on our diesel, but one which nevertheless necessitated its removal from the train. While there were plenty of diesels in the vicinity none was immediately available, and to minimise delay in getting the train away again the locomotive controller gave us the first thing that was ready, a steam 'Pacific', the *Duchess of Rutland*.

The fresh driver and fireman, who were to take the train through to Glasgow, were very upset. Knowing the condition into which so many steam locomotives had deteriorated by that time, the driver told the controller he would not be responsible if they lost a lot of time. The inspector who had accompanied me down from Euston asked if I wished to continue on the footplate, because I was hardly dressed for riding steam; but I decided to go through with it, and he produced an overall 'slop' to cover up my ordinary clothes. When I climbed aboard, and stowed myself in the right-hand corner of the cab, if anyone had told me I was

about to log the fastest run I had ever yet made from Crewe to Carlisle I am afraid I should have told him not to be silly. Yet so it turned out. The engine, despite the prevailing conditions, proved to be in good shape; the crew, Messrs Purcell and Keen of Crewe North shed were a grand pair, and to crown it all we had an absolutely clear road. Only at the final approach to Carlisle did we sight an adverse signal, and then it cost us a mere half-minute in running. The log of the journey gives no more than a background to a most exhilarating experience:

4:04 pm Crewe to Carlisle

Distance miles		Schedule (min)	Actual m	s
0.0	Crewe	0	0	00
24.1	Warrington	23½	23	05
35.8	Wigan	35½	34	32
51.0	Preston	53½	50	46
72.0	Lancaster	75½	71	31
78.3	Carnforth	81	76	40
91.1	Oxenholme	94	89	05
104.2	Tebay	111½	104	30
109.7	Shap Summit	120	111	59
123.2	Penrith	133	125	00
141.1	Carlisle	151	141	30

The load also was no featherweight, being 12 of the latest coaches, well filled, a gross trailing load of 455 tons behind the tender.

In other publications I have described this grand run in extensive technical detail. It did not at any time involve any gargantuan outputs of power such as those tabulated earlier in this chapter; but it was a joyous experience, as much for the driver and fireman as far me, in being able to win back so much of the time lost by the unexpected engine change at Crewe. So far as individual feats of performance were concerned, our maximum speed before Warrington was 77½ mph; we ran at 77 mph on dead-level track between Preston and Lancaster, and on the mountain section our minimum speeds were 40 mph at Grayrigg and 30 at Shap Summit. The maximum for the whole journey, 80 mph between Penrith and Carlisle on falling gradients, was of course easy to attain. It was not until the Class '47' and '50' diesels came upon the scene, with an engine horsepower of 2,750, that I recorded a faster overall time from Crewe to Carlisle, and the circumstances in which this truly splendid steam run was made rendered it particularly memorable.

Turning finally to locomotives of the East Coast route it is a fitting acknowledgement of the fame achieved by the Class 'A4' streamlined 'Pacifics' that no fewer than six, out of the class total of 34, should be preserved, in various parts of the world. The first of those decked in Garter Blue for working the Coronation train in 1937, the *Dominion of Canada*, is appropriately in the Railway Museum at Delson, near Montreal, while the one named after

The southbound 'Elizabethan', non-stop from Edinburgh to Kings Cross leaving Peascliff Tunnel north of Grantham, hauled by 'A4' Class 'Pacific' No 60011 Empire of India *(the late M.W. Earley).*

the great wartime leader *Dwight D. Eisenhower* is in the USA, at Green Bay, Wisconsin. Two others, *Bittern*, and the *Union of South Africa*, are treasured possessions at Dinting, and the Lochty Railway, in Fife; but the most travelled of them, so far as operational mileage since preservation is concerned, is that named after Sir Nigel himself and happily carrying the original number, 4498. But it is with their last days in regular revenue-earning service, rather than preservation, that I am concerned in this chapter, and it must be admitted that the most famous of them all, *Mallard*, was at one time something of a controversial engine. Her achievements, not forgetting her vicissitudes, were variously regarded: with the utmost enthusiasm by the Gresley fans; with thinly veiled derision by those whose partisan sentiments lay elsewhere; and with intense interest by those who probed deeply into the whys and wherefores of the mechanical behaviour of locomotives.

That *Mallard*'s world-record breaking flight in July 1938 ended in complete failure of the machinery could be put down to the extreme conditions to which it was subjected; but when, much against the advice of those who then knew best, she was put on to represent the Eastern Region in the Locomotive Interchange Trials of 1948, and suf-

The 'A4' named after the designer before withdrawal for preservation Sir Nigel Gresley, *then numbered 60007, at Grantham, after having worked 'The Northumbrian' from Kings Cross* (Kenneth H. Leech).

fered two complete failures on the road, the 'Ranks of Tuscany' were ready enough to jeer openly. It seemed to justify the arguments that had been put forward in the anti-Gresley campaign waged during the time of his immediate successor on the LNER. But after a speed during which both 'A3' and 'A4' 'Pacifics' were under something of a cloud, the arrival of a 'new broom' at the head of affairs in Doncaster, and the application of precision methods in the repair and resetting of the conjugated valve motion for the inside cylinder on these engines, wrought a positive transformation and both classes saw steam out on the East Coast route in a blaze of glory. There are many points to be recorded in a later chapter of this book which deals with the general subject of steam locomotive preservation, but just now it is their ordinary working life, and its conclusion that claims attention.

In those closing years *Silver Link, Mallard, Sir Nigel Gresley,* not to mention the non-streamlined *Flying Scotsman, Papyrus* and others were much in demand for specially chartered trains, and many spectacular performances were put up. But the ultimate in 'A4' 'Pacific' running came on an otherwise ordinary occasion, when *Mallard* herself was on the 2 pm Anglo-Scottish express from Kings Cross. There were no special preparations, no inspector riding on the footplate, and the engine crew did not know that an expert recorder was travelling on the train. He, in turn, did not even know the names of the driver and fireman. What transpired was the result of devotion to duty by a keen crew handling an engine that was still, in 1963, in superb condition. *Mallard*

Left *'The Elizabethan' nearing the end of its northbound non-stop run, near Monktonhall Junction hauled by the 'A4 Pacific' now preserved on the Lochty private railway, No 60009* Union of South Africa (E.D. Bruton).

Below The Flying Scotsman *in her penultimate state as a regular traffic engine, before fitting of twin-orifice blast pipe* (British Railways).

Right *The northbound 'Elizabethan' crossing the swing bridge at Selby on the one-time main line, now no longer used. The locomotive is the 'A4 Pacific' No 60017* Silver Fox (Leslie Overend).

was, in fact, finally withdrawn from service not long after this run. The train was then allowed 111 minutes, start to stop, for the 105.5 miles from Kings Cross to Grantham, and on this particular day the load was one of 11 coaches, 390 tons tare, and about 415 tons with passengers and luggage. Before the start it would have been known to the crew that two severe speed restrictions for permanent way work would have to be observed, both in fast-running locations, and that harder running than normal would be needed if Grantham was to be reached on time; but what they did not expect was a dead stand, in the face of adverse signals, for nearly 2½ minutes at Langley Junction, between Knebworth and Stevenage. As a result the train passed Hitchin 4½ minutes late, and with both the expected speed restrictions still to come.

A characteristic spell of 'A4' running followed, on the generally favourable stretch north of Hitchin, and here the 19.8 miles on to St Neots were covered at an average speed of 84.2 mph. Then came the first of the engineering speed restrictions, to 18 mph; but, although the recovery was brisk, and a maximum of 84 mph was clocked up descending the Abbots Ripton bank, speed was then restricted to 60 mph over the Fenland stretch, and the approach to Peterborough was hindered by another signal check. So, despite the enterprising work that had gone before, Peterborough itself was passed three minutes late, in 83 minutes for the 76.4 miles from Kings Cross, and with the worst of the temporary speed restrictions to come—a lengthy 20 mph just when speed would be piling on to get some impetus to climb the long bank to Stoke Tunnel. It was of

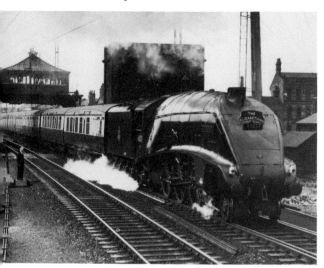

time, with 29.1 miles to go, most of it uphill, and a speed restriction intermediately that was going to cost at least 2½ minutes in running.

Whatever fame *Mallard* may have achieved on her lightning downhill dash in 1938 I feel it was completely surpassed by the superlative performance of these unknown footplate men on that day in 1963, and it was fortunate beyond measure that so critically expert a recorder was travelling in the train. On the vital uphill length he was clocking every milepost, and the times from Peterborough onwards are tabulated below.

Above Little Bytham on the continuous gradient of 1 in 200 speed was being sustained absolutely at 80 mph, a tremendous effort that involved an equivalent drawbar horsepower of 2,450, surpassed only slightly, and on a very few occasions by the maximum achievements of the LMS 'Duchess' Class engines, which had the advantage of a rather higher nominal tractive effort. It was fitting that in this Indian summer of steam it should have been *Mallard*, of all engines, to blazon such a record on the roll of fame, to match her earlier world record for maximum speed.

course in coming down this same gradient that *Mallard* had been pounded up to 126 mph just quarter of a century earlier. Now she had only 28 minutes left, if Grantham was to be reached on

Distance from Kings Cross miles		Schedule time (min)	Actual time m s	Speeds (by chronograph) mph
76.4	PETERBOROUGH (pass)	80	83 00	20*
79.5	Werrington Junc	85	87 22	62
—			pw slack	20*
84.8	Tallington		94 11	69
88.6	Essendine	94	97 16	78
92.2	Little Bytham		99 58	82
96.0	Milepost 96		102 45	80
97.1	Corby Glen		103 34	82
100.1	Stoke Box	105	105 51	78
102.0	Milepost 102		107 18	83
105.5	GRANTHAM (arr)	111	110 39	—

*Speed restrictions

7. The main line electrics

The Kent Coast electrification, provided for in the Modernisation Plan, was the first on the Southern Region, or for that matter on its predecessor the Southern Railway, to provide for the complete elimination of steam traction. While in keeping with foregoing practice it could be anticipated that all the regular passenger services of both local and main line categories would eventually be maintained by multiple-unit trains, the important Continental services via Folkestone and Dover were in a different class, particularly in regard to the heavy through freight service operated via the Train Ferry routes. At the outset of the Modernisation Plan it was therefore determined that provision would have to be made for the operation of a number of trains of heavy formation, passenger and freight, by electric locomotives. There was, of course, no question of departing from the existing system of electric traction, which had been standard on the Southern for so many years; and with dc traction and third-rail current collection there would necessarily be many places with gaps in the conductor rails. This factor, which did not affect multiple-unit trains because of the wide spacing apart of the pick-up shoes, had already been faced in the electric locomotives built for the Newhaven services, and is described in Volume 2 of this work, Chapter 11. The principle of having a booster set, with a heavy flywheel with enough stored energy to keep the booster set running when the locomotive was passing over gaps in the conductor rails, had proved successful enough to be adopted for the new locomotives proposed for the Kent Coast electrification. But in the short space of time that had elapsed since

O.V.S. Bulleid and Alfred Raworth had produced CC-1, for the Newhaven route, a vast amount of technical evolution had taken place and, whereas the earlier locomotives had a nominal horsepower of about 1,500 and weighed 99½ tons, the new requirement was for 2,500 horsepower. Yet S.B. Warder, Chief Electrical Engineer of the British Transport Commission, and W.J.A. Sykes, Chief Mechanical and Electrical Engineer of Southern Region, produced between them a locomotive of the B-B type to do the job, which had an all-up weight of only 77 tons. At the time of their introduction, at the end of 1958, the new Southern locomotives of the 'E5000' series were by far and away the most powerful single units running on British Railways. In making this assertion, and having regard to the nominal rated horsepower of the Southern 'E5000' Class which is only 2,500 against the 3,300 horsepower of a 'Deltic', some reference is needed to the hard realities of available horsepower at the drawbar at varying train speeds.

The accompanying diagram has been prepared to show the comparative performance of various well-known steam, diesel, and electric locomotives. In the first two cases the graphs are based on data obtained in dynamometer car and stationary plant testing by British Railways; the electric graphs relating the original Bulleid-Raworth 'CC' Class No 20003 to the new 2,500 hp B-B are based on data supplied to me by Mr Sykes, and it was made clear to me that the rated horsepower bears no relation to the actual drawbar horsepower developed on the road. Whereas the actual dhp of a diesel-electric is usually not more than about 70 or 75 per cent of the

Left *Southern Region: One of the 'E5000' Class 2,500 hp electric locomotives of 1958, No E5002, on a Charing Cross to Folkestone and Dover express near Tonbridge (British Railways).*

Right *The all-Pullman 'Golden Arrow' continental boat express for Dover Marine, near Hildenborough hauled by electric locomotive No E5015 (original numbering) (British Railways).*

Top right *Southern Region: 750v ac electric locomotive 2,500 hp side elevation.*

Above right *Graphs showing equivalent drawbar horsepower plotted against speed for steam, diesel and electric locomotives.*

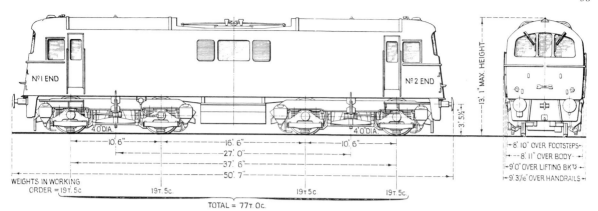

NO1 END NO2 END

4'0"DIA. 4'0"DIA.

WEIGHTS IN WORKING
ORDER = 19T. 5c. 19T. 5c. 19T 5c. 19T. 5c.

TOTAL = 77T. 0c.

13' 1" MAX. HEIGHT

3' 5½"

10'.6" 16'.6" 10'.6"
27'.0"
37'.6"
50'.7"

8'.10" OVER FOOTSTEPS
8'.11" OVER BODY
9'0" OVER LIFTING BKTs
9'.3/16" OVER HANDRAILS

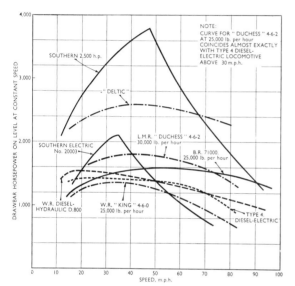

rated value, with electric motors the power rating is calculated on temperature rise, and it depends upon how hot one is prepared for the motor to run. During a test run with one of the new Southern locomotives, on which a train of 695 tons was taken up the 1 in 132 gradient eastward of Canterbury at a sustained speed of 60 mph(!), the equivalent drawbar horsepower was 2,920, or 17 per cent *greater* than the nominal power of 2,500. In explanation of the rather unusual shape of the electric power curves in the diagram, the torque on the road wheels remains constant during the period of acceleration, while by the stepping process on the controller more and more resistances are being cut out. On the new Southern locomotives the climax was reached at about 48 mph after which, with all resistances cut out and control changed over to weak-field, the edhp falls rapidly. But at that peak it was no less than 3,800.

A very detailed technical description of these new locomotives was contained in the March 1959 issue

Left *One of the original Southern 2,500 hp dc electric locomotives of 1958, now all withdrawn, here seen in 1974 on a mixed freight for Dover, approaching Petts Wood Junction. These locomotives, equipped for third-rail current collection also had a pantograph for use in yards* (Brian Morrison).

Below right *Southern Region. Electro-diesel locomotives, general arrangement* (GEC).

of *The Locomotive,* to which readers may be referred, and some personal experiences of my own in the drivers' cabs will give some impressions of actual work on the road. My own runs were made on passenger trains, but their utilisation was mainly on goods trains, and certain special facilities had to be introduced. It was necessary, for example, to electrify the access lines to certain large yards; and to avoid the risk of staff, ordinarily used to moving freely and rapidly among tracks, by night as well as day, from coming inadvertently into contact with the live rails, overhead wires were installed. As with the older 'CC' type locomotives, double-pan pantographs were fitted on the roofs, so that current collection could be changed from third-rail to overhead when entering yards. The braking equipment had to be somewhat complex, to permit working of trains that might be either air or vacuum equipped. The locomotives themselves were air braked, with apparatus for controlling vacuum-fitted trains through an air-vacuum proportional valve.

My first run in the cab of one of these locomotives was on the inward-bound 'Night Ferry' train. It was then at the height of its popularity and towards the end of the steam era it was nearly always double-headed. When I went down to Dover overnight, ready for a start at 7.20 am next morning, I recalled an earlier expedition for the same purpose, not long after the post-war restoration of the service. It then took the normal boat-train route via Tonbridge, but after electrification the Chatham route was used throughout except that in the London area the train took the Catford loop line. It is a much harder route than the old South Eastern main, including the long initial pull out of Dover up to Shepherds Well, another from Canterbury up to Milepost 57, and worst of all the severe Sole Street bank, by which the line climbs from Rochester out of the Medway valley. But even with a very heavy train of 620 tons the locomotive was working some way below full power on all of these ascents, and in each case was

accelerating from a low initial speed. The controller had a total range of 33 notches and the results in the three cases were:

Location	Gradient	Notch	Speed mph	edhp
Shepherds Well	1 in 132	27	45	2,120
Milepost 57	1 in 132	27	44	2,100
Sole St bank	1 in 100	30	43	2,200

It was interesting to experience the effect of passing over the gaps in the conductor rails, when the locomotive was working hard, at relatively low speed. In the Kentish countryside there are many level crossings and, although the booster generator continued to supply the traction motors, the supply, when crossing the gaps, was considerably less than what was normally being taken from the conductor rails on these heavy climbs, and the result was a gentle backward surge as the gaps were crossed. Despite two signal checks we passed Swanley Junction, 60.7 miles from Dover, exactly on time, in 82 minutes; but we were entering the London suburban area at the time of the heaviest rush-hour traffic, and did not get a clear road. The last 18¾ miles from Swanley to Victoria took 32¼ minutes and we were a little over four minutes late on arrival.

The return working of the Dover men assigned to the 'Night Ferry' was on the outward bound 'Golden Arrow' Pullman, and in the summer of 1962 it was subjected to a notable acceleration, to cover the 78 miles from Victoria to Dover Marine in 82 minutes. In view of the complexities of the first part of the journey, over the old Chatham line, with many permanent speed restrictions, it needed skilful work, even with so powerful an electric locomotive, to cover the initial 14.9 miles to Orpington in 19 minutes. Although with the booster set in operation the current supply to the motors was maintained in crossing the numerous gaps, the driver used skill in manipulating the controller to avoid the slight surges one felt on the locomotive working the 'Night Ferry' train. The easing back of the controller on the 380-ton 'Golden Arrow' gave a faultless ride over the gap sections. A similar technique with such a load as 620 tons, on a 1 in 132 gradient would have resulted in loss of time, and the surges that we felt in the cab would probably have been imperceptible further down the train. On the 'Golden Arrow' we had a permanent-way slowing to 20 mph near Paddock Wood, but were keeping closely to schedule time. The maximum speed was 80 mph on the level near Headcorn and we passed Folkestone Junction, 72 miles, in exactly 'even time'. With a leisurely run down through the Warren, amid the ever-famous White Cliffs, we arrived at Dover Marine almost a minute early, in 81 minutes 10 seconds from Victoria. Because of changes in the traffic pattern in Kent, all the 2,500 hp electric locomotives have now been withdrawn.

In February 1962 came the first of the 'electro-diesel' locomotives, built for use on the Southern Region at Eastleigh works. While the complete elimination of steam was a major objective in the Modernisation Plan, not all the secondary lines would be electrified, and the novel concept was evolved of having medium-powered motive power units which could be used as straight dc electrics or as diesel-electric. The general layout of these interesting locomotives can be seen in the accompanying diagram. The four traction motors, reference 7, are each of 400 hp, and take current direct from the conductor rails, when on electrified track. The master controller, which of course has duplicate controls at each end of the locomotive, has two main power handles, one for diesel operation and one for straight electric working. Changeover from one to the other is made simply by returning one handle to the lock-off position and releasing the other from it. The diesel engine has relatively low power, of only 600 horsepower, because it was generally considered that the work called for on non-electrified lines would be of no more than a light nature. A total of 49 electro-diesel locomotives was originally built, all but one of which are still in service today.

The Modernisation Plan for British Railways, launched at the beginning of 1955, included in its proposals the electrification of the main lines from Kings Cross to Doncaster (and possibly to York), in addition to the major project of Euston to Liverpool and Manchester, including the loop line through the Black Country, serving Birmingham and Wolverhampton. But at the time the Plan was launched it was not certain what system of electric traction would be used. In May of the previous year, for the first time since 1925, the annual meeting of the International Railway Congress Association was held in London, and as one of the delegates I had many opportunities of hearing the divergent views held on what emerged as one of the crucial subjects on the agenda: the advancement of electrification. That it should have been so thoroughly aired in a

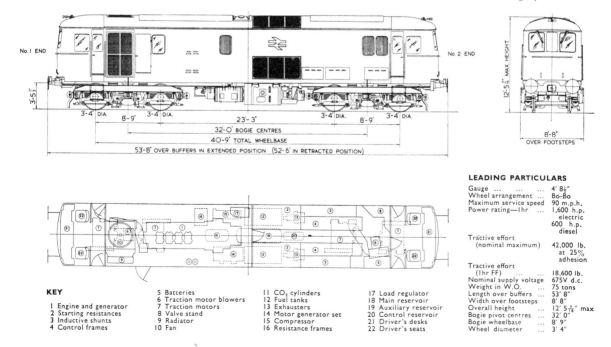

LEADING PARTICULARS

Gauge	4' 8½"
Wheel arrangement ...	Bo-Bo
Maximum service speed	90 m.p.h.
Power rating—1hr ...	1,600 h.p. electric
	600 h.p. diesel
Tractive effort (nominal maximum)	42,000 lb. at 25% adhesion
Tractive effort (1hr FF)	18,600 lb.
Nominal supply voltage	675V d.c.
Weight in W.O. ...	75 tons
Length over buffers ...	53' 8"
Width over footsteps ...	8' 8"
Overall height	12' 5 7/8" max
Bogie pivot centres ...	32' 0"
Bogie wheelbase ...	8' 9"
Wheel diameter ...	3' 4"

KEY

1 Engine and generator	5 Batteries	11 CO₂ cylinders	17 Load regulator
2 Starting resistances	6 Traction motor blowers	12 Fuel tanks	18 Main reservoir
3 Inductive shunts	7 Traction motors	13 Exhausters	19 Auxiliary reservoir
4 Control frames	8 Valve stand	14 Motor generator set	20 Control reservoir
	9 Radiator	15 Compressor	21 Driver's desks
	10 Fan	16 Resistance frames	22 Driver's seats

Above *Southern Region electro-diesel locomotive BR Class '73' No 73123 on freight for the LM Region approaching Clapham Junction, Brighton line* (Brian Morrison).

Left *A Southern electro-diesel No 73136 working diesel, passing Kensington Olympia, West London line, on a train of coal hopper wagons from Wimbledon to Acton* (Brian Morrison).

Below *An electro-diesel No 73113 working a train of tank cars from Earley to Hoo, near New Eltham* (Brian Morrison).

Above *Express passenger duty for a Southern electro-diesel: locomotive No 73124 on a Weymouth to Waterloo boat train approaching Clapham Junction* (Brian Morrison).

Right *An electro-diesel in heavy mineral traffic: locomotive No 73126 on a coal train from Hither Green yard to Tonbridge, passing Stone crossing halt* (Brian Morrison).

Below *A Co-Co 1,500v dc electric locomotive No 27001* Ariadne, *for the Manchester-Sheffield line, built 1954* (C.J. Marsden).

forum of international experts was fortuitous at a time when British opinion seemed to be undecided. It was nevertheless not generally realised that already in Great Britain one quarter of the total passenger train mileage was electrically operated, a striking commentary upon the activities of Southern Region and its third-rail dc system. But it had been generally agreed at the time of the Weir report on electric traction, in 1930, that this system was unsuitable for long-distance main line application and, until developments in France in the early 1950s led to some re-thinking, it had been generally assumed that 1,500 volts dc with overhead line current collection would be the future British standard. It had already been installed on the Manchester–Sheffield–Wath scheme of the former London and North Eastern Railway, and a start had been made on its installation on the suburban lines from Liverpool Street, Great Eastern line.

Delegates to the IRCA gathering in London learned that: 'The investigations of the reporters show that for all practical purposes the only systems suitable for extensive railway application are:

Direct current	1,500 volts
Direct current	3,000 volts
Alternating current	Low frequency at 11/16 kv
Alternating current	Standard frequency at about 25 kv

Mr S.B. Warder, then Chief Officer, Electrical Engineering, British Transport Commission, concluded his own report thus:
'There seems to be insufficient information at present to confirm any definite superiority of any of the four main systems in all respects which would permit any one to be preferred over the others under conditions at present obtaining. The evidence at present available suggests that it is unlikely that in the foreseeable future one system will prove to be the best for all railways having regard to their very diverse characteristics. In any case, such superiority, wherever it exists, is unlikely to be sufficient to justify the cost of replacing an existing system of the other three types considered, with the one having only a marginal advantage. On most lines the choice between systems can only be made by detailed comparative estimates, taking all the special factors on the lines concerned into account'. And, after digesting this masterpiece of non-committal verbage, the conference passed on to other topics.

While the fog of uncertainty still hung over British Railways at the time of the introduction of the Modernisation Plan, some guidance as to the way ahead came as a result of a convention on electrification at 50 cycles, single-phase ac organised by the French National Railways, at Lille, in May 1955. There the equipment of the largely freight line from Lille, through Metz and Strasbourg to Basle, was discussed particularly in respect of the imminent opening of the first section, between Valenciennes and Thionville. Before the year was out French precepts and early experience with this newly equipped line had turned the scale with the British Transport Commission, and in the dawn of 1956 it was announced that all new electrification schemes on British Railways other than those on Southern Region would be on the 25 kv 50-cycle ac system. The announcement went so far as to omit the Western Section of the Southern Region from lines that were to remain third-rail dc, thus predicting that when the time came to electrify the line to Southampton and Bournemouth that also would

Left *A Continental design that influenced the wheel arrangement for the LM 25 kv electric: the Bern-Lötschberg-Simplon Ac '4-4' Class* (BLS Railway).

Right *A further influence: a French Co-Co type 1500v dc electric, '1700' Class, one of which attained a maximum of 205 mph* (G.F. Fenino).

be 50-cycle ac. Two main points were made for the decision: first, that many fewer sub-stations and a lighter and thus cheaper overhead line would be required; and secondly, that although individual electric locomotives might be a little more expensive, if French experience were to be borne out on British Railways, ac locomotives with rectifier-fed dc motors were expected to be able to haul loads 60 per cent greater than a modern dc locomotive of the same weight. On the other side of the balance sheet was the cost of raising money for overline structures to give the required extra clearance.

To make comparison with what was to follow on the London Midland Euston line it must be recalled that the 1,500-volt dc electric locomotives on the Manchester–Sheffield–Wath line, referred to and illustrated in Volume 2, Chapter 11, were of the the the Bo + Bo type, had an all-up weight of 87.9 tons, and a rated horsepower of 1,868. They were primarily freight locomotives. In 1954 a Co + Co version of the design was introduced having six 415 horse-power traction motors, total 2,490 horsepower. These latter, of which only seven were built, were intended for express passenger work, and had a maximum permissible speed of 90 mph. One of these was displayed in an exhibition of modern British locomotives at the time of the IRCA conference in London in 1954. At the time they were the only electric locomotives in the country permitted to exceed 70 mph. They were massively built, and had a total weight of 102 tons.

For the London Midland main line electrification a single class of mixed-traffic locomotive was envisaged, so that maximum utilisation could be obtained by arrangement of diagrams covering both passenger and freight duties. The original speci-

fication did not stipulate any actual ratings, but set out the duties in passenger and freight service that were then thought to be the maximum the electric locomotives would have to perform, as mentioned in Chapter 1. There were two only of these, as follows:

1) 'The locomotive to be capable of hauling a 475-ton express passenger trailing load from Manchester (London Road) to London (Euston) with a balancing speed of 90 mph on level tangent track and a maximum running speed of 100 mph. The average speed is 67 mph with one stop of 1 minute, and 4 miles at 15 mph additional speed restrictions for track maintenance';

2) 'The locomotive to be capable of hauling a 950-ton freight train between Manchester (Longsight) and London (Willesden) at an average speed of 42 mph with a maximum speed of 55 mph. The locomotive will also have to work 500-ton express freight trains (fully fitted) at a maximum speed of 60 mph over this section. The locomotive to be capable of making three consecutive starts with the 950-ton train up to 20 mph on a 1 in 100 gradient, and to be capable of working without damage to the equipment with this train for 10 miles at 10 mph on any part of the route'.

The specification having been laid down, however, the situation within British Railways was rather extraordinary. Prior to 1955, when the haulage requirements for a new locomotive had been laid down there had always been a huge bank of solid experience to draw upon, whether the design was to be done at Crewe, Doncaster, East-leigh or Swindon; but in 1956-7 there was nothing! No-one on the British railways had any experience of ac locomotives, nor of two-axled bogies required to run beneath them smoothly and safely up to 100

Left *The first 25kv ac electric locomotive for the London Midland Region, No E3001, with AEI motors, built 1959, now locomotive No 81001* (British Railways).

Below *One of the original electric locomotives (now Class '81') running at high speed with a 12-coach train, on the West Coast main line near Wolverton* (Britsh Railways).

Right *Two of the Crewe-built 25kv electric locomotives with AEI traction motors, Nos E3077 and E3083 now Class '85', standing in Crewe station* (British Railways).

mph. Warder decided at once to play safe so far as the traction motors were concerned; these were to be dc fed through ac to dc rectifiers, of which there was ample experience in the electrical industry, if not necessarily in locomotives. Invitations were therefore give to five separate manufacturers to submit designs for a Bo + Bo type of electric locomotive of approximately 80 tons overall weight that would meet the traction requirements. The only strict instruction was that all should have identical controls for the driver, so that a man could step on to any one of them and drive away, so to speak, without having to make any self-adjustments for incidental differences. The contracts for the first 55 locomotives were placed as follows:

Original numbers	Builder	Later Class	Later number
E3001-23	AEI (BTH Rugby)	81	81001-23
E3024-35	English Electric	83	83001-12
E3036-45	General Electric	84	now withdrawn
E3046-55	AEI (Met Vick)	82	82001-8*

*Two of the original damaged beyond repair in accidents

There then followed a batch of 40, original running numbers 3056 to 3095, built at Crewe Works, with AEI (BTH Rugby) traction motors. All five varieties had a nominal horsepower rating of 3,300. The overall weights varied between 73 and 79.6

tons and compared to the 'E5001' Class dc locomotives on the Southern, having a weight of 77
tons, the new LM units fulfilled the French prediction of a tractive power substantially greater for
the same weight, though not perhaps to the extent of
60 per cent. In this case it was about 35 per cent or
45 per cent on the one-hour rating of motors.

Just as the design of the new locomotives had
provided some problems that were novel to the
engineers so also, it was realised, would it be for the
crews that would have to handle the new power in
service; and an interesting way of providing some
pre-instruction was found. Metropolitan Vickers
had on their hands the second of the gas-turbine
electric locomotives built for trials on the Western
Region, and an order was given to the firm for its
rebuilding as a 25 kv straight electric. It was not to
be considered in any way as a prototype, but as a
means of providing a locomotive that would have
some of the characteristics of the new power and
which could be used for driver training. The
changes to the locomotive involved the removal of
the turbine with its air-filter units, fuel tanks and
control gear; lowering the roof of what had been the
gas turbine compartment to accommodate the
pantograph, and the special air-blast circuit-
breaker; and the conversion of the cabs to left-hand
drive. The mechanical parts remained practically
unchanged, and of the six original traction motors
four were retained, together with their blowers,
exhausters, main compressors, and the battery with
its manoeuvring feature on the original locomotive.
As on the new standard locomotives then in production, the dc traction motors were supplied
through mercury arc rectifiers, though by reason of
the removal of two traction motors the tractive

power of the locomotive was accordingly reduced.
Nevertheless, the availability of this unit, roughly a
year before delivery of the new standard Bo + Bo
locomotives was expected was an asset in training
the crews. The Stockport avoiding line, via Styal,
was the first section on which electrification was
completed, and it was there that the experimental
running was carried out.

The first of the new locomotives to be completed,
one of the order for 24 placed with the British
Thompson Houston Company of Rugby, recently
combined with Metropolitan Vickers of Trafford
Park to form the Traction Division of Associated
Electrical Industries, was delivered to the London
Midland Region at the end of 1959. The manufacture of the mechanical parts had been sub-
contracted to the Birmingham Railway Carriage
and Wagon Company. The general layout of the
equipment can be studied from the accompanying
drawings, from which it will be seen that the central
portion of the roof is lowered to accommodate the
pantographs and the main circuit breaker, though
this is not apparent from a lineside view of the new
locomotive. To improve the appearance of the
stepped roof a glass-fibre fairing, moulded to the
shape of the corner radius, extended for the full
length between the raised portion over the two cabs.
The locomotive was attractively finished in blue,
with the British Railways' emblem and with the
number in raised, stainless steel characters.
Recollections of the Gresley streamlined 'A4'
'Pacifics' of pre-war days would result in the colour
being described as 'Garter Blue' though this was not
mentioned in any of the official descriptions.

To anyone who had studied the specifications of
earlier British non-steam locomotives a point about

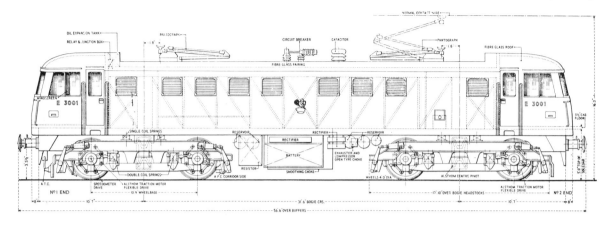

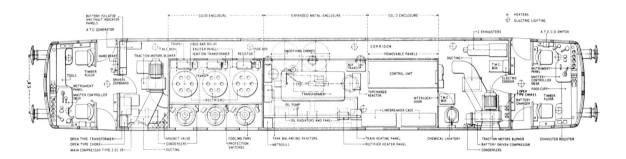

the new 25 kv electrics that would intrigue any engineer was how it had been possible to make such a marked reduction in the overall weight. There were no massive frames below the main body, and as will be seen from the drawing there appeared to be no framing at all. Actually the complete body of the locomotive was designed as a weight-carrying structure. Each side of the body took the form of a deep lattice girder, with diagonal and vertical 'I' section members to which the sheet-steel skin was attached. This latter was of No 12 standard wire gauge 0.104 inches thick. The two sides of the body were braced together at roof level with a series of formed members, and this made a rigid box structure of great strength but of minimum weight for the support of the main frame, through which the traction and buffing loads were transmitted, and on which the electrical equipment was mounted. The cab roof was a double-skin glass-fibre moulding. At the cab front there was a three-piece screen, the driving panels of which were fitted with pneumatic wipers. The screens incorporated a layer of transparent gold film in the laminations which formed an electric heating element to act as a de-icer and de-mister.

Above *25 kv ac locomotive, London Midland Region, No E3001, built by AEI Traction Division* (Railway Magazine).

Above right *One of the British Railways standard 25kv electric locomotives, designed as a result of experience with the first 100, supplied by various contractors, No E3164, originally classed 'AL6', later Class '86'* (British Railways).

Below right *A more recent photograph of one of the first batch of 25 kv ac electrics, No 81007 (originally No E3007) entering Lancaster Castle station with a Carlisle to London parcels train, in 1974* (Derek Cross).

Turning now to the main business of the loco-motive, current at 25 kv, 50 cycles per second, collected from the overhead line is passed through the air blast circuit-breaker on the roof to the main transformer which, as will be seen from the drawing is located almost exactly amidships. Thence ac current at reduced voltage is passed to the three rectifiers, which in these original locomotives were of the mercury-arc type. Load-sharing reactors were provided to ensure that the current passing from the transformer was shared equally between the three rectifier units. In view of the high power being transmitted, special attention had to be paid to the cooling arrangements, both for the transformer and the rectifier units. While the standard line voltage for the London Midland main line electrification was 25 kv it was at first thought there would have to be sections energised at no more than 6.25 kv, because of limited electrical clearance overhead. The locomotives had to be designated to operate at full power on either, and this was done by arranging the main transformer windings so that the connections could be switched to suit one line voltage or the other. The four traction motors on each locomotive had the following characteristics:

Continuous rating	975 volts
	700 amperes
	847 horsepower
total for locomotive	3,300 horsepower
One-hour rating	975 volts
	760 amperes
	920 horsepower
total for locomotive	3,680 horsepower

From reference to the diagram reproduced on page 102, in respect of earlier locomotives, it will be appreciated that at peak notching the horsepower would be considerably greater than 3,680; in fact

the maximum tractive effort at peak notching was quoted at no less than 48,000 lb. If this took place at 50 mph such a pull would be equivalent to about 6,000 horsepower.

Very careful attention was given at the design stage to the bogies and the method of suspension. The idea of having a locomotive that was to run at speeds up to 100 mph continuously, and which had no carrying wheels, struck many older locomotive engineers as grounds for concern; but adoption of the Alsthom system of rubber cone pivot body suspension, radius-arm guided axle-boxes, and flexible link drive to the wheels was some reassurance, because it had been successfully used in some of the latest Continental electric locomotives, that also had to travel fast. On these it had been noted that they gave good riding characteristics, while reducing unsprung weight. The four-wheeled bogies, which were of the underslung equalising beam type, were welded steel fabrications of minimum weight for amply adquate strength. The bogie frame was supported on four nests of double-coil helical springs, from the low-level equalising beams. Shock absorbers were fitted, and the rise of the primary springs under high-speed running conditions was checked to maintain adequate clearances in all conditions. While the locomotives supplied by the various contractors during the year 1960 varied in the details of both electrical and mechanical equipment, there were 20 of basically the same design ready for the opening of the first stage of the London Midland main line electrification in September 1960, between Manchester and Crewe. Some of the greatest variations were to be seen in the bogie design, shown on the separate drawings. The 20 locomotives then available included examples from each of the four contractors mentioned earlier.

This first section had hardly been brought into operation when, as a result of a Government inquiry into schemes of railway capital investment, the whole project of the extension southwards from Crewe was halted, and the London Midland Region was faced with the horrifying prospect of having its 25 kv electrification confined to that section already opened, with the possible addition of the line between Liverpool and Crewe, on which work was already well advanced. Fortunately this defeatist attitude did not last for too long, though long enough to throw production programmes into something of a disarray; and early in 1961 the then Minister of Transport announced to the House of Commons that the electrification scheme southwards from Crewe to Euston was to go ahead. It was in this period of uncertainty that I had my first run in the cab of one of the new locomotives, on the 9.20 am 'West of England Express' from Manchester. The ordinary load was augmented by a second electric locomotive that was being hauled 'dead', and the gross trailing load was one of 475 tons. The train engine, on which I rode, was one of the English Electric Vulcan batch, built at Newton-le-Willows, No E3026. From the stop at Wilmslow we made a fast run as far as Sandbach, passing that station, 14.3 miles, in 13 minutes, after attaining a maximum speed of 93 mph. After that an engineering slack to 40 mph prevented a better time than 20¾ minutes for the 18.8 miles from Wilmslow to Crewe. I remember being impressed with the smooth and steady riding of the locomotive at maximum speed.

By the end of 1964, when electric working had extended as far south as Rugby, the London Midland Region had accumulated a wealth of experience in the running of the five varieties of high-speed electric locomotive, all having a nominal continuous power rating of 3,300 horsepower. The actual variations in the form of traction motor and flexible drive may be summarised as follows, using the original class designations (below).

It was then that British Railways designed their own standard version, which was introduced in 1965, and was at first known as Class 'AL6'. Authority was given for 100 locomotives of the new design, some built at the Vulcan works at Newton-le-Willows and others at Doncaster. The principal changes from the preceding units lay in the use of axle-hung traction motors, rectifiers of the semi-conductor silicon type, instead of mercury arc, and rheostatic braking, controlled from the driver's

Class	Running Nos	Builder	Traction motor	Flexible drive	Total weight (tons)
AL1	E3001-23	AEL (BTH)	847 hp	Alsthom quill	79.6
AL2	E3046-55	AEI (MV)	847 hp	Alsthom quill	78.4
AL3	E3024-35	English Electric	740 hp	SLM resilient	73.0
AL4	E3036-45	General Electric	750 hp	Brown Boveri spring	76.5
AL5	E3056-95	BR Doncaster	BTH 847 hp	Alsthom quill	79.0

One of the 'AL6' ac electrics hauling a train of Ford car components from Halewood (Merseyside) to Dagenham: locomotive No E3129 (British Railways).

brake valve. The feature of design that caused some surprise and not a little criticism was the use of a traction motor that was axle-hung. While this resulted in much simplification mechanically in that there was no need for a flexible drive from the motors to the axles, the design nevertheless involved a considerable amount of unsprung weight. Tests had been carried out in 1960–1 at speeds of up 100 mph with a locomotive that had been so equipped, and it satisfied both civil and mechanical engineers; so work went ahead with a production batch of 100 locomotives.

8. Ac electric locomotive performance: a general survey

When, in March 1967, the full electric high-speed inter-city service was introduced between Euston, Liverpool and Manchester, together with that to Birmingham and Wolverhampton, the London Midland Region had a total of 200 high-power electric locomotives, all rated for a maximum speed of 100 mph. It should be mentioned that, in addition to the 95 contract-built locomotives of Classes 'AL1' to 'AL5' listed in Chapter 7, there were a further five, numbered E3096 to E3100, incorporating various modifications, some of an experimental nature. When doing the 'field work' for my book *Britain's New Railway* in 1965, which I wrote at the express invitation of Sir Henry Johnson, then General Manager of the LM Region, I saw, at first hand, a good deal of the performance of the new locomotives; while as author of the monthly feature 'Locomotive Practice and Performance' in *The Railway Magazine* I was, for a time, well-nigh swamped with a correspondence relating to the experiences of readers on the new trains, that provided data covering tens of thousands of miles travelling. The reaction to the new trains from the stop-watching enthusiasts was unanimously favourable, while the soaring traffic receipts were a gratifying indication of the travelling public's warm appreciation.

In this book I am, of course, primarily concerned with the locomotives as motive power units; but the new service which their performance made possible was of so revolutionary a character, in its entirety, that it would be taking altogether too one-sided a view to attribute the whole of its success to the 'power to pull'—and run!—of the locomotives. The feature that stamped the new service as profoundly different from any other accelerated timetable previously introduced on the railways of Britain was that it was not a case of giving a few prestigious trains preferential treatment in speed; the entire service was given a tremendous boost-up. It had to be so. With the intensity of traffic to be provided, all the express trains had simply got to travel at the same speed. And the timetable of 1967 was only a beginning. Throughout the 'off-peak' hours there were departures from Euston at each hour, followed by trains at five and 15 minutes past. When the service was further developed to provide a connectional pattern with the newly systematised North East to South West service via the Midland route, the departures from Euston were re-arranged in what are now termed 'flights' of no fewer than six

trains leaving within half an hour, at 40, 45, 50, and 55 minutes past the hour, on the hour, and at ten minutes past, with five out of the six trains leaving within five minutes of each other, and continuing so to Rugby. This 'flight' sequence was repeated hourly throughout the day, in what were still euphemistically described as the 'off-peak' periods.

With five trains following each other at five-minute intervals, all running to schedules that required continuous running at 90 to 100 mph, it will be appreciated that the closest and most sophisticated integration of locomotive and track-side equipment was essential to ensure safe running. The line itself was provided with multi-aspect colourlight signals throughout, sited so as to give adequate warning if any reduction of speed was required, and all locomotives were fitted with the British Railways standard form of automatic warning developed from the principles established earlier on the Great Western Railway, but incorporating an inductive link-up between locomotive and track, instead of the contact ramps used on the GWR. In both variations of the basic principles, provision was made for an automatic application of the brakes if a driver inadvertently, or through some sudden emergency, failed to acknowledge receipt of an audible warning. It is now 17 years since this intense high-speed service was inaugurated, and there has been not a single accident due to the close headway running and the high speed of all trains.

Before passing on to a more general appreciation of London Midland electric running in the early years, summary details of some notable individual runs may be appended. With the exception of No 3, which was a special run for members of the Locomotive Club of Great Britain, all were on ordinary service trains, and were logged by several different observers. On certain runs there were slight excesses beyond the official maximum speed limit of 100 mph, although none at more than 106 mph; but on all runs the speed restrictions at various intermediate locations like Rugby and Stafford, and the lesser ones at Berkhamsted, Weedon, and Atherstone were all most carefully observed. Run No 7 was on the 16.05 Glasgow express, before electric working extended north of Weaver Junction, and was one that I observed personally, when travelling from Euston to Wigan. It was an occasion of which I retain vivid memories.

It was a murky November day in 1966 when

Above *An impressive parade of eight of the new electric locomotives outside the depot at Crewe in July 1961* (British Railways).

Right *Training the drivers: the training simulator showing the driving seat and the instructor's control panel on back of the driver's partition* (British Railways).

Below *Euston, February 1972: Class '86' (then 'AL6') locomotives E3147 on 1H42 for Manchester, and E3139, 1S75 for Glasgow* (Derek Cross).

atmospheric conditions were sufficiently bad for all internal air services from London to be cancelled, and the first-class accommodation on the 16.05 Scottish express was crowded with disgruntled would-be air travellers who had been given rail tickets in lieu. Many of them had perforce to overflow into the second-class part of the train. I had a driver's cab pass, so was no more than a witness of their discomfiture. Before we started the fog had closed in considerably, but with the assurance of the audible signals in the cab we went out of London as on the fairest of days and were doing 100 mph not more than ten miles out of Euston. It should not be forgotten that another express had left the terminus five minutes before we did, and was ahead of us all the way to Crewe. Fog or no fog we drew gradually ahead of time, and passed Rugby, 82.6 miles, nearly three minutes early, in 60 minutes 40 seconds from Euston. Soon after that however it became clear that we were close on the tail of the preceding train, from successive signals showing the 'double-yellow' indication; and our driver eased the speed a little. Nevertheless, it was not until we were approaching Crewe that we were appreciably delayed by adverse signals. Having passed Betley Road, 153.3 miles, in 116½ minutes, doing 102 mph, we were in good time to make a punctual arrival when the final sequence of signal checks began.

By the summer of 1968 such a vast accumulation of logs of LM electric locomotive performance compiled by many different correspondents was swelling my files that it was fairly evident the initial brilliance of the running between Euston and Crewe was being fully maintained. Even those pen-friends of mine who were inclined to take a habitually cynical view of all British Railways' activities could find little to grumble about, and my own personal experiences, whether riding in the driver's cab or not, were uniformly excellent. Yet the thought occurred to me that, while the favourable evidence was massive, few enthusiasts—save those with cynical turn of mind—would take the trouble to copy out details of poor runs, or of occasions when the traffic regulation was faulty and the close succession of fast trains was subjected to considerable delay. It seemed that a day-long observation of a typical day's running might yield some interesting data, to supplement the closely detailed timings of the running of individual trains sent to me by correspondents. The London Midland Region accordingly arranged for me to spend the best part of a busy summer day in the control room of the power signal box at Rugby, from the windows of which I could observe the passage of all trains. Also, because of the extended geographical area controlled by this large panel box, I could see, on the illuminated track diagram, the approach of the trains for some time before they actually passed in front of the windows, and could appreciate the problems in regulation that sometimes faced the controller in the case of southbound trains converging upon Rugby from the Birmingham and the Trent Valley lines simultaneously. While this was of great interest to me from my lifelong association with signalling, and operating problems, in this book it is the overall picture of running on the down line and the assessment of electric locomotive capacity that provides the compelling feature.

In addition to the train in which I travelled down to Rugby, the running of 16 express passenger trains was noted from the signal box, with the results set out in the accompanying table. With the

Left *Manchester Piccadilly: electric locomotive No 86006, in September 1976, after arrival with the 06.55 from Euston* (Brian Morrison).

Right *Close-up of a Class '85', No 85008, on an up van train near Rugby* (Brian Morrison).

Ref No	Route	Coaches	Load Gross trailing (tons)	Loco Class	No	Distance miles	Sched min	Actual m s	Net time min	Av sp mph
1	Stockport–Euston	12	430	AL6	3141	183.0	151	145 07	139	79.0
2	Euston–Stockport	12	420	AL6	3147	183.0	151	139 07	134	82.0
3	Euston–Weaver Junction*	10	400	AL6	3169	174.3	—	128 30	121	86.6
4	Crewe–Euston	12	420	AL6	3135	158.0	120	110 55	111	85.5
5	Stafford–Bletchley	14	530	AL5	3089	86.9	65	63 33	63½	82.2
6	Bletchley–Euston	14	530	AL5	3089	46.7	40	37 25	37½	74.6
7	Euston–Crewe	11	415	AL6	3196	158.0	121	123 21	118	80.3

*Passing time, on non-stop run to Liverpool

LM Region: Euston–Rugby summer 1968

Euston depart	Destination	Rugby Scheduled	Actual	Av speed from last stop (mph)	Load coaches
10.00	Manchester	11 03½	11 03	78.7	12
10.05	Glasgow	11 08½	11 05	82.6	12
10.15	Manchester via Birmingham	11 22½	11 18½	87.5*	10
10.35	Holyhead	11 42½	11 40	82.8†	12
11.00	Liverpool	12 03½	12 03½	78.0	11
11.05	Barrow-in-Furness	12 10½	12 08½	78.0	12
11.15	Liverpool via Birmingham	12 18½	12 16	81.3	13
13.00	Liverpool	14 03½	13 59	84.0	12
13.05	Blackpool	14 14½	14 12	77;0†	12
13.15	Liverpool via Birmingham	14 18½	14 14	84.0	12
14.00	Manchester	15 03½	15 00½	82.0	12
14.05	Glasgow	15 08½	15 06½	80.6	13
14.15	Manchester via Birmingham	15 18½	15 15½	82.0	11
15.00	Liverpool	16 05½	16 02	80.0	12
15.05	Holyhead	16 12½	16 11	79.5†	12
15.15	Liverpool via Birmingham	16 18½	16 17½	79.3	11

*Average speed from Watford Junction stop.
†Average speed from Bletchley stop.

exception of the 10.15, 10.35, 13.05 and 15.05 departures from Euston, all trains in the table were non-stop to Rugby or beyond. It will be seen that of the 16 trains observed not one was as much as a minute late, and the actual average speeds from the last stopping station make an impressive record of high-speed travelling. From the control room look-out I was not able to note the numbers of the individual locomotives concerned, but the majority were of Class 'AL6', later to be known as Class '86'. On that particular day there were no temporary speed restrictions on the down line between Euston and Rugby. In fact my own journey down by the 8.45 Irish Mail must have been one of the fastest of the day. From leaving Watford Junction on time we passed Kilsby Tunnel North Location, 61.2 miles, in 41 minutes 39 seconds, and would have reached Rugby in about 47 minutes, 3½ minutes early, but for a brief signal stop outside. Our net average speed from Watford was 83 mph with a load of 12 coaches, for a gross trailing load of 450 tons.

It was about this same time that the original class designations, 'AL1', 'AL2' and so on were changed, and they became Classes '81', '82', '83', '84', and '85'. When the 100 new locomotives of Class '86' became available they were put on to the hardest and fastest duties, though the former

'AL5s', now Class '85', continued to be used on many important duties. During the transition period, when the line was electrified as far south as Nuneaton, and engines were changed there, I had some interesting runs with the earlier classes, summary details of which are set out in the table below. Run No 1 was interesting in that the maximum speed of the whole trip, 86 mph, was attained when climbing the 1 in 177 gradient of Madeley bank, while No 4, on the same service, was a very fast run following a late start from Crewe. On some of the runs I was in the cab, and noted with pleasure the very smooth riding of the locomotives. The clarity of the writing in the rough note books I carried was a testimony to the absence of vibration. It was not the same when I came to ride Class '86'.

The decision to specify the Bo + Bo wheel arrangement for the ac electric locomotives of the London Midland Region was undoubtedly influenced by the outstanding success of the 'BB9200' Class on the French National Railways which, although lighter and nominally less powerful than the 'CC7100' Class, with the Co + Co wheel arrangement turned in such a magnificent performance that the two classes came to be used almost indiscriminately on the very fast and heavy express train services of the South-East Region, the former PLM line. On the London Midland Region, while

LM Region: the intermediate stage

Ref No	Section	Distance (miles)	Loco Class	No	Load gross trailing (tons)	Sched (min)	Actual m s	Average Speed (mph)
1	Crewe–Nuneaton	60.9	81	3004	445	51	49 03	74.5
2	Liverpool–Crewe	35.6	83	3031	445	41½	37 00*	62.2*
3	Nuneaton–Stafford	36.5	85	3056	455	32½	30 06	72.9
4	Crewe–Nuneaton	60.9	85	3061	415	51	44 30	82.2
5	Crewe–Rugby	75.5	85	3095	435	69½	66 48†	72.0†

* Net time 34¼ minutes.   † Net time 63 minutes.

the very high power-weight ratio of all the new electric locomotives was held up as a mark of their advanced design, coupled with the fact that all their weight was available for adhesion, if comparison was to be made with the steam locomotives that had preceded them (and still more so to the diesel-electric designs of the intervening period) a total weight of around 80 tons was not over-generous for locomotives capable of developing 5,000 horsepower when accelerating. It was, however, not a tendency to wheel-slip which proved a major point of criticism of the new locomotives.

Of the original 55 that were contract-built, Classes 81-4, and referred to in the previous chapter, the 12 in Class '83', and the ten in Class '84' proved the least reliable. When experience in running the service showed that it could be satisfactorily operated with fewer locomotives than were regularly available it was decided to take Classes '83' and '84' out of traffic to await possible modification. Although the extent of the troubles with them were not made public, it may be noted that these two classes had a different form of flexible drive from that used on Classes '81', '82' and '85'. It was also to avoid altogether the complications of the flexible drive that the '86' Class were built with axle-hung motors. This was not done without a considerable amount of design investigation, and consultation with the civil engineers on the likely effect of such a design change on the track. Those with recollections of earlier investigations into the interaction of locomotive design and its effect on track, and underline bridge structures might have imagined that an electric locomotive, or a diesel for that matter, with no reciprocating machinery would have had a minimal effect upon the track, other than that of dead weight. The axle-loading of the London Midland electric locomotives, not exceeding 20 tons, was in any case considerably less than that of the largest steam locomotives previously in use on the West Coast main line.

Left *The 12 noon ex-Euston passing Tebay at high speed hauled by locomotive No 86036 in June 1974* (Brian Morrison).

Top right *The 11.10 (Sundays only) Glasgow to Euston near Lamington, hauled by locomotive No 85001 in August 1974* (Morrison Bryce).

Above right *Early morning in Upper Clydesdale: an overnight sleeping car express, Euston to Glasgow, near Abington, hauled by locomotive No 83015 in August 1975* (Derek Cross).

Right *A heavy southbound parcels train approaching Warrington hauled by locomotive No 85025, followed by No 81001. The latter, with no pantograph raised was probably being hauled 'dead'* (C.J. Tuffs).

Above *The overnight Dover-Stirling 'Motorail' passing Crawford at high speed hauled by locomotive No 86018 in August 1965* (Derek Cross)

Left *Southbound Anglo-Scottish express entering Carlisle Citadel hauled by locomotive No 81015 in August 1981* (T.H. Noble).

Below right *A picturesque broadside view of the 13.10 Glasgow to Euston 'Electric-Scot', south of Beattock (October 1983) hauled by No 85005* (T.H. Noble)

When the Class '86' locomotives first took the road there was to be noted a subtle difference in their riding from Class '85', and all the earlier experimental types. There was a pronounced bouncing action in the cab. I have several times previously told the story of the jocular remark of the driver of one of the '86's on leaving Wilmslow on a non-stop run to Euston ('Ride her, cowboy!') And we certainly did have what would be technically described as a 'poor vertical ride'. Drivers who had been nurtured on steam, weathered the war years, and suffered the time of post-war austerity thought nothing of it. There was nothing dangerous in the action; no terrifying side-to-side yawing as with the Western Region diesel-hydraulics—just a good deal of bouncing. The '86' Class were indeed popular with their crews for the complete mastery they had over any task set to them south of Liverpool and

Manchester; and in the course of my business travelling I had many superlative runs with them. But of course the making of fast runs is not the 'be-all and end-all' of satisfactory locomotive performance, taken in its broadest sense; and with the intensity of the service, particularly between Rugby and Euston, and continuous running at 90 to 100 mph by so many trains, it was realised that the track was taking a terrific hammering. That it took the engineers of the London Midland Region, and indeed of the British Railways Board, something by surprise is now a matter of history.

In the autumn of 1970 my great friend T.C.B. Miller, a locomotive engineer trained under Sir Nigel Gresley on the LNER and by that time Chief Engineer (Traction and Rolling Stock) of the British Railways Board, was elected to the Chairmanship of the Railway Division of the Institution of Mech-

Hammer-blow effect at 6 rps

Railway of origin	Engine Class	Max axle-load (tons)	Speed (mph) at 6 rps	Max combined load per axle at 6 rps (tons)
LNWR	'George V' 4-4-0	19.15	87	33.2
Midland	'Compound' 4-4-0	19.75	87	23.4
Midland	'2P' 4-4-0	17.5	90	29.3
Caledonian	'60' 4-6-0	19.3	78	31.0
LMS	'Royal Scot'	20.9	87	21.2
GWR	'Castle'	19.7	86	23.1
LNER	'A3' 4-6-2	22	86	24.7
Southern	'Lord Nelson'	20.65	85	23.2

anical Engineers, and on two notable occasions he laid bare some of the problems that had faced them over the track behaviour of the Class '86' electrics. The first was his Chairman's address to the IMechE, Railway Division, and the second a paper he entitled '*Running on Rails*' which he read to the Permanent Way Institution. In the latter he opened thus: 'Most of us thought that when the steam locomotive gave way to the diesel and electric locomotive our troubles were over. There would be no out-of-balance in the wheels, so no hammer blow. There would be lots of wheels, so weights would be low and well distributed'. But then he went on to say: 'I doubt if my friends in the Civil Engineer's Department would agree that all their hopes of an easier life on the permanent way at any rate, have been realised—possibly very much the contrary'.

Inevitably, his comments came round to the Class '86' locomotives, and to a comparison between their unsprung weight and that of other British non-steam locomotives. The relevant figures were:

Unsprung weight per axle (tons)

Diesel-electric Class '47'	3.55 tons
'Deltic', diesel-electric	3.3 tons
Class '85' LM ac electric	2.7 tons
Class '86' LM ac electric	4.25 tons

On the face of it the higher unsprung weight of Class '86' should not have caused undue difficulty or damage to track, even at speeds up to 100 mph. After all it should have been a steady load, in contrast to the pulsating hammer-blow of a reciprocating steam locomotive. As a matter of interest the values of hammer-blow recorded in the celebrated investigations of the Bridge Stress Committee in the 1920s may be quoted, for certain famous steam locomotive classes working on the West Coast main line. The above figures were given in the Committee's report for a speed of six revolutions per second, which, on account of the varying driving wheel diameters of the locomotives concerned, involved some variation in actual speed on the line.

While one can express astonishment at the severe effect upon the track meted out by relatively small and obsolescent designs of locomotive it must be added that, at the time they were built, the balancing was done by methods calculated to give a smooth ride, rather than with any collateral consideration for effect upon the permanent way. The more modern designs were vastly better. With the above figures in mind and appreciating that the 'dynamic augment' to the dead load was a rapidly pulsating one, it is not surprising that the change from steam to diesel and electric locomotives was expected to result in a considerable improvement.

In his address to the Railway Division of the Institution of Mechanical Engineers Mr Miller explained how the change to axle-hung motors came to be made in progressing from Class '85' to Class '86'. He said:

'In the first instance all five locomotive types evolved for the London Midland electrification were provided with fully sprung motors. Tests carried out with an axle-hung version, to measure the vertical dynamic loads downstream of rail joints, produced the rather unexpected conclusion that given the same track conditions there was little difference between the dynamic loads caused by axles having similar total loads but having an appreciable difference in the amount of unsprung weight involved. Add to this the desire to check rising first costs and savings resulting from the use of axle-hung motors, combined with the obvious desire to check main-tenance expenses, and the almost inevitable outcome was the Class '86' locomotive.'

The impression that all was not well in the riding of Class '86' led to further consideration, and Mr Miller referred to the close study that had been made in the years 1969–70 of the dynamic loads imposed on the rails at high speed. He explained how 'the wheels of a vehicle inflict a blow upon the rails at every discontinuity in the top surface of the rail, be it an ordinary joint (such joints are fast being reduced in number as welded rail is being progressively installed), or an insulated joint which is introduced to divide the rails for track circuiting purposes, or at any point or crossing in the track where a wheel has to 'jump' a gap. The force of the impact is greater if the gap to be jumped is wide, or if the running-off and running-on rails are not level, or if a joint is not adequately supported.'

Suspicions as to the effect of the Class '86' locomotive led to the question being referred to the Research Department, and in October 1970 a series of tests was made at speeds of up to 125 mph with several different types of locomotive. The site chosen was on the down main line just north of Cheddington station, near the foot of a long descending gradient of 1 in 335, and on straight track. The Research Department provided load-

The 11.50 Glasgow to Nottingham express near Lanark Junction, hauled by locomotive No 86315 in May 1982 (T.H. Noble).

measuring base-plates which were fitted to six sleepers, two of them before a rail joint. The track was otherwise continuously welded, and on concrete sleepers. The locomotives tested were of Classes '85' and '86', plus a 'Deltic' borrowed from the East Coast route for test purposes. In comparison with the unsprung weights per axle of 2.7 and 4.25 tons for Classes '85' and '86' the 'Deltic' figure was 3.3 tons. As was to be expected, Class '85' proved the best, and '86' by far the worst, with the 'Deltic' somewhere in between. But, as Mr Miller explained in his address to the Railway Division of the Institution of Mechanical Engineers: '. . . the force does not exert itself on the rails alone but also on the wheels and axles and on all the equipment that is attached to them. If such equipment is attached without the intervention of any form of shock-absorber, such as a spring or block of rubber, then the impact will be the more severe, and this is particularly damaging so far as axle-hung traction motors are concerned.'

To those who knew Class '86' only from experience of travelling in trains hauled by them, and who could thus appreciate to the full the regularity, speed and reliability of the service provided, it might seem rather graceless to disparage the locomotives on a technicality in design, which to the ordinary traveller had not the slightest effect. But the beating that the track was taking was like some insidious disease, which, if not checked at source can in all suddenness erupt to catastrophic levels; and on a railway lead to such a situation that it required the imposition of severe speed restrictions. Fortunately it was suspected, diagnosed, and eventually remedied by the rebuilding of the '86' Class locomotives. At this stage, however, I must pay tribute to them as the remarkable motive power units that they were. There can surely have been very few locomotive classes that have amassed such an aggregate of brilliant high-speed mileage in so short a time from their first introduction, and in concluding this chapter reference must be made, in some depth, to a few selected performances of outstanding quality. That the official speed limit of 100 mph was exceeded on many occasions, even when the trains concerned were running ahead of time, may be taken as a measure of the confidence of the crews in the machines put at their disposal.

The first of these runs was on an up express from Birmingham allowed only 16½ minutes for the 18.9 miles from New Street to Coventry, start to stop, and then 56½ minutes for the 76.5 miles on to Watford Junction. The first was a sharp enough timing for so short a distance, particularly in that one cannot really open up until the complicated start out of New Street station has been negotiated.

The second section involved a start-to-stop average speed of 81.3 mph. With a 12-coach train, representing a gross trailing load of 430 tons, locomotive No E3193 took 4½ minutes to cover the first 3.8 miles out of Birmingham, to Stechford; the speed was then 83 mph and it rose rapidly to 105 mph at Hampton-in-Arden. An easy finish brought the train into Coventry just 15 seconds inside schedule time. Then, on restarting, there began a most remarkable exhibition of the capacity of these locomotives. In addition to the normal speed restrictions at Rugby, Weedon, Wolverton and Leighton Buzzard, there were temporary slowings to be observed, to 23 mph before Rugby, and to 45 mph between Leighton and Cheddington; yet so vigorously was the locomotive driven that despite a concluding signal check this very fast schedule was accurately observed. On no fewer than seven separate occasions in this run of 76½ miles the speed attained or crossed the 100 mph mark. The succession of maxima were 103, 110, 100, 105, 102, 103 and 100 and, allowing for the three out-of-course checks, the net time for the journey was 53½ minutes, an average from start to stop of 85.8 mph.

Another run, with one of the heavy Anglo-Scottish expresses electrically hauled south of Crewe, provides a remarkable example of how this most famous of the railways built by Robert Stephenson had been upgraded to provide a modern speedway. On this run there were no temporary restrictions below the statutory 100 mph, though the permanent restrictions to 80 mph over the curves at Weedon, Wolverton and Linslade Tunnel north of Leighton Buzzard were then still in force. The run was logged in great detail by a pen-friend who recorded the passing time at no fewer than 41 locations between Rugby and South Hampstead, a distance of 80.2 miles. This latter station was passed in 53 minutes 53 seconds from the start at Rugby, and over the 77.9 miles from Hillmorton relay room to South Hampstead the speed averaged 92½ mph. More notably, however, this fine performance was achieved with no more than marginal excesses over 100 mph. Four times on the run my friend noted 100½ mph, once 101, and at two other locations a brief rise to 102 and 103 mph. The regular speed restrictions were carefully observed, and the high average speed was made possible by the rapidity with which the locomotive accelerated this heavy train to something near to line maximum speed after the restricted length was cleared. A much abbreviated log of the journey will give a good impression of the overall result. The '86' Class locomotive was No E3164, and the gross trailing load 510 tons.

From a number of runs in the driver's cabs of these

Distance (miles)	Actual time		Average speed (mph)
	m	s	
0.0 Rugby	0	00	
4.35 Kilsby Tunnel North End	4	56	51.9
12.82 Weedon	10	21	93.5
22.75 Roade Junction	16	52	91.5
35.85 Bletchley	25	31	91.1
50.80 Tring	35	28	90.1
65.10 Watford Junction	44	11	99.0
77.2 Willesden Junction	51	37	97.7
80.2 South Hampstead	53	53	79.8
—	sig checks		—
82.5 Euston	63	57	—

locomotives, and observing the degree to which they were habitually run well below their maximum capacity, it had often occured to me what kind of overall times could have been attained if one of them had been run as near to all-out as the track conditions permitted. The question was to some extent answered on an occasion in the summer on 1972 on the 16.05 Glasgow express from Euston. In order to pick up a party of distinguished visitors arrangements were made for the train to stop specially at Stafford, and to ensure punctual running north of that station as far as possible, instructions were given for the train to be worked at higher speed than normal from Euston so as to compensate for the effect of the additional stop. A locomotive inspector rode in the cab to invigilate and, because the train would be leaving London only five minutes after the 16.00 train to Manchester, instructions were given to this driver also to run harder than usual to keep out of the way of the Scottish express. The former train, taking the

North Staffordshire line, would be diverging at Colwich. The result so far as the 16.05 train was concerned was a remarkable run. Details taken by an expert recorder show that care was taken to avoid anything but the merest margin of excesses over the line maximum speed of 100 mph, but with excellent enginemanship the train drew gradually ahead of time until the arrival in Stafford station was seven minutes before the schedule time of passing through, having made a start-to-stop average speed of 88.7 mph from Euston. The locomotive was No E3116 and the gross trailing load 390 tons, for 11 coaches.

The intermediate average speeds are interesting in that they show a performance, with a good paying load, practically up to the limit of the road, with speed restrictions as then enforced.

It will be seen that, after passing Rugby six minutes ahead of time, there was a fairly close adherence to the booked point-to-point times. Although the regulations required reductions of speed to 80 mph

LM Region: 16.05 Euston—Stafford

Distance (miles)	Sched time (min)	Actual		Av speed (mph)
		m	s	
0.0 Euston	0	0	00	—
5.4 Willesden Junc	7	6	31	49.8
17.4 Watford Junc	15	13	50	98.7
31.65 Tring	24½	22	22	100.3
46.65 Bletchley	34½	31	39	97.0
59.75 Roade Junc	43½	39	52	95.1
69.75 Weedon	50	46	03	96.8
—		slight signal check —		
82.55 Rugby	60½	54	26	91.5
97.1 Nuneaton	71	64	50	84.0
110.0 Tamworth	79½	73	08	93.3
116.25 Lichfield	83½	76	57	99.8
121.0 Armitage	86½	79	58	94.6
127.15 Colwich Junc	90½	83	53	94.0
133.5 Stafford	97½	90	27	—

Two Class '86' electrics, coupled in multiple, Nos 86033 and 86318, hauling a southbound load of steel coil from Ravenscraig, near Motherwell in October 1983 (T.H. Noble).

at Leighton Buzzard, Wolverton and Weedon, to 60 mph at Rugby, and to 70 mph at Atherstone, the power of the locomotive was such that with very rapid subsequent recovery of speed the running average over the 121¾ miles from Willesden to Colwich was 94.3 mph—a remarkable testimony both to the capacity of the '86' Class locomotives and to skilful driving.

9. Multiple-unit express trains

The evolution of the multiple-unit stop-go fixed-formation local into a corridor main line express with Pullman cars and other restaurant facilities began with the electrification of the main line to Brighton, in 1932; and there is much to be written about post-nationalisation developments on the Southern Region later in this book. But, I can hear some readers asking, are extended references to multiple-unit trains of any kind—express or otherwise, diesel or electric—appropriate in a book about locomotives? It really depends upon how strait-laced is our definition of a locomotive. Today, when the motive power of an ever-increasing number of British express trains is contained in vehicles that have other functions as well, the multiple-unit type of train has come to present a major field of study into high-speed motive power. However, from the traffic handling point of view, the fixed-formation train, which is becoming increasingly common on some of our busiest passenger routes, is by no means ideal in meeting the pronounced fluctuations in traffic volume at times of peak traffic. In this chapter I am discussing trains introduced in the early 1960s which made possible substantial accelerations of service.

At the outset, however, there is a point about modern railway terminology. What is an 'express' train? At one time a train did not have to run very fast to carry the Railway Clearing House lamp headcode for an express passenger train: one lamp immediately above each buffer on the front of the locomotive. A notable instance was that *all*

passenger trains on the Mallaig extension of the West Highland, on which speed was subject to an overall limit of 40 mph for nearly all its length, were accorded this status . Now, in the modern multiple unit-fleet, I know that in some quarters a train is not considered an 'express' unless its equipment is rated to run at 90 mph. In this chapter, however, I have taken the term 'express' in its more general form and included some train-sets classified as 'high-performance', rather than 'express'.

The introduction of the first of these networks, from Glasgow along the north bank of the Firth of Clyde to Helensburgh, in 1960, was very far from a success story; in fact, after a rather serious mishap in which some passengers were injured, the new electric trains were withdrawn entirely in December of that year and steam traction was reinstated. In this project it is important to appreciate that British Railways was breaking fresh ground in the field of railway electric traction. These were equipped on the dual high-voltage ac overhead system using 25 kv, 50 cycle, single-phase ac on the outlying lines, but 6.25 kv through the inner suburban area, because of restricted clearances of tunnels and bridges. A neutral section divides each 25 kv line from the adjoining 6.25 kv line and the change-over is carried out automatically. This system, although provided for in the original decision of the British Transport Commission to adopt the 50-cycle single-phase ac system, had not been put into practical operation until the Glasgow project; and then it was for the first time anywhere in the world.

Left *When the Clyde electrics were first introduced in 'Caledonian blue'; one of the new trains waiting at the junction with the West Highland line, at Craigendoran Junction* (British Railways).

Right *Scottish Region: one of the Clyde Class '303' three-car sets, repainted in the later standard colours, leaving Dalmuir in 1983, on the Balloch-Airdrie service* (T.H. Noble).

But it was not in this novel feature that defects developed and caused the accidents in December 1960 that led to the withdrawal of the entire fleet of the Glasgow electrics.

There had been lesser incidents prior to the explosion which injured a guard and several passengers on December 13, but it was after a fire in one of the trains on December 17 that the whole fleet was withdrawn from service. Until then it had been thought that the trouble was due to over-heating of the transformers whereby the single-phase high-voltage ac line voltage was reduced prior to rectification into dc at 975 volts for the traction motors. But examination of several transformers revealed that the coils of the secondary windings were badly distorted, evidently by severe electo-magnetic forces of a magnitude greater than anything anticipated by the designers. Once this defect was laid bare it was relatively easy to see how it had led to serious trouble. Distortion of the coils would have put strain upon the insulation, leading to its breakdown, and then, of course, to severe arcing, with the obvious risk of fire and explosion. The situation was serious enough for Brigadier Langley, the Chief Inspecting Officer of the Ministry of Transport, to issue an interim report as early as February 1961. He pin-pointed the trouble as being inadequate strength in the secondary winding structure to withstand the electro-magnetic forces resulting from heavy traction current conditions.

It is a measure of the surprise and concern caused by these early failures that reference to them has preceded an actual description of the trains themselves. The electric service was restored at the beginning of October 1961, and has performed admirably ever since. The trains themselves, which were built by the Pressed Steel Co Ltd, are in three-car sets, the middle vehicle of which is powered. The traction motor voltage is 975, and there is a motor to each axle, with a one-hour rating of 220 horsepower. Both the trailer cars have driving ends. The trains were attractively finished, in Caledonian locomotive blue, and with a lavish provision of windows; with a view out ahead from the front seats of the driving trailers, a journey in them is a very pleasant experience. The cars were skilfully designed for maximum passenger accom-modation, with seating for 83 in each trailer, and for 70 in the motor cars. There are, of course, pro-visions for coupling in multiple, so that one can have a six-car, or nine-car train as required to deal with maximum traffic requirements. The maxi-mum service speed is 75 mph.

In May 1960 I was one of an invited party making a trial trip from Glasgow to Helensburgh, but nothing in the way of speed was attempted because the aim was to view various objects of engineering interest, and there were frequent stops. It was not until after the lines on the south bank of the Firth of Clyde had been electrified, in June 1967, that there came an opportunity of riding in the cab, and taking some detailed notes of the running. In wintry weather, some eight months after the inauguration of the service, the 10.40 from Glasgow to Wemyss Bay comprised no more than a single three-car set, though the performance would have been identical had we had six or nine cars. We were stopping only at Paisley and Port Glasgow, and then the two intermediate stations on the Wemyss Bay branch. Real express running was required as far as Port Glasgow, and any such on

this line always puts me in mind of that hectic summer of 1899 when train-steamer competition between the Caledonian, and the Glasgow and South Western Railways for the tourist and residential traffic from Glasgow to the resorts across the Firth of Clyde rose to its zenith. Then, the 4.08 pm Caledonian train was booked to run the 26.2 miles from Glasgow to Gourock Pier in 32 minutes. Seeing that the start out of Glasgow was slow, that a dead slowing was required through Paisley, and that the last few miles through the tunnels and curves beneath Greenock had to be run cautiously, this was a fairly hot schedule for that period, and the Caledonian had to spare one of their 'Dunalastair' Class 4-4-0s from its crack Anglo-Scottish duties to work the train. One could take not a second over 24 minutes to cover the 20.3 miles to Port Glasgow if time was to be kept and speed was

not to be uncomfortably high on the sharply curved concluding length.

It has been worth while recalling what was needed on this super-prestige train of old—so 'prestige' that it did not last long!—in view of what is now done daily by the modern 'Blue Electrics'. As far as Port Glasgow there is not a gradient worth mentioning, though the start must necessarily be slow, over the curves and junctions across the River Clyde to join the one-time Glasgow and South Western line, at Shields. Then we got away well, on the straight and level line past Ibrox, quickly attaining 70 mph; but it was not far to our first stop, at Paisley, and power was shut off, allowing the train to coast freely. I found this was a regular driving technique with the 'Blue Electrics', to work rapidly up to 70 mph and then coast. On the complete 26-mile run between Glasgow and Gourock it is not unusual for power to

Left *A Class '303' electric multiple train, Balloch to Airdrie in picturesque surroundings by Bowling harbour, in November 1983 (T.H. Noble).*

Below left *One of the later Glasgow Area three-car sets of 1979, Class '314' at Bowling (GEC).*

Right *A good impression of the Class '314' three-car sets, working on the Argyll line through Glasgow, from Motherwell to Dalmuir via Glasgow Central low level, here seen near Kelvinhaugh (T.H. Noble).*

Below *A '314'-Class three-car set, Motherwell to Dalmuir, beside the Firth of Clyde at Bowling—March 1982 (T.H. Noble).*

be on for no more than 11 or 12 minutes of the journey. On the continuation of my own westward trip from Paisley we were up to 60 mph in just over one mile from the start and then sustained 71 to 73 mph, passing Langbank, 8.9 miles in 8¾ minutes. Then, as before, power was shut off and we coasted for three miles until the brakes were applied for the stop at Port Glasgow. Our overall time from Glasgow Central was only 23 minutes, including the slowing down and restarting from the stop at Paisley, which lasted 43 seconds. The start-to-stop run for the 13 miles from Paisley to Port Glasgow took only 12 minutes 55 seconds. The branch line to Wemyss Bay traverses some very hilly country, and no further fast running was possible; but I was impressed by the way the very steep gradient from the junction was climbed, attaining a speed of 47 mph on a grade of 1 in 67.

By 1960 the trauma of route modernisation had settled upon the West Coast main line south of Crewe. The preparations for electrification have been likened to building a new railway over the track of the old one, and the heavy engineering work involved was requiring the imposition of many temporary speed restrictions, and not infrequent diversion of important express trains via the Grand Junction line south of Stafford, and via Northampton, south of Rugby. Timekeeping often was chaotic despite decelerated schedules, and the 'image' of the railway, in the eyes of regular travellers, was sinking ever lower. So far as Liverpool was concerned there was not much that could be done about it, but for Manchester there was the alternative of the Midland route, then of course in full commission. It was then that the concept was formed of putting on a luxury high-speed train,

Above *The short-lived Midland Pullman Manchester to St Pancras at speed near Loughborough* (C.J. Marsden).

Left *The down midday Midland Pullman in very characteristic Midland surroundings and signalling* (C.J. Marsden).

specially to attract the frustrated regular business clientele of the Euston route. This train was aimed primarily at the cream of the 'executive' business, and was to be all-Pullman first class only, and diesel-propelled. It was, indeed, in its general formation, the prototype of the high-speed trains of the present time, though very different in the details of construction. But having formed this idea it was decided from the outset to extend it, and authority was obtained for five of the new trains to be constructed, three to include some third-class accommodation. These latter were for the Western Region. While this book is primarily concerned with engineering matters it is, nevertheless impossible to pass over the marketing policy which guided the introduction of Pullman trains on the Western Region, and which proved so unhappily wrong.

The Midland Pullmans in the speed and travel amenities they provided were certainly welcomed by the upper echelon of first-class passengers. The overall timing of 3 hours 10 minutes between Manchester Central and St Pancras, with a very convenient stop at Cheadle Heath to pick up passengers from outer residential districts, was the fastest that had ever been scheduled between London and Manchester, LNW route included; and the trains were well patronised from the outset. I remember however, with much amusement, the reaction of a senior Westinghouse colleague of mine travelling by the 6.10 pm down from St Pancras who, having reserved his seat and paid the fairly substantial Pullman supplement, was very surprised at having to pay for his dinner as well! On the Western Region, however, reaction to the new trains was rather different. Former Great Western men with long memories may have recalled what happened when a Pullman limited express was introduced between Paddington and Torquay, running in addition to the well-established and very popular 'Torbay Limited'. The prospect of luxurious travel, albeit at no higher speed, failed to attract patrons away from the ordinary trains, and the Pullman did not last long. No one wept any salt tears over its passing. It had been an 'extra', not supplementing or replacing an existing service; but in 1960 it was another matter altogether on the Western Region, at any rate so far as the Bristol service was concerned.

At first running non-stop from Temple Meads via Badminton, and then after a few months being diverted and calling additionally at Bath, it was injected at the height of the morning peak traffic to London, at a time when there had been fast, well-patronised, and notably punctual expresses to Paddington. No regular traveller, and there were not a few who commuted daily, would dream of having to reserve a seat, let alone pay a Pullman supplement, for a relatively small improvement in journey time. Between the principal morning and evening business-run both the Bristol and the corresponding train from Birmingham made return midday runs, as the Midland Pullman did from St Pancras to Nottingham; but these were not particularly well patronised. From occasional journeys on the evening train from Paddington to Bath I came to realise that with a few patrons there was a certain 'snob-value' in travelling down by Pullman; but I am afraid that the majority of travellers, accustomed to the 'honest-to-goodness' service that the Western Region had inherited from the Great Western Railway, regarded the 'Blue Pullmans' as something of an imposition. Their attitude was to harden considerably as time went on. However, I must now revert to the engineering aspects of the job.

When the trains were under construction I had occasion to visit a very senior engineering officer of the British Transport Commission who, in confiding to me some features of their design, expressed the view that when they went into traffic they would 'be quite something', to quote his exact words. When details were released the railway and technical journals carried pages of description of the interior decor, which though a little austere to those of us who remember the sumptuous cars of the old Southern Belle were nevertheless attractive, and included many features designed to add to passenger comfort, particularly in the first class. They were the first trains in Great Britain to be fully air-conditioned with controlled temperature and humidity, and it was stated that particular care had

been taken over the reduction of noise. The vehicles were heavily insulated against external sound and heat, with the windows double-glazed, and having fully adjustable venetian blinds between the glasses. The floors were suspended on rubber pads, and insulated. So far, so good.

In the published descriptions it was stated that: 'for maximum passenger comfort, the train has Metro-Schlieren type bogies incorporating helical springs and hydraulic dampers. In each of the four driving bogies the two separate electric traction motors are fully suspended, and the transmission from each motor to the respective axle is by a quill drive. The driving bogies are situated at the trailing end of each motor car, and at the leading end of the adjacent vehicle—that is, the kitchen cars in the six-car trains and the additional parlour cars in the eight-car units. A new type of permanent coupling is used between the cars which absorbs both buffing and drawing loads, and was designed for these Pullman trains to provide a smooth pick-up on starting and stable riding at high speed'.

It was evident that an immense amount of care and thought had been put into the design of these trains, and there is no doubt that the first impression upon entering one, even to the most die-hard Western Region traveller, was pleasurable. There was certainly plenty of power to pull. Six-car and eight-car trains were alike in having two 1,000 horsepower MAN 12-cylinder diesel engines, supplied by the North British Locomotive Company direct-coupled to a GEC composite main and auxiliary generator. The main generator supplied direct current for the traction motors, while the auxiliary supplied current for such functions as starter-battery charging, control circuits, air compressor for the brake system, driving-cab heaters, and so on. These trains were the first in Great Britain to have the Westinghouse two-stage electro-pneumatic system of braking. At that time British Railways had not yet decided upon the general adoption of air-braking instead of vacuum; but these being fixed-formation set trains there was no question of coupling to other vehicles, at any rate when in ordinary service, and so the air-brake could be used. The principle of the two-stage brake needs some explanation, particularly in the evidence it gave that British Railways was not falling into the trap that the London and North Eastern Railway had done in 1935, when they had introduced a train of such speed potential that it could not be stopped within the safety parameters that had to be made.

Brake power in the ordinary way is dependent upon the friction between the brake shoes and the wheel treads; but what is not sometimes appreciated is that the coefficient of friction varies according to the speed of rubbing. As speed increases so the coefficient decreases, and a higher brake force can be applied without risk of skidding the wheels. With the hitherto-traditional fixed brake layout the force was limited by the coefficient of friction at lower speeds. Just after the end of the Second World War the Westinghouse high-speed two-stage brake was developed to overcome this difficulty, and it was first applied to the new multiple-unit electric trains on the Netherlands State Railways in their post-war reconstruction programme. They had a special form of switch that cut in at a predetermined running speed of the train and, through an electro-pneumatic control, this caused an increased air pressure to be applied in the brake cylinders. On the Dutch trains the higher degree of braking was cut in at 37 mph. As fitted to the 'Blue Pullmans' it meant that in round terms the train could be brought to rest from 90 mph in about the same distance that an ordinary train would need from 70 to 75 mph.

My own first experience of the 'Blue Pullmans' was on the Manchester run, when I was privileged to ride in the cab of the 8.50 am up, through to St Pancras, on a wet morning in August 1960. The train was booked to run non-stop over the 181.3 miles from Cheadle Heath in 179 minutes. There was a total of 14 minutes recovery time in this schedule, so that if working at maximum recovery one could expect a time of 165 minutes to St Pancras or an average speed of 65.2 mph; but on the occasion of my travelling there was only one out-of-course slack near Bakewell, and such was the time allowance that we passed Ambergate on time, and ran ahead of it thenceforward to London. The loaded weight of the six-car train was about 310 tons and, with diesel engines having a rated horsepower of 2,000, even in making a time of 86¾ minutes over the 99.1 miles from Leicester to St Pancras, full power was used for no more than 15¾ miles of this distance. For the most part we were working at seven notches out of the maximum of ten on the controller, and often coasting on the downhill stretches. The most impressive part of the run was in mounting the long initial climb up to Peak Forest, much of it on gradients as steep as 1 in 90. Driving up this once-toilsome grind of an incline the quiet effortless ascent was something then quite new to me in railroading. It was the same sort of feeling that one gets sometimes taking a powerful car up some hill that is hallowed with memories of youthful struggles on a push-bike! Rain was driving across the high moors, but with the screen wipers in action we had perfectly clear vision of the line ahead, and the gloomy aspect of the hills, the low cloud, and the dive into the very mountainside at Dove Holes Tunnel—all at nearly 60 mph—seemed to

emphasize the complete mastery of this train over wild nature.

Later in the journey, in more level country and at speeds of around 80 mph, we swept along with smoothness and a very slight buoyancy. There was little sensation of speed. But these, it must not be forgotten, were early days with the 'Blue Pullmans'. When conditions were at their worst on the Euston route the Midland Pullman provided the fastest available service from London to Liverpool, and in the autumn of 1960 I once did the journey in 4 hours 4¼ minutes. The Pullman was then due into Manchester at 9.21 pm, and I continued by the 9.30 pm diesel multiple-unit train over the Cheshire lines route. The 34-mile journey took no more than 43¾ minutes including a 1½-minute stop at Warrington and one of one minute at Widnes, but at times the riding of the four-coach set was terribly rough. At that time we hoped, and believed(!) that such riding of multiple-unit trains at speeds of 70 mph or so would be confined to the older semi-fast services; but not so many months were to pass before those of us who had occasion to use the Bristol Pullman began, sadly, to have other ideas.

The introduction of these trains was greeted with no particular enthusiasm by many of the older Western Region men. At first it was perhaps the natural attitude towards the long-held idea of what an express train should be, and I remember well the cynical looks of a gathering of them at Bristol on the day of the 'Invitation Run' to Reading and back on September 6 1960. I was one of those favoured with an invitation for that demonstration trip; and we certainly made some fast running, especially on the return, when the 70.9 miles from Reading to Bath were covered in 54 minutes start to stop.

On that occasion, after some restricted speed at the start, we ran the 49.8 miles from Cholsey to Corsham at an average speed of 89.3 mph. The maximum service-speed of these trains was 90 mph, although they could run a good deal faster; but on that occasion, when we had some civic dignitaries as well as important railway officers on board, the absolute maximum was 91 mph. The speed was, indeed, controlled with remarkable accuracy despite the varying gradients on the way. But, in view of all the publicity given to the features of design intended to give a well-nigh perfect ride, I cannot say that I was altogether impressed, and when I came to travel by the train in regular service, early in November 1960, I was truly shocked. The train was the 7.57 am up from Bath, and the 'juddering' began as the speed built up to the full 90 mph approaching Chippenham. Between there and Wootton Bassett it was horrible. We eased down a little before Swindon, and between there and Didcot, where we averaged 80 mph, it was more comfortable. But it became very rough again around Goring, and when we tried to pour out coffee it just went everywhere except into our cups! On the London side of Reading there were several checks, and I have a note made on passing Iver: 'riding still rough, even at 60 mph'. Because it was convenient for business appointments—not for choice!—I used the train many times in the first six months of 1961, and with regular patrons its rough riding became something of a joke. There was a 'wag' who used to call out 'fasten your seat belts!' as we left Bath.

The timekeeping was generally reliable, although the booked speed of 65.3 mph from Bath to Paddington was not exactly heroic for a train on which so much care and design expertise had been showered. But in view of the riding I was glad that the scheduled average speed was no higher. Just over 20 years ago, when the 'Blue Pullmans' were continuing their tempestuous progress, I wrote in *The Railway Magazine*:

'Not long ago, I had occasion to make some journeys in the multiple-unit electric trains of the Netherlands Railways. I was in the company of a number of English railwaymen, none of whom had any professional connection with rolling stock, and comment was universal on the excellent riding qualities of these trains. In Great Britain multiple-unit trains are not famed for their good riding, whether it be local railcar sets, express electrics, or the so-called "luxury" diesel Pullman trains. There are some notable exceptions, but they are certainly in the minority, and in the light of experience abroad, the British traveller naturally asks why this should be so. The Dutch trains which are freshly in my mind at the moment seemed to ride more solidly on their springs; they were not so lively, or bouncy, as British multiple-unit trains, and some of my railway friends questioned whether they had a lower centre of gravity. This might be a partial explanation in the case of diesel railcar sets, or even of some of the Southern electrics; but it would not explain that peculiar shuddering effect that one experiences in the Blue Pullmans.

'It is one of the characteristics of increasing years to look at the experiences of bygone days through rose-tinted spectacles, and becoming inured to modern "luxury" travel, as exemplified by the "Bristol Pullman", I have sometimes fallen to wondering whether the locomotive-hauled Pullmans of former days, not to mention such trains as the ordinary Anglo-Scottish expresses by both East Coast and West Coast routes, were really as smooth-riding as one now recalls them. Then, for a time, the blue Pullman train was withdrawn for overhaul, and we had instead a train of old-style Pullman cars, locomotive hauled. I was not wrong after all! It was once again a real pleasure to travel Pullman, and to feel that one was getting something more than mere speed for the supplementary fee. Now, alas, the blue train is back, and is continuing its purgatorial progress . . .'

What the root cause of our discontent was, I never fully discovered. At the time it was said that the wheel diameter of the Schlieren bogies had been changed from the standard used in Switzerland, to a wheel size then standard on British Railways, and that this had upset the dynamics of the bogie. Whether this was so, or not, I cannot confirm, nor

One of the original six-car diesel express Trans-Pennine sets, used between Hull and Liverpool (British Railways).

is there much point in prolonging the story of an unhappy episode in the history of British rolling stock. The 'Blue Pullmans' were withdrawn from the St Pancras–Manchester run in 1966, after completion of the electrification of the Euston route, and from the Western Region route to Birmingham and Wolverhampton in March 1967. Thereafter, for another six years they were used on the Bristol and South Wales services. Their final withdrawal came on May 4 1973, and on the following day the Western Region organised a commemorative tour. The final leg of this tour, over the 133 miles from Newport, passed slowly, to Paddington occupied no more than 99 minutes, an average of 80.6 mph, though not exceeding the statutory '90' to which those trains had always been limited. That they could *run* there was never any doubt.

Another enterprising service, worked entirely by multiple-unit express trains, is that over the former Great Eastern line, between Liverpool Street and Clacton. Here again the timings are very sharp for, although maximum speeds up to 90 mph are permitted on the main line, there is an upper limit of 75 mph on the branch between Colchester and Clacton. Against the total distance of 65.2 miles to Thorpe-le-Soken the scheduled running times total up to no more than 68 minutes including such start to stop bookings as nine minutes for the 9.5 miles from Shenfield to Chelmsford, and 12 minutes for the 13.1 miles from Witham to Colchester. The trains themselves, which are made up to a maximum of 12 cars, comprise two different types of

four-car set, one including a buffet/griddle car and one without any refreshment facilities. Each four-car set has a driving-trailer car at each end, a non-driving motor-brake second, on which all the motive power is mounted, and one trailer which in one class of set is a griddle/buffet car, and in the other is an open second saloon. A 12-car train with one of the former class of sets, and two of the second class provides seating for 108 first-class and 464 second-class passengers with an additional 32 seats in the buffet car. The total tare weight of such a set is 504 tons, or about 540 tons loaded. Each of the three power cars has four 282 horsepower GEC-type traction motors, making a total of 3,384 horsepower for a 12-car train. Such an impressive installation of power is well reflected in the running performances of these trains, seeing also that with traction at 2.5 kv 50 cycles, the actual output during the process of 'stepping' can considerably exceed the nominal capacity of the motors.

This feature is shown in details of an actual run logged early in 1964, in which some of the sharp point-to-point bookings previously mentioned were markedly improved upon. In the early stages of a run down from Liverpool Street with a 12-car train, delays had caused the initial run of 20.2 miles to Shenfield to take $29\frac{1}{4}$ minutes, instead of 23 minutes; but some remarkable running followed on to Colchester (see table below).

The start-to-stop average speeds were thus 70.5 68.5, and 71.2 mph which were of an almost unprecedented vigour, even with modern electric

Distance (miles)	Section	Time start to stop schedule min	Time start to stop actual m s	Maximum speed (mph)
9.5	Shenfield–Chelmsford	9	8 06	89
8.9	Chelmsford–Witham	9	7 49	90
13.1	Witham–Colchester	12	11 03	90.5

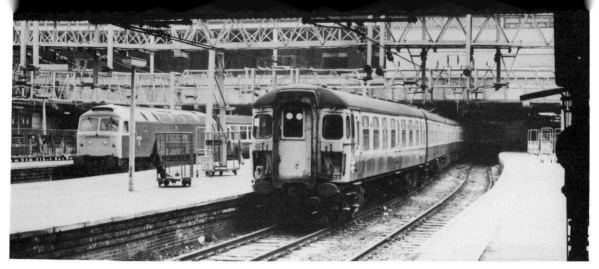

Above left *Manchester-Hull Trans-Pennine express approaching Rotherham* (C.J. Marsden).

Above *At Liverpool Street, in July 1983: in centre the 12.50 express to Clacton, made up to two Class '309' four-car electric multiple unit sets (a Class '47' diesel in the background)* (Brian Morrison).

Below *Great Northern electrification: the first of the four-car outer-suburban sets, introduced in 1975* (GEC).

traction. In each case the train was running at, or near 90 mph in less than four miles from the dead start. Details of the latest developments in the multiple-unit electric trains of the Southern Region are given in a later chapter of this book. Brief mention should also be made of the Swindon-built six-car multiple-unit diesel sets for the express service between Glasgow and Edinburgh, via the former North British main line. These were similar to the Trans-Pennine sets, except that the diesel engines were of 150 instead of 230 horsepower. The balancing speed of these trains on level track was about 70 mph, and on this account, by some reckoning these should not be classified as 'express' trains.

It is very different in the case of the Class '312' electric multiple-unit set trains introduced for the longer distance commuter services on the Great

Left *Express for Royston, made up of two '312' Class four-car sets, in the historic No 10 platform at Kings Cross* (Brian Morrison).

Below *Royston to Kings Cross express between the north and south tunnels at Welwyn* (Brian Morrison).

Bottom *One of the new St Pancras-Bedford electric multiple unit trains '317' Class on arrival in St Pancras Station* (Brian Morrison).

Right *Electric multiple unit train, consisting of two Class '317' four-car sets leaving St Pancras for Luton* (Brian Morrison).

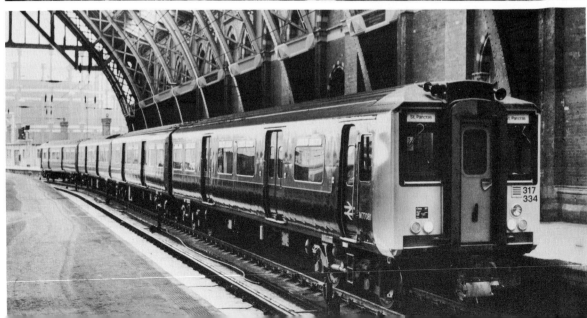

Eastern and Great Northern lines of the Eastern Region, and the more recent Class '317' for the St Pancras–Bedford electric service. As in the case of the Clyde electrics, there is one power car in a four-car set train, but Classes '312' and '317' have four traction motors each of 270 horsepower, and have a rated maximum speed of 90 mph. Not long after the Great Northern service was introduced I saw for myself the entirely new standards of performance that had been established by these trains. On a train made up of two four-car sets I noted a time of exactly 22 minutes, start-to-stop, for the 27.6 miles from Kings Cross to Stevenage,

achieved by an almost record start up the steep gradients out of the terminus to pass Finsbury Park, 2.5 miles, in just three minutes, and a sustained speed of 82 mph up the continuous 1 in 200 ascent from Wood Green to Potters Bar. On a return journey the start from Stevenage was again very fast, passing Woolmer Green, 4.1 miles in five seconds *under* four minutes. Then, over the ensuing 21 miles to Finsbury Park, the speed averaged 89.3 mph, and a very carefully made descent of the final incline completed the run in 22¾ minutes. This, it will be appreciated, represented entirely new standards in outer suburban running.

10. Major developments for non-electrified routes

At the conclusion of Chapter 4 of this book, brief reference was made to the introduction of the Brush Type '4' diesel-electric locomotives, following upon the successful working of the prototype *Falcon*; but before passing on to extended reference to the design and performance of this ultimately very large class, now well known as '47', much more than a mere passing reference must be made to another important prototype which preceded the *Falcon* and the *Lion*, namely the English Electric gas turbine 'GT3'. After proving trials on the stationary testing plant at Rugby, this remarkable locomotive took the road for running tests in 1961, first between Leicester and Marylebone over the former Great Central line, and later between Crewe and Carlisle. It was built at the Vulcan Foundry, by that time a part of the great English Electric group, and had been designed by J.O.P. Hughes, Chief Mechanical Development Engineer of the company. Through my membership of the Institution of Locomotive Engineers I came to know Hughes well, and some time before the locomotive was completed he confided to me many features of its design.

The thinking behind this far-sighted project was that with a suitable turbine cycle and simple transmission the advantage of a gas turbine in terms of power-weight ratio, its ability to burn low grade fuel, with ease of maintenance and high availability, could outweigh the disadvantage of gas turbines in railway traction, that of high fuel consumption when they were working at less than full power. If this could be demonstrated by 'GT3' in ordinary service, the gas turbine could become a serious rival to the diesels. In passing, it was more than once remarked how broadminded must have been the top management of English Electric to finance a project with such an object in view, in the light of their heavy commitment to diesel-electric traction. In designing 'GT3' Hughes felt it was essential that the mechanical design of the locomotive should be as simple as possible, with one final drive mounted

Below *Gas-turbine No3—principle of the locomotive* (Institution of Locomotive Engineers).

Above right *General layout of 2,700 hp gas turbine 4-6-0* (Institution of Locomotive Engineers).

Below right *'GT3'—Longitudinal section through the power unit* (Institution of Locomotive Engineers).

Below far right *'GT3'—Diagram of gear trains in the transmission gearbox* (Institution of Locomotive Engineers).

Filtered air is compressed in six axial stages and one centrifugal to the ratio of 4.8:1. It then passes, via diffusing trumpets, into an outer casing and thence through ducting into a heat exchanger. The compressed and heated air is then delivered into twin combustion chambers, fuel oil is pumped in (continuously) and the mixture ignited, the resulting expanding gases provide sufficient energy to drive first a 2-stage charging turbine which rotates the compressor and secondly a 3-stage power turbine which, through flexible couplings and gearing, rotates the main driving axle, and thus the six driving wheels. The initial start is by an electric motor which disengages itself when the compressor becomes fully turbine driven, ie, at some 2,700 rpm.

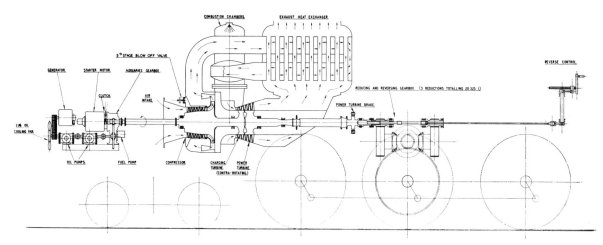

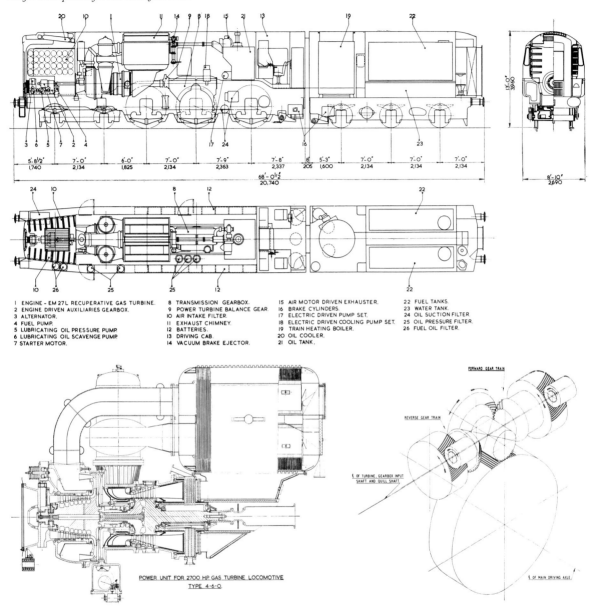

1 ENGINE - EM 27L RECUPERATIVE GAS TURBINE.
2 ENGINE DRIVEN AUXILIARIES GEARBOX.
3 ALTERNATOR.
4 FUEL PUMP.
5 LUBRICATING OIL PRESSURE PUMP.
6 LUBRICATING OIL SCAVENGE PUMP.
7 STARTER MOTOR.
8 TRANSMISSION GEARBOX.
9 POWER TURBINE BALANCE GEAR.
10 AIR INTAKE FILTER.
11 EXHAUST CHIMNEY.
12 BATTERIES.
13 DRIVING CAB.
14 VACUUM BRAKE EJECTOR.
15 AIR MOTOR DRIVEN EXHAUSTER.
16 BRAKE CYLINDERS.
17 ELECTRIC DRIVEN PUMP SET.
18 ELECTRIC DRIVEN COOLING PUMP SET.
19 TRAIN HEATING BOILER.
20 OIL COOLER.
21 OIL TANK.
22 FUEL TANKS.
23 WATER TANK.
24 OIL SUCTION FILTER.
25 OIL PRESSURE FILTER.
26 FUEL OIL FILTER.

POWER UNIT FOR 2700 HP GAS TURBINE LOCOMOTIVE
TYPE 4-6-0.

direct to one coupled axle in a rigid wheelbase, thus avoiding all the complications of flexible drive on to axles carried on bogies. The locomotive was evolved as a simple 4-6-0, with a separate corridor tender containing the fuel supply and a train heating boiler.

Hughes was to read a paper on the construction of the locomotive at meetings of several scientific societies; but a month before the first of these was presented, at Derby, in December 1961, he invited me to join him on a footplate run from Crewe to Carlisle. It was a novel experience to ride on a locomotive that was to all outward appearances a 4-6-0, but on which the 'firebox front' was replaced by a plain steel casing finished in ultra-modern style in light mottled grey, and on which the 'corridor' ran through the middle of the tender, with fuel tanks on either side. Before describing some incidents in the course of a very fine run, however, some of the salient features of the design itself must be discussed.

Hughes' paper presented to the Institution of

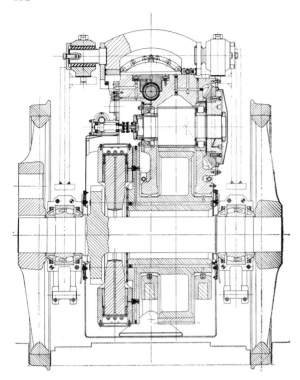

Locomotive Engineers in April 1962 was a master-piece of engineering scholarship and lucid description. The general layout of the locomotive and tender may be studied from the accompanying diagram, from which it will be appreciated how neatly the various components were disposed in the necessarily limited space available within the limits of the structure gauge. Hughes was a past-master in the field of gas-turbine design, and the longitudinal section drawing of the power unit reproduced herewith provides evidence of a beautiful piece of work. From the general layout drawing it will be seen that the power unit was located vertically above the rear pair of bogie wheels, with the transmission gearbox driving directly on to the middle pair of coupled wheels. How the power from the horizontal shaft of the main turbine was transmitted to the main driving axle is shown in a diagram of the gear trains, while a further detailed drawing shows a transverse section through the transmission gearbox. The care and skill taken in the design of all these components was reflected in the notable freedom from failure experienced when the locomotive was on its running trials out on the line. Between Crewe and Carlisle the tests terminated at Upperby Yard, 140.2 miles from Crewe, and about three-quarters of a mile short of Carlisle station. The schedule time laid down for a non-stop run was 174 minutes in each direction, and provided an ample recovery margin.

So far as actual performance goes, a striking comparison was quoted in the discussion on Mr Hughes' paper in London, bearing on the time taken to attain the balancing speed of 70 mph on level track. The second of the Southern diesel-electric locomotives No 10202, hauling a trailing load of 399 tons, attained this speed in just over seven minutes, while 'GT3' practically equalled this acceleration despite hauling a load of 638 tons behind the tender—a remarkable advance in power. Some further details were also quoted of comparative ascents of the Shap Incline, as follows:

Power	Steam	Diesel-electric	Gas turbine 'GT3'	Gas turbine 'GT3'
Class of Loco	'Duchess' 4-6-2	EE 2,000 hp Class '40'	'GT3'	'GT3'
Load, coaches	11	12	12	15
Speed (mph)				
at Tebay	77	68	75	—
at Summit	37	25	42	34
Time (min)				
for 5.5 miles	6¼	8¾	6	8

On the run that I enjoyed in the cab of 'GT3' a slight leakage in the fuel system made it undesirable

Above left *'GT3'—Transverse section through transmission gearbox* (Institution of Locomotive Engineers).

Below *The English Electric gas turbine locomotive 'GT3' on a trial run, climbing Shap* (Derek Cross).

to work the locomotive at full power on the heavy gradients of the North Country; but even working at no more than seven-eighths full the running was impressive enough, with a time of 6¼ minutes from Tebay to Shap Summit, and initial and concluding speeds of 77 and 40½ mph with 12 coaches. The driver, a regular Crewe North top link man, said he thought the locomotive was equal to a 'good Scot'; but I have never personally known or heard of a climb of the Grayrigg and Shap inclines by a 'Royal Scot' either of the original type, or as rebuilt, to come anywhere near what 'GT3' did when I rode in the cab, even though it was working at no more than seven-eighths full power. On Grayrigg bank the climbing was the more impressive in that we were checked to 20 mph at the very foot of the incline, near Milnthorpe, and had to work back into speed on the gradient. On the lengthy stretch at 1 in 131 above Oxenholme we attained 52 mph and, with a trailing load of 385 tons, this represented an output of about 1,600 equivalent drawbar horsepower. In response to some points in the discussion on his paper to the Institution of Locomotive Engineers Mr Hughes gave details of a remarkable climb from Carlisle to Shap Summit with a trailing load of 458 tons, on which the 30½ miles from Upperby Yard to the summit signal box took no more than 42 minutes, against the 52 minutes of the test schedule. It would have taken good work on the part of a 'Duchess' Class 'Pacific' steam locomotive to surpass such a climb as this.

Promising as these results were, however, the enterprise of English Electric in building this fine locomotive was not followed up. On only one of the test runs from Crewe to Carlisle was the dynamo-

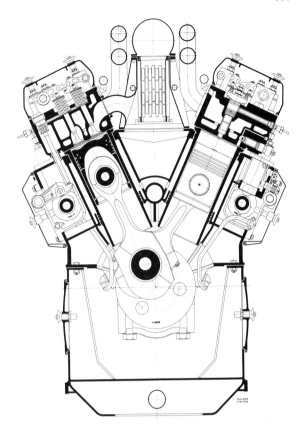

Above right *Cross-section of the Sulzer 'LVA24' engine, fitted on certain of the Class '47' locomotives, instead of the in-line type standard on the majority of the class* (Sulzer).

Below *Test with 'GT3', Carlisle to Crewe passing over Tebay troughs* (Derek Cross).

meter car used, and by the end of 1962 it was evident that, for non-electrified routes other than those of the Western Region, British Railways had settled upon the Brush Type '4' diesel-electric, later known as Class '47', as the future standard for quantity production. To some it seemed strange that, while the Brush *Falcon* prototype had the Bristol-Siddeley-Maybach engines, the new standard type had the Sulzer '12 LDA 28C' engine that had been used on the rival BRC&W project, the *Lion*. Certain traffic men, notably Gerard Fiennes, then Chief Operating Officer of British Railways, felt that 2,750 horsepower was not

enough, in view of what was coming forth with the electric locomotives on the London Midland Region. Fiennes indeed, who was planning for major accelerations all round, asked for 4,000 horsepower; but J.F. Harrison, who was then Chief Mechanical Engineer, would not be moved beyond the 2,750 horsepower of the new Brush-Sulzer Class '47'. He felt that in cases of exceptional loading one could always resort to double-heading, which with diesels coupled in multiple could be done without the necessity for a second crew.

Technically, the principal difference between the *Falcon* and the standard Class '47' was that, while the former had two engine units, each developing 1,400 horsepower and mounted on a single frame, Class '47' was a single-engined job, of the 12-cylinder twin-bank type, with a rated output of 2,750 horsepower. Great importance in design was given to the reduction of total weight. A super-structure design for the locomotive body was evolved using techniques suggested by the aircraft side of the Hawker Siddeley-Brush organisation. A stressed skin construction was the lightest that could be adopted and a triangular framework was evolved for the front ends of the locomotive for transferring buffing loads to the body sides over the top of the side doorways in the cab. Torsional rigidity of the structure was obtained by the incorporation of bulkheads, and also by the careful design of those roof sections over the ends of the locomotive next to the cabs. The boiler compartment and the radiator structure are the sections which were designed to provide the torsional resistance. The accompanying 'exploded' view gives a good impression of the general arrangement of the locomotive. The companion drawing shows how considerably the layout

of the machinery differed from that of the *Falcon* — also built by Brush.

The locomotives are carried on two single-piece cast steel bogies of the Commonwealth type, each equipped with three axle-hung traction motors continuously rated at 368 horsepower, providing a total horsepower per locomotive of 2,208. The superstructure weight is taken on large, flat centre-pivot plates on the bolsters, which in turn are mounted on four helical coil-spring nests carried on two spring links. The axles run in roller-bearings. In view of the strictures placed on the use of axle-hung traction motors in the case of the Class '86' electric locomotives, discussed in previous chapters of this book, it is interesting to compare the values of unsprung weight per axle with those of contemporary high-power locomotives:

Locomotive	Max axle load (tons)	Max speed (mph)	Unsprung weight per axle (tons)
Diesel-electric Class '37'	17.8	90	3.35
Diesel-electric Class '47'	19.8	95	3.55
Diesel-electric 'Deltic'	18.0	100	3.3
Electric Class '86'	20.5	100	4.25

I rode many thousands of miles on Class '47' loco-motives, on all Regions of British Railways except the Southern, and found them invariably smooth-riding and comfortable whatever the terrain and the speed.

Basic details of these locomotives, as first introduced, are:

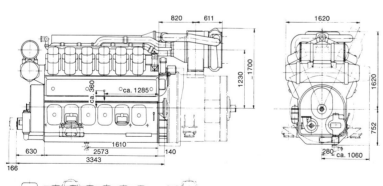

Left *General proportions of the Sulzer 12LVA24 engine of 3,000 hp* (Sulzer).

Above right *One of the Class '47's (original number D1815) and two tone green livery on a test special in April 1965 southbound near Shap station* (Derek Cross).

Right *A Class '47', since electrification No 47013, working a southbound train of empty car carriers, near Beattock summit in 1974* (Morrison Bryce).

Weight in working order	114 tons
Tractive effort (max)	55,000 lb
Tractive effort (cont at 27 mph)	30,000 lb
Wheelbase (total)	51 ft 6 in
Bogie wheelbase	14 ft 6 in
Bogie pivot centres	37 ft 0 in
Width overall	9 ft 2 in
Height overall	12 ft 9⅜ in
Length overall	63 ft 6 in
Length over buffer beams	59 ft 10½ in
Minimum curve negotiable	4 chain
Maximum permissible speed	95 mph
Fuel tank capacity	850 gallons
Boiler water-tank capacity	1000 gallons

When first introduced they were finished in a handsome livery of two-tone green, consisting of olive-green bodywork with a broad band of a lighter shade of green around the waist. This style, the result of collaboration with the Design Panel of the one-time British Transport Commission, was later superseded by the 'electric blue' with yellow nose livery which, however desirable from the practical working point of view, was not nearly so attractive aesthetically. There were eventually more than 500 of Class '47' built at intervals between 1962 and 1967.

It became common knowledge that initially British Railways had a good deal of trouble with

Above *Last day before the change to electric traction: Class '47' diesel No 47459 on the 15.55 (Sundays) Glasgow to Euston (Morrison Bryce).*

Left *A Class '47' working a Blackpool to Paisley special express over the former G&SW line between Sanquhar and Kirkconnel in 1973 (Morrison Bryce).*

Below *West Coast expresses diverted to the Settle and Carlisle line: Sundays only Glasgow to Manchester train near Cotehill, hauled by No 47454 in March 1975 (Morrison Bryce).*

these locomotives, as indeed they had experienced earlier with the Peak Class, referred to in Chapter 4 of this book. While part of the trouble arose from the uprating of the standard Sulzer engine from 2,200 horsepower, first to 2,500 in the Peaks, and then to 2,750 on Class '47', there were some who felt that the troubles might have been lessened if more attention had been given to training the shed staffs in the totally different maintenance procedures necessary with diesels, as compared to steam. It may be noted in passing that in 1927 Sulzer Brothers had given up the 'V' type of engine for the in-line type, and that all those supplied for the British Type '4' locomotive, whether made in Switzerland or by Vickers, at Barrow-in-Furness, were of the latter type with two banks of cylinders. Even though the firm had reverted to the 'V' type in 1960, with a new range designated LVA 24, as distinct from LDA 24 in the British locomotives, the latter remained standard on British Railways. Teething troubles apart, and with replacement of faulty components, Class '47' proved capable of excellent performance on the road, and has certainly withstood the test of time.

My first experience on the footplate of one of these locomotives was on the 1 pm Anglo-Scottish express from Kings Cross, and from this it appeared that, with a trailing load of 405 tons (11 coaches), the balancing speed in a 1 in 200 gradient when working at maximum power was about 71 mph. This seemed rather low for a locomotive of 2,750 nominal horsepower, but in correspondence Mr J.F. Harrison gave me some interesting figures as to the way the power of the locomotive was absorbed:

Air and rolling resistance of coaches at 11¾ lb per ton	900
Gravity resistance on 1 in 200	850
Gravity resistance or 114-ton locomotive	240
Air resistance of locomotive at 8;15 lb per ton	176
Rolling resistance of locomotive at 4.5 lb per ton	99

This makes a total of 2,265, and the difference between this figure and the rated 2,750 is accounted for by the overall efficiency of the locomotive installation, generally reckoned at about 80 per cent. In this particular instance it was 82½ per cent. The value of air and rolling resistance of the coaches quoted as 11¾ lb per ton is equal to the most up-to-date British Railways test figure for a train travelling against a light breeze of 4½ mph blowing at an angle of 45 degrees to the track.

The accompanying table sets out details of certain examples of maximum performance that I have noted personally; in all except No 6 I was in the driver's cab. The first three were all in the course of a single return trip to Inverness by the 'Clansman' service, with the same locomotive, and gave consistent results on the steep gradients of the Highland line. The fourth was what appeared to be an exceptional performance on *The Royal Scot* train. The speed was sustained at a shade over 60 mph on the 1 in 131 section of the Grayrigg bank and had not fallen below 58 mph after the final two miles at 1 in 106. The last five miles of this lengthy incline were covered in 4 minutes 50 seconds; an average speed of 62 mph. It was this same locomotive that provided the seventh example, of an attained speed of 88 mph on level track between Garstang and Lancaster. It should be added that the speed in all cases was recorded by stop-watch, and not from the locomotive speedometer, and were cross-checked by reference to the point-to-point times read from a second independent watch. The figures quoted in this table are enough to establish the Brush Class '47' as a very successful locomotive.

When Gerard Fiennes was Chief Operating Officer of British Railways, and asked for a 4,000 horsepower diesel-electric locomotive, he received a

Class '47' diesel-electric locomotives: Examples of maximum performance

Ref No	Speed (mph)	Load, gross trailing (tons)	Gradient 1 in (rising)	Location	Equivalent drawbar horsepower
1	32½	420	60	Highland Line	1,900
2	38	420	70	Highland Line	1,950
3	42	420	80	Highland Line	1,970
4	60	465	131	Grayrigg bank	2,200
5	71½	410	200	GN Main Line	1,955
6	86	385	880	GW Uffington (westbound)	1,622
7	88	465	Level	Galgate (LNW)	1,705

rather 'crusty' answer from the Chief Mechanical Engineer. But the seeds had been sown and at the end of 1967 Hawker Siddeley-Brush produced a 4,000 horsepower prototype, the *Kestrel*, which could be broadly described as a 16-cylinder version of the standard '47' Class. An important difference from the great bulk of the latter class is that *Kestrel* had the V-type of diesel engine, the 16 LVA 24 instead of the in-line double-banked LDA 24. But, prior to the completion of *Kestrel*, five locomotives of Class '47' has been built by Brush and supplied to British Railways with the new 12 LVA 24 engine. These five locomotives, all stationed at Sheffield, had already enjoyed a very satisfactory and intense spell of utilisation by the time *Kestrel* was completed.

In 1965, with the approaching completion of the London Midland electrification from Manchester and Liverpool to Euston, and the prospect of finance being made available for the continuation of the electrification northwards to Carlisle and Glasgow still remote, it was felt that to continue north of Crewe with comparable standards of speed to those about to be established south of that centre would require diesel-electric locomotives of 5,000 horsepower, and the proposition was put to Brush. The best that could be put forward using existing well-tried components was a 4,0000 hp locomotive using the standard Sulzer 16 LVA 24 engine.

Although *Kestrel* was not quite what British Railways had asked for in the first place, it was a remarkable locomotive. It was the most powerful single-engined unit in the world, though the actual

tractive power was not in proportion to the nominal output of the 16 LVA 24 diesel engine. Whereas the Class '47' had traction motors of 368 horsepower, making a total of 2,208, against the engine horsepower of 2,750, *Kestrel* had six motors of the same design but uprated to 515 hp — a total of only 3,075 hp. The ratio of traction-motor horsepower to engine horsepower was thus 77 per cent as against 81 per cent in Class '47'. Nevertheless, it was a remarkable piece of locomotive design, and one that seemed not a little venturesome in that it put a locomotive of such power on to as few as six axles. The designed speed was 110 mph continuously, with a maximum of 125 mph. The accompanying perspective drawing shows the general layout of the locomotive. Not only had the weight been reduced to a minimum, compared to the 114 tons of Class '47', but the overall length was no more than 3 feet longer — 66 feet 6 inches. *Kestrel* was finished in a distinctive two-tone colour scheme of yellow and brown, with the Hawker-Siddeley emblem at each end on the side below the driver's window.

In asking for a diesel-electric locomotive of 4,000 hp Gerard Fiennes had in mind the limited platform lengths at Kings Cross, where to meet the need for maximum utilisation of the coaching stock it was necessary for an incoming train and its locomotive to remain in the platform while unloading, cleaning

General arrangement drawing of the Kestrel *4,000 hp diesel electric locomotive* (Brush).

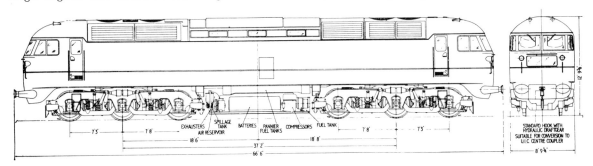

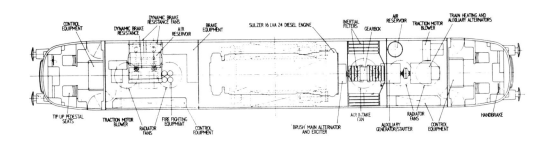

Above *The notable Brush prototype locomotive* Kestrel *as built* (Brush Elec. M/Cs Ltd, G. Toms Collection).

Below *Part-sectioned perspective drawing of the* Kestrel (Brush).

and reloading took place. and there had to be sufficient length for the outgoing locomotive to back on, couple up and stand clear of the fouling point before departure. As Fiennes pointed out, the Chief Mechanical Engineer's suggested alternative of double-heading on the most severe duties would in such conditions encroach on the platform space between the buffer stops and the outer fouling point by two coach lengths, and this of course would be quite unacceptable. At the time *Kestrel* was introduced an interesting comparison was made of its capital cost, maintenance charges, and fuel costs, with its equivalent in multiple heading, with references to two Type '3' locomotives, and three Type '2's used on the same duties. All were somewhat hypothetical, because no existing Type '2' or Type '3' was authorised to run at the design speeds of *Kestrel*. Nevertheless the comparison was interest-

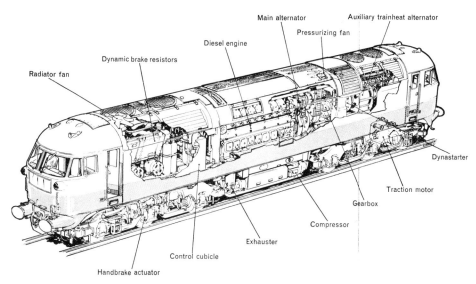

Main alternator
Auxiliary trainheat alternator
Pressurizing fan
Diesel engine
Dynamic brake resistors
Radiator fan
Dynastarter
Traction motor
Gearbox
Compressor
Exhauster
Control cubicle
Handbrake actuator

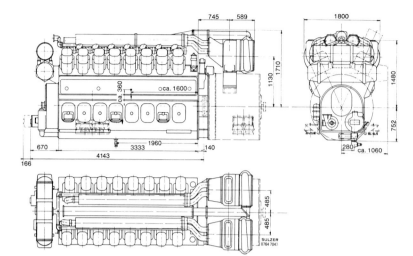

Left *General proportions of the Sulzer 16 LVA 24 engine of 4,000 hp as installed in* Kestrel *(Sulzer).*

Below *The Brush* Kestrel *prototype on its first demonstration press run from Marylebone in January 1968* (Brush Elec M/Cs Ltd, G. Toms Collection).

Right *The Brush* Kestrel *prototype on a 20-coach trial train between Crewe and Carlisle in 1968* (Brush Elec M/Cs Ltd, G. Toms Collection).

Below right Kestrel *on heavy mineral train trials. Unfortunately a full load for the locomotive's potential could not be taken because the train would have been too long for BR sidings!* (Brush Elec M/Cs Ltd, G. Toms Collection).

ing. It showed that two Type '3's would have a capital cost 80 per cent of that of three Type '2's, with a maintenance cost of 70, and a fuel cost of 95 per cent. The corresponding percentages for the one *Kestrel* against three Type '2's were 60, 45 and 85. As regards overall length, the variations were 154 feet 6 inches using Type '2' and 123 feet with Type '3', both showing a great increase over the 66 feet 6 inches of *Kestrel*.

What *Kestrel* could actually do in the way of power output seems never to have been fully demonstrated on British Railways. Although her axle-loading was less than that of the largest and most powerful steam locomotives, she was introduced just at the time when the London Midland Region was experiencing the severe effects on the track caused by the Class '86' electric locomotives; and, although the unsprung weight from the axle-hung traction motors of *Kestrel* was not much greater than that of Class '47', when added to a 21-ton axle-load the total effect was considerably more. After some preliminary running the Chief Civil Engineer of British Railways forbade the use of the locomotive in passenger service. This of course was a great disappointment to the builders, who were hoping that the great power would be a selling point for overseas railways. It had in fact been designed so that by exchange of bogies it could be used on routes having different rail gauges. In its original form it ran a considerable mileage in heavy mineral service, but was subsequently taken into the Brush works for modification to bring the weight down to an

acceptable level for passenger service. This was achieved by use of a different type of bogie. From the late summer of 1969 the locomotive went into service on the East Coast main line between Kings Cross and Newcastle, although I did not receive any details of its running. It was also tried in the West Coast route north of Crewe, though here the only references to its working came from a source subsequently found to be unreliable. After completing about 125,000 miles of running on British Railways it was withdrawn and, after modification to the Russian 5 foot gauge, was sold to the USSR Railways, in 1971. So ended a notable experiment.

In following the Brush developments from the '47' Class through to the departure of the *Kestrel* for foreign parts, I have drawn somewhat ahead of events elsewhere in Great Britain. In 1962, not very long after the Brush Electrical Company had produced the prototype Type '4' locomotive *Falcon*, which in some ways was the progenitor, the English Electric Company built their prototype, known as 'DP2'. Incorporating none but well-tried components this could be described as a Type '4' version of the very successful Type '3' locomotive from the same company, now Class '37', and introduced in 1961. These, like 'DP2', had the same equalised-type bogies, with swing bolsters and three motorised axles as in the 'Deltics'. The engines, in both 'DP2' and Class '37', were of the English Electric 'CSVT' type, with cylinders arranged in V-formation. Class '37' had 12 cylinders giving a maximum output of

1,750 horsepower, whereas 'DP2' had 16 cylinders. The latter was actually the same engine as used in the Class '40' diesel-electric locomotives of which 200 were at that time in service on British Railways. On this class the engine was rated at 2,000 horsepower, but by the application of inter-cooling it was uprated to 2,700 in 'DP2'.

Basic data regarding these two closely related designs are:

	Class '37'	**'DP2'**
Wheel arrangement	Co-Co	Co-Co
Weight in working order (tons)	103	105
Tractive effort max (lb)	55,000	50,000
Length overall (ft-in)	61-6	69-6
Width overall (ft-in)	8-11⅝	8-9½
Height overall (ft-in)	12-10½	12-9⅜
Max permissible speed (mph)	90	90
Fuel tank capacity (gal)	920	900
Boiler water tank capacity (gal)	800	640
Engine, GEC type	'12 CSVT'	'16 CSVT'
Power rating	1,750 hp	2,700 hp

At the time 'DP2' was built, the company was in full production with Class '37', which eventually totalled 308 locomotives. Both these designs, like the 'Deltics', had the characteristic English Electric 'nose' cabs, which gave a stylish and distinguished appearance to them. When R.C. Bond was Chief Mechanical Engineer of British Railways he strongly favoured this design, and considered it not only decorative but essential to have some projection forward of the driver, as a protection in case of accident. But the Design Panel of British Railways thought otherwise, and the 'Deltics' and Class '37' were the last to have this feature.

Class '37' was introduced as a mixed-traffic unit but from the outset these locomotives were put into first-class express duty on the Great Eastern line and did excellent work on the fast Liverpool Street–Norwich express. They took over the jobs of the Class '40' 2,000 hp English Electric diesels and although rated at no more than 1,750 hp appeared to do equally well, if not actually better. On one particular run with a nine-coach train of 325 gross trailing tons the 46.3 miles from Norwich to Ipswich were covered in 40¼ minutes start to stop, with a maximum speed of 87 mph through Stowmarket. The train was checked by signal in getting away from Ipswich, but made good time from Manningtree onwards. Then after making the last stop, at Colchester, a very fast run up to London followed passing Stratford (47.7 miles) in 41¼ minutes. But for a signal stop outside the terminus, Liverpool Street (51¾ miles) would have been reached in 46¼ minutes. More recently, Class '37' locomotives have distinguished themselves in express mineral train service in South Wales, working three together in multiple-unit on 2,700-ton iron ore trains. Detailed reference to these duties, in company with other heavy freight activities, is made in a later chapter of this book.

The 2,700 horsepower English Electric prototype, 'DP2', went into regular service, and without any trouble immediately began to amass an impressive total of high-speed express passenger mileage, between Euston, Crewe and Carlisle, regularly averaging about 4,000 miles per week. In view of the impending completion of electrification between Euston, Liverpool and Manchester, it was then transferred to the East Coast route, and continued in a similar trouble-free spell of activity, including complex diagram working. In the summer of 1963 she was regularly running 5,270 miles a week between Kings Cross and Edinburgh, going down each weekday on the 10.10 am, due at Waverley at 4.30 pm, and returning during the night on the 10.30 pm up, arriving at Kings Cross at 5.24 am. It was only on Sundays that there was a lay-over for 11 hours for maintenance purposes. In the autumn of 1963 'DP2' was put on to a daily diagram that involved running from Kings Cross to Leeds and back, and then from Kings Cross to Grantham and back, a daily mileage of 583, and it was while she was on this working that I had the privilege of a ride in her cab, on the 'Yorkshire Pullman' non-stop from Doncaster to Kings Cross. We had a load of 11 cars — a gross trailing load of 460 tons. The train was then booked to cover the 156 miles in 158 minutes, and although we experienced a hampering series of checks there was some splendid running intermediately; indeed, despite three slowings to 20 mph for permanent way work, signal checks to 10, 25, 20 and 25 mph, and one dead stop, we passed Finsbury Park three minutes early, in 150 minutes for the 153.4 miles from Doncaster. A final signal stop, however, made us three minutes late on arrival at Kings Cross. A careful reckoning shows that the aggregate effect of the numerous checks was to incur a loss of 27 minutes in running, which left a net time of 134 minutes and a start-to-stop average speed of exactly 70 mph from Doncaster to Kings Cross.

I was very impressed with the performance of this locomotive. On the favourable stretches of line restraint had to be applied to avoid exceeding the designed permissible maximum speed of 90 mph, but the adverse lengths were climbed as though the gradients scarcely existed, with such an average speed as 81 mph up the eight miles from the Trent Valley up to and through Peascliffe Tunnel. On several occasions my observations confirmed that the locomotive was working up to the designed optimum, with an equivalent drawbar horsepower of 2,150 at 80 mph. It only remains to be added that, despite the intense utilisation to which this prototype locomotive had already been subjected, with a well-nigh impeccable record of reliability, 'DP2' was still riding perfectly, and was altogether a very enjoyable locomotive on which to travel. The successful working of this locomotive led to British

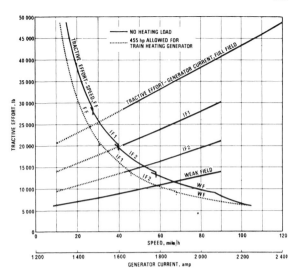

Right *Performance characteristics of the Class '50' diesel-electric locomotives* (GEC).

Below *General arrangement drawing and plan of the Class '50' locomotive* (GEC).

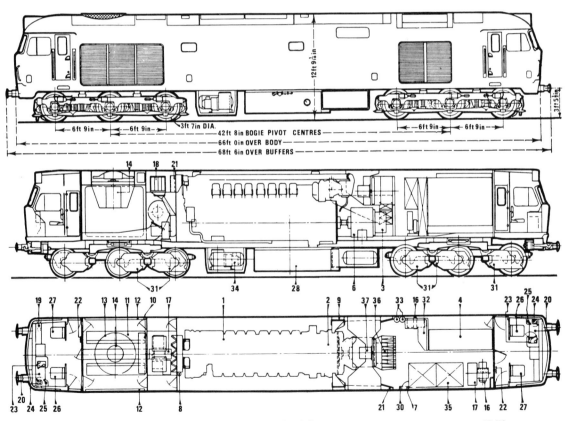

1. Engine 16 CSVT
2. Main generator EE 840
3. Auxiliary generator E 911
4. Main equipment frame
5. Batteries
6. Train heating generator
7. Urinal
8. Engine fuel supply unit
9. Engine air ducting
10. Radiator header tank
11. Radiators
12. Radiator shutters
13. Radiator fan
14. Radiator fan motor
15. Compressor WTG 3VC75
16. Exhausters
17. Traction motor blowers
18. Air filters
19. Sand fillers
20. Driver's desk
21. Air filters
22. Handbrake
23. Master controller
24. Automatic air brake valve
25. Independent air brake valve
26. Driver's seat
27. Assistant's seat
28. Main 1,000-gal fuel tank
29. Main fuel tank gauge
30. Urinal flush tank
31. Traction motors EE 538
32. Brake equipment
33. CO_2 bottles
34. Air reservoirs
35. Dynamic brake
36. Air filter (equipment compartment)
37. Fan motor

Below *Liverpool and Manchester to Glasgow express on the Shap Incline, hauled by Class '50' diesel No D437, at a time before the electrification was completed* (Morrison Bryce).

Below right *Aberdeen-Euston express approaching Carstairs in 1970 before electrification and when the signalling was still semaphore. The train is hauled by Class '50' diesel No D409 (original numbering)* (Derek Cross).

Railways placing an order for 50 with the same diesel engine and traction motors, but incorporating in their controls a number of features that were new. These arose from the continuing demand for increased power output per ton of total locomotive weight, combined with the consistently high standard of reliability that had been demonstrated in 'DP2'. Superficially the new locomotives, first introduced in 1967, differed from 'DP2' by having a flat-ended superstructure, carrying roof-mounted route indicators, and by BR specification eliminating the characteristic English Electric nose cab — regrettably, in the opinion of many.

Apart from outward appearances however, the new locomotives, at first numbered D400 to D449 and later becoming well known as Class '50', were equipped with automatic tractive-effort control, dynamic braking, inertia filtration, and slow-speed control. It is important to appreciate what these

novel features involved, and what it was hoped to achieve by the incorporation in a locomotive that had basically the same power plant as 'DP2'. First, as to tractive-effort control, the range of performance of a diesel-electric locomotive is extended by progressively weakening the field current in the traction motors as the train accelerates, and it is important that this process is accurately controlled. On Class '50' electronic time-delay units are used in the associated control circuits, to give a precise control of the field-weakening switches. A 'closed loop' system of control is used to regulate the tractive effort, diesel engine load and train speed in response to the electrical signals from the driver's manipulation of the control handle. The system is able to control wheel-slip automatically, so that, if the available adhesion could not sustain the tractive effort selected by the driver, the automatic tractive-effort control imposes a lower value. This was expected to give considerable advantage in starting heavy trains by giving more precise control over the power equipment, in addition to quickly controlling wheel-slip. To minimise wear on brake blocks and brake rigging, the locomotive design includes electro-mechanical dynamic braking, control of which is integrated with the purely mechanical braking on the train. The two forms of braking, the one on the locomotive and the other on the train, are controlled by the driver with a single brake handle.

The Class '50' locomotives were designated mixed traffic, but while they were originally allocated to the West Coast main line to work on the non-electrified sections between Weaver Junction and Glasgow they were also fitted with a slow-speed control. For precise working in the speed range below 3 mph, as required for the 'merry-go-round' coal trains, the driver can pre-set the speed, and the control system will maintain that value constantly, regardless of gradients or trailing load. This is an arrangement similar to that fitted to some of the latest French electric locomotives, though on some that I have ridden the constant speed control is operated at full express-train speed. The accompanying diagram shows the performance characteristics of the 'D400/50' Class, and it will be seen that they approximate to those of 'DP2', except that the production batch of 50 had a maximum designed speed of 105 mph. The maximum actually permitted on any part of the West Coast main line

north of Crewe was 100 mph, and at the time of their introduction there were not many lengths where this was authorised. The general arrangement and plan of the locomotive is shown herewith, and it will be noted that the overall length of 68 feet 6 inches over buffers was only 1 foot short of the 4,000 horsepower *Kestrel*, and that it had an all-up weight of 117 tons.

The new locomotives were introduced at a time when it was still doubtful whether financial authorisation for the extension of the London Midland electrified system from Weaver Junction northwards to Carlisle and Glasgow would be forthcoming, and they were all allocated to the West Coast main line. Except that they had a maximum service speed of 100 mph, there was little difference between them and Class '47', as far as tractive units were concerned. In any case, when I first rode on them in the winter of 1968–9 the only section over which running at 100 mph was permitted was the electrified portion between Crewe and Weaver Junction. Five instances of high-power output that I noted in the course of some runs between Crewe and Glasgow are tabulated overleaf, all with the locomotives working at full power.

These instances, it will be seen, are closely similar to my observations on the Class '47' locomotives.

On the run to which the first two examples in the table refer, the train had to make a special stop at Oxenholme, and the total time over the complete ascent from Carnforth to Shap Summit was

Location	Gradient 1 in	Trailing load gross (tons)	Speed (mph)	Estimated edhp
Grayrigg bank	133	450	53½	1,970
Shap Incline	75	450	40	2,040
Auldgirth (G&SW line)	200	450	69	1,960
Law Junction	100	415	48	1,850
Thrimby Grange	125	415	57	1,930

lengthened accordingly; but on another trip, on which the gross trailing load was heavier by one coach, totalling 495 tons, the climbing was unchecked and the 31.4 miles, in which the train was lifted 885 feet in altitude, were covered in 29¼ minutes, at an average speed of 64.3 mph. The initial speed passing Carnforth was 87 mph and Shap Summit, at an altitude of 915 feet above sea level was topped at 41 mph. An analysis of the dynamics of this fine performance indicates that the

Below left *Inauguration of the accelerated diesel service north of Crewe: the two Class '50's, D437 and 447 coupled in multiple, at Crewe, setting back on to 'The Royal Scot' which has been electrically hauled from Euston* (British Railways).

Bottom left *Twin-diesel haulage on the Caledonian line, locomotives D443 and D415, on a northbound express* (British Railways).

Below *Euston-Glasgow express hauled by Class '50' diesels D423 and D440, in multiple, passing Beattock station at high speed, before it was closed, and the signalling changed to multi-aspect colourlight* (Derek Cross).

Bottom *The down 'Midland Scot', from Birmingham, leaving Carstairs for Glasgow, having detached the through carriages for Edinburgh—a load for the two Class '50' diesels of only seven coaches. The locomotives are D424 and D427* (Derek Cross).

average value of the equivalent drawbar horsepower during this strenuous half-hour was around 2,000, clearly an all-out performance. So far as spectacular running in the North Country is concerned, and in some way preparing us for what electrification would eventually bring, in the summer of 1970 a notable acceleration of all the passenger train services north of Crewe was made by using the Class '50' locomotives in pairs, coupling them in multiple unit. The objection to double-heading diesel-electric locomotives of such a length as 68 feet 6 inches over buffers, which was cogent enough in the confined space at Kings Cross, did not apply on the West Coast route, because there was ample platform space at Crewe where the change from

Above *A Class '50' diesel on a Glasgow-Euston express in September 1975 on a Sunday when the electricity was switched off. Locomotive No 50029 is seen here near Wandelmill in the upper Clyde valley. (Morrison Bryce).*

Left *An impressive study of a Class '50' diesel in the latest style of painting with the large BR 'Logo' and name. All the Class '50' locomotives have now been named after famous ships of the Royal Navy: No D50004 as shown is* St Vincent *(British Railways).*

Below *A Euston-Glasgow express in 1971 diverted to the former G&SW line, with Class '50' diesels Nos D415 and D420 here seen near Closeburn (Derek Cross)*

Class '50's, on the Western Region in Cornwall, locomotive No 50042, since named Triumph, *on an up express from Penzance, in the tin-mining country east of Camborne* (GEC).

electric to diesel haulage took place, and at Glasgow Central.

With 5,400 horsepower in the engine room and at least 4,000 at the drawbar, the power available was roughly equal to that of the ac electrics south of Crewe, and the accelerations timetabled reduced the journey time over the historic 141 miles of the northern division of the one-time London and North Western Railway between Crewe and Carlisle to the level two hours, or 120½ minutes to be exact. But the principal innovation was the scheduling of a time of 51½ minutes over the 62.8

miles of the mountain section between Carnforth and Carlisle, with the uphill section covered as rapidly as the downhill. Moreover, the demands of the timetable were modest compared to what a pair of Class '50' diesels could actually do when making up lost time. Before the year 1970 was out I had a record of a run on which a 13-coach train with a trailing load of 455 tons behind the second locomotive was taken from Carnforth to Carlisle in 45½ minutes: 22 minutes for the 31.4 miles up to Shap Summit and 23½ minutes for exactly the same distance down to Carlisle. The lowest speeds were 78 mph on the Grayrigg bank and 65 mph at Shap Summit. Such running was a good foretaste of what could be expected when the line was electrified, and one 5,000 hp electric locomotive replaced two diesels.

11. Dc electrification: developments on Southern Region

The historic decision, in 1923, by the management of the newly constituted Southern Railway to standardise upon the low-voltage dc system of electrification with third-rail current collection, in preference to the 6,600-volt single-phase ac system recommended by Sir Philip Dawson and adopted for its celebrated 'Overhead Electric' by the London Brighton and South Coast Railway, was to have continuing repercussions as the modernisation of British Railways proceeded. In the second volume of this work the ingenious, if somewhat inelegant use of a large flywheel to maintain continuity of supply to the traction motors of electric locomotives when passing over gaps in the conductor rails was described, while in Chapter 7 of this volume reference is made to the introduction of the electro-diesel type of locomotive and to the need for electric locomotives used for yard duties to have both third-rail and overhead means of current collection. The projected extension of the electrified network to Southampton and Bournemouth, and perhaps even to Weymouth, posed some new problems for Southern Region, even as to what form the system of electrification should take. At one time quite serious consideration was given to not extending the third-rail dc system beyond Woking, and utilising the 25 kv 50-cycle ac system with overhead-wire current collection for the westward extensions. But, when preliminary considerations made it clear that electrification could be justified financially only as far as Bournemouth, any thoughts of ac traction beyond Woking were dropped.

The problem was complicated by the relative density of traffic between London and Bournemouth on the one hand, and on the continuation to Weymouth on the other. In steam days it had been traditional, from the time of the London and South Western Railway, for the principal express trains from London to have sections, usually of four coaches, for Weymouth, which were detached at Bournemouth Central, and taken forward separately, after which the main part of the train proceeded to the terminal station of Bournemouth West. The question was how this facility could be best provided, or improved upon, with electric traction between London and Bournemouth. It would be easy enough to attach a diesel-electric locomotive to the one or two four-car trailer sets forming the Weymouth portion, leaving the electric locomotive, after some shunting, to work the remaining part of the train round to Bournemouth West. But Southern operating philosophy was moving towards the elimination of light-engine movements, and in this light the principle of propelling seemed to offer a very neat solution. While appreciating that there would be many purely engineering questions to be faced, the basic concept was so attractive that a practical solution was sought with energy and foresight. The idea was formed of having a high-powered four-car electric motor unit at the buffer-stops end of a train at Waterloo, propelling a further eight cars as far as Bournemouth Central. There a diesel-electric locomotive equipped for push-pull operation would

Left *Southern Region: 12-car multiple unit express train, gangwayed throughout, Ramsgate to Victoria passing Bickley Junction, December 1981* (Brian Morrison).

Above right *Propelling tests on Southern Region: diagram of eight-coach test train and electro-diesel locomotives* (Institution of Locomotive Engineers).

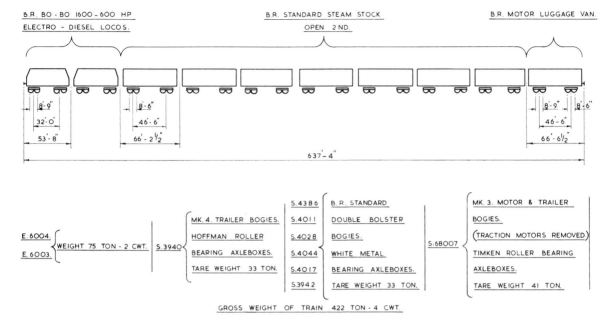

couple to the leading end and take four or eight trailer cars on to Weymouth. For the return journey the trailer cars would be propelled by the diesel, and at Bournemouth Central buffered up to couple with the electric motor unit to continue to Waterloo.

The problems seemed to lie in the mechanics of propelling a lengthy train at high speed, and to meet the proposed new electric timetables 'high speed' meant legislating for 100 mph. The project might well have seemed venturesome were there not examples in other countries of fast propelling, notably on some outer suburban services around Paris, where lengthy trains were propelled by steam locomotives up to the one-time maximum legal speed in France, of 75 mph. How the investigation was tackled on the Southern Region was described in a fascinating paper presented to the Institution of Locomotive Engineers in April 1965 by W.J.A. Sykes, then Chief Mechanical and Electrical Engineer of Southern Region. The work involved finding the answers to two important questions:
a) Were there any adverse or dangerous effects, either in the vehicles or on the track, resulting from the propelling of a 12-coach main line express train at speeds of up to 100 mph?
b) What was the best method of remote control of diesel and electric locomotives, over train line cables which had necessarily to be compatible with the control of multiple-unit electric stock?

From this clear definition and subdivision of the problem it was clear that the one question was purely mechanical, and the other electrical.

With regard to the first, whereas in pulling a train the tension forces in the drawgear provide longitudinal guiding to each coach, in propulsion the forces are compressive, and would be at a maximum between the locomotive and the first coach. A comprehensive series of tests was organised to investigate the effects experienced by this first coach in high-speed propelling conditions. The first test train consisted of two standard electro-diesel locomotives of the type described in Chapter 7 of this book, seven open second-class coaches of standard steam stock, and a motor luggage van, as used on some boat train workings, but with the traction motors removed. This enabled the two electro-diesel locomotives at the rear end of the train to be remotely controlled from the motor luggage van, with the seven coaches of steam stock in between. The total weight of the train, including the two locomotives, was 422 tons. It will be realised that this assembly of vehicles was nothing more than an experimental 'hook-up'. A standard Southern Region 27-way control line cable was laid through the train vestibules to connect the locomotives with the luggage van, which was to be used as a driving trailer.

The electro-diesel locomotives, when coupled in multiple, were under a method of electrical control that renders the acceleration characteristics identical whether hauling or propelling. It was deduced that the sideways component of the tractive effort at the drawgear should be the same in either direction of running, but of opposite direction: the actual

Above *Southern Region: 12-car multiple unit express set, empty coaches, passing over the viaduct leading to Folkestone Harbour station to form the 17.40 boat train to Victoria, May 1981* (Brian Morrison).

Left *In sidings at Dover Priory, May 1981: Motor luggage van No 68007 and just ahead, a four-car express multiple unit set after arrival from London Victoria* (Brian Morrison)

Right *Propelling tests: records on 186 chain curve at speeds of 95 to 100 mph* (Institution of Locomotive Engineers).

magnitude of this sideways component will reach its maximum on the sharpest curve and decrease almost to zero on straight track. The coach next to the locomotives would naturally sustain the greatest drawbar pull in the direction of travel, and it was assumed that this coach would also sustain the greatest sideways forces. Consequently instrumentation was applied to measure the lateral forces on this coach. The first set of tests was carried out on the Eastern Section, between Tonbridge and Ashford, where the long straight lengths of line permitted running up to 100 mph, and the slight curves enabled the effects of propelling at maximum speed to be observed. All eight axleboxes on the coach next to the locomotives were fitted with a lateral force measuring device, and tests were made at 10 to 15 mph round a 10-chain curve (radius of 220 yards) and at 95 to 100 mph round an 186-chain curve (radius of 4,100 yards). It was found that lateral forces when propelling were marginally higher, though in general there was very little to choose between the two conditions.

This first group of tests had shown that eight-coach trains could be safely propelled at the speeds contemplated on the electrified Bournemouth line; but, while such trains were then expected to be adequate for most normal requirements, at peak holiday periods relief trains made up to 12 cars were expected to be necessary, and a further series of tests were made. This time there was a complication that did not make the two sets of trials truly comparable. The coaching stock that could be made available was not that normally hauled by steam locomotives, but was taken from electric multiple-unit express trains. Two similar electro-diesel locomotives and a similar motor luggage van were used at opposite ends of the train, but the intervening 11 vehicles comprised two four-car express sets, with the traction motors rendered inoperative, and one four-car express set from which the motor coach was removed. The ensemble, including the two locomotives, and the motor luggage van, made up an extremely heavy total load of 595 tons, and with it the two locomotives, worked at their maximum

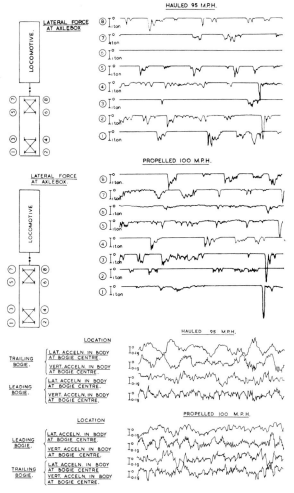

Below *Southern Region: Diagram of 12-coach propelling test train* (Institution of Locomotive Engineers).

capacity, could not exceed 88 mph. But the tests, though not carried up to the highest speed desired, were enough to show once again that there was no appreciable difference in the lateral forces experienced when hauling and propelling. No safety problem was considered to exist and the Chief Inspecting Officer of Railways at the Ministry of Transport formally signified his agreement to the propelling of trains up to a maximum of 12 coaches at speeds of up to 90 mph.

At the time these tests were conducted, in the summer of 1964, the haulage was provided by electro-diesel locomotives, and the second part of the investigation was in respect of the remote control of locomotives over train line cables from the distant end of a 12-car train. In the paper he presented to the Institution of Locomotive Engineers, Mr Sykes said that the problem was to connect in multiple four different types of motive power:

 a) multiple-unit dc electric stock;
 b) resistance-controlled dc electric locomotives;
 c) booster-controlled dc electric locomotives;
 d) type '3' diesel-electric locomotives.

It seemed from this that there was an intention to employ locomotive haulage between Waterloo and Bournemouth, with the locomotive at the London end of the train. There was adequate space in the platforms at Waterloo for one electric locomotive which would presumably have been one of the 2,500 hp class. These were not then arranged for multiple-unit work, but had a multi-notch control. As things eventuated however an even more elegant solution was arrived at. For the Waterloo–Bournemouth stage the propelling unit was not a locomotive at all, but a four-car multiple-unit set with two power cars, each having four traction motors of 365 hp. The total horsepower available was thus 2,920. This ingenious arrangement meant that the overall length of the train did not exceed

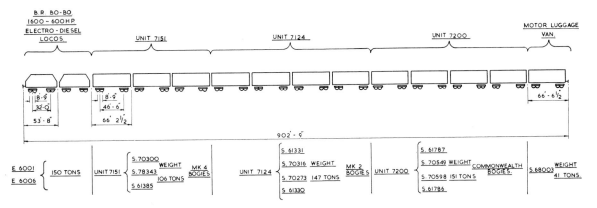

that of the 12-cars. The leading car at the country end was a driving trailer equipped for remote control of the two power cars at the rear end; but all the remaining vehicles were trailers. The standard make-up of the four-car trailer units is: driving trailer second; trailer first; trailer brake second; driving trailer second. These are known as Class '491' (4-TC). The four-car power units have the following make up: motor second; trailer brake first; trailer buffet; motor second. They are Class '430' (4-REP). The tare weights are 132 tons (4-TC) and 173 tons (4-REP). With traction motors totalling up to 2,920 hp there is ample power to propel, or haul, a 12-car train of 437 tons tare at 90 mph on level track.

The more complex aspects of the business of propelling trains came in connection with the diesel-powered part of the operation between Bournemouth and Weymouth. On the electric part the method of control was the same as that for a multiple-unit electric train, except that all the power was at one end. Control from a driving trailer vehicle, as on the down journey to Bournemouth, was standard practice. The novelties arose when a diesel-electric locomotive had to be remotely controlled, from the far end of a multiple-unit train, which though having no powered axles had all the equipment for its inclusion in an electric train. On the multiple-unit electric stock constituting the largest batch of vehicles likely to be involved, the system of control was by direct wires over a 27-way control cable, and because of this the direct wire system between driver and power car was selected as the transmission link of command. The first series of experiments was made to devise means of adapting the standard 27-core cable, by the imposition of simple codes that receiving equipment on the loco-motive could interpret. Using this technique, and superimposing a coded control, meant that the 27-core cable could still fulfil its normal function, when normal multiple-unit electric working was in progress.

Coded control, however, could not be directly applied to a diesel-electric locomotive. Unlike multiple-unit trains these have a large number of tractive-effort, or power notches, and for push-pull working it was necessary to combine these into the minimum number of groups that would be compatible with a reasonably flexible control. The actual diesels allocated to the Bournemout-Weymouth push-pull run were of the former 'D6500' Class, Type '3', now Class '33'. They have the Sulzer 8 LDA 28 engine of 1,550 horsepower, with Crompton Parkinson traction motors. When first introduced in 1960 they worked on some of the Kent Coast express trains prior to full electrification. At the present time 16 of them are equipped for push-pull working. Their maximum permissible speed is 85 mph. An electric multiple-unit train has only four tractive-effort steps of power control, and the power controls of the diesels were grouped accordingly, with facility for the actual locomotive control to notch automatically through the intermediate stages between the four main 'commands' from the remotely positioned driving trailer car. There were other features of diesel-engine control that had to be modified to suit remote control, before the necessary experimental running could be commenced.

One of the difficulties experienced, surprisingly, by the locomotive engineers of Southern Region was the limited availability of stock that could be modified. A six-car train was formed from two express-type motor coaches and four trailers taken from the old Brighton and Eastbourne express stock of 1930. The motor control and traction motors were removed, and these two vehicles were converted to driving trailers, to be located at each end of the six-car train. But apparently there was some

Southern Region: 12-car multiple-unit express train, Waterloo-Portsmouth service, with Class '423' (4-VEP) set leading (British Railways).

difficulty over fitting up the Type '3' diesel-electric locomotive with the necessary equipment for remote control. To install what was termed the 'translator unit', by which the electrical signals from the remote end of the train were to be converted for controlling the generator and engine of the locomotive, was going to take some considerable time, and to have even one of these locomotives out of traffic was unacceptable to the operating department—such apparently was the intensity of their utilisation. So the 'translator' had to be mounted in one of the coaches. There were some complications in coupling up, but it had the desired effect of keeping the locomotive out of service for the minimum of time. Running tests were carried out first between Wimbledon and Farnborough, and then between Victoria and Dover, in the course of which operation of the brakes as well as the traction control gear was examined. The results were sufficiently encouraging for the construction of a new six-car prototype set train to be authorised and work put in hand in 1965.

Mr Sykes' paper was read and discussed at meetings of the Institution of Locomotive Engineers in Derby, Glasgow, Manchester, and York, in addition to its original presentation in London. Among members there was naturally a slight uneasiness over the whole principle of propulsion of trains at high speeds, or in some track configurations at any speed. One speaker questioned the taking of lateral forces during the tests only on the vehicle immediately ahead of propelling locomotives; he thought that the flange forces and riding of the leading vehicle would be particularly important. Another speaker wondered if Mr Sykes would feel happy about propelling 12 coaches round the Borough Market Junction curves (just outside

London Bridge) in the rush hour with flange forces which might rise to 3¾ tons. In his reply Mr Sykes said: 'The leading vehicle in a propelled train experiences the least disturbance from the propelling force; whether it is pushed by one vehicle —a well-tried practice—or by 11, and no difference in riding is felt by the passenger. Speeds both hauled and propelled are dependent on factors such as windage and track voltage: comparisons have been made as nearly as possible at the same point in the track in each case but there is insufficient evidence in the tests from which to deduce differences in train resistance'.

Having listened to the original presentation of the paper, and read the reports of the discussion at the four provincial centres as which it was read, it can be well imagined with what interest I made a trip in the driver's cab from Waterloo to Weymouth and back, when the electric service as far as Bournemouth had been inaugurated, in the summer of 1967. The make up of a 12-car train differed from that used on the Portsmouth line on which the four-car units all included motor equipment, four 225 hp traction motors to each four-car set. Thus a 12-car train had a total of 2,700 horsepower. The new Bournemouth trains, as previously mentioned, were powered by one Class '430' four-car unit (4-REP) with a total of 2,920 horsepower. On my own westbound journey the second 4-TC set was minus one trailer car, so that we had only 11 cars from Waterloo. As far as Bournemouth I rode in the driving trailer at the leading end of the train, with our 2,920 horsepower to propel a train of 404 tons tare. It should be explained that the Bournemouth expresses are subject to the suburban third-rail current of 660 volts as far out as Brookwood, 28 miles from Waterloo. From there transition to the new standard of 750 volts is made in steps of about 25 volts at a time at successive sub-stations.

Although we were closely following a semi-fast train through the outer suburban area and running under restrictive signal aspects, I could already

Southern Region: 12-car multiple-unit express, Charing Cross to Dover Priory, on the viaduct abreast of Waterloo main station (Brian Morrison).

appreciate the smoothness of running at the front end of the train, particularly when rounding the curve through the platforms at Clapham Junction; and, once the preceding train was diverted, speed quickly mounted to 90 mph near Weybridge. At this speed the riding was exceptionally smooth and quiet, without any suspicion of any lateral yawing that I thought might possibly be felt at high speed. After passing Clapham Junction the curves in the line are very slight, and the restriction of 75 mph through Woking station and junction is unconnected with curvature. While still working on 660 volts, the recovery from this speed on the continuous rise at 1 in 300 to Milepost 31 was relatively slow, although an acceleration to 84 mph represented an output of about 2,000 horsepower.

Beyond Farnborough on level track speed rose to 96 mph. In describing the journey at the time I wrote: 'The riding was almost unbelievably smooth. I have never experienced anything as good on any other kind of motive power unit, anywhere'. So far as my own travels are concerned, that statement remains as true today as when I wrote it, now nearly 17 years ago. It may be that the Bournemouth electrics are not quite so smooth as they were when new; but, so far as the theory of propulsion is concerned, they certainly justified all that was predicted for them when first introduced.

West of Basingstoke there is plenty of variation in the track alignment on which the behaviour of the propelled leading vehicle could be observed. First of all came the slight curves and crossings at Basing-

stoke itself, and then the left-hand turnout at Worting Junction, where the West of England line diverges from the Southampton route. At 65 mph the latter junction was negotiated with perfect smoothness. We had a good spell of 90-mph running downhill towards Winchester, and in the environs of Southampton negotiation, at slow speed, of the very sharp right-hand curve at Northam Junction. Here I recalled the doubts of the man who wondered what it would be like propelling round the curves at Borough Market Junction. Northam is equally severe, though not so long, and in the leading car I was not conscious of any squealing or grinding action that would suggest excessive wheel-flange friction. Despite the slight signal checks experienced on the way down, which between them accounted for about 24½ minutes running time, we kept the scheduled allowance of 70 minutes for the 79.2 miles from Waterloo. The net average speed was 71 mph. The continuation through the New Forest provided further opportunities for observing the riding of the propelled coaches, because the line included many curves on which speed is restricted to 60 mph, or less, and fast running has to be made intermediately in order to keep scheduled time. The fluctuations in speed within a space of barely 20 minutes were 40, 75, 65, 82, 60, 90, 60 and 67 mph and the 28.7 miles from Southampton to Bournemouth Central took 26½ minutes start to stop.

At Dorchester Junction: a Class '3' diesel No 33105 with an eight-car train, forming the 10.34 service Weymouth to Waterloo in October 1983 (Brian Morrison).

Only the leading 4-TC set was going forward to Weymouth, and to this was attached one of the Type '3' diesel-electric locomotives, now Class '33'. No more than six minutes are allowed for change-over of the controls and, with the locomotive leading, the run to Weymouth was no different from a conventional journey. There was however one big difference. Instead of the smoothly silent driving trailer of the electric train we had a noisy, rough-riding diesel! So far as tractive effort was concerned, with 1,550 horsepower 'under the bonnet' and a gross trailing load of no more than 140 tons, no very great power output was involved; but with station stops at Poole, Wareham, Wool and Dorchester, and smart start-to-stop timings, there was no chance of dawdling on the way. The total distance from Bournemouth Central to Weymouth is 34.9 miles and our running time added up to 43 minutes; except on the short run between Bournemouth and Poole. Speed was rapidly accelerated to well over 70 mph on each stage. The return journey was made with the same locomotive and coaches, in this direction propelling. Again there was some fast running between station stops including a maximum of 80 mph within the ten-mile run from Dorchester to Wool. The riding in the leading coach, the 'driving trailer', was good, though in view of the incessant curvature on this part of the line not so impeccably smooth as on the run down from Waterloo to Southampton. Nevertheless the going was excellent by all ordinary standards, and seemingly effortless.

The run up from Bournemouth to Waterloo, with the full 12-car train and the 2,920 horsepower unit leading, was quite uneventful. In the driving cab

the travelling was again delightfully smooth and quiet, because the motors in the four-car power unit are not under the leading vehicle. We had some impressive examples of power output on the long continous rise at 1 in 250 to Litchfield Tunnel. From slightly restricted speed through Eastleigh, speed was worked up first to a steady 86 mph on the gradient; and then after signal delays through Winchester there was an acceleration from 30 to 85 mph on the gradient. This indicated an output of about 2,300 horsepower: an excellent and impressive performance. Because of signal checks at the conclusion, the overall time from Southampton to Waterloo slightly exceeded the 70 minutes scheduled for the run of 79.2 miles; but the net time was not more than 67 minutes. Taken all round, the Southern Region electrification to Bournemouth and its diesel extension to Weymouth was highly successful, in the improved train service offered to the public, and in the vindication of the principles of train dynamics in propelling lengthy trains at speeds of up to 100 mph.

The introduction of the multiple-unit electric trains as the principal form of coaching stock on the Bournemouth route brought a haulage problem so far as trains other than the regular London express and semi-fast services were concerned. For part of their journeys some of these had to run over non-electrified routes, but when on the Bournemouth line they had to run up to the very high standards expected from the new multiple-unit trains. Slower running would have been difficult to fit into the timetable. Use of a pair of electro-diesels would probably have met most requirements, but these locomotives could not be spared from their existing

Above *Southern Region: the propelling operation near Weymouth, with a 4-TC driving trailer unit, propelled by a Class '33' diesel No 33103 near Upwey* (Brian Morrison).

Above right *Southern Region: one of the larger electrodiesel locomotives converted from the 'E5000' Class electric to become Class '74', on train of coal empties Tolworth to Acton, approaching Clapham Junction in August 1973* (Brian Morrison).

Right *Southern Region: one of the Class '74' electrodiesels, No 74003, working a train of empty coaching stock from Waterloo into Clapham yard* (Brian Morrison).

Bottom right *Southern Region: one of the latest type multiple unit outer suburban trains, Class '508', with four 110 hp traction motors per four-car set, used on the western section from Waterloo* (GEC).

duties. It so happened, however, that changed conditions on the Eastern Section of Southern Region were making a number of the 2,500 horsepower, 750-volt dc electric locomotives of the 'E5000' Class surplus to requirements, and in consultation with the English Electric Company the proposal was formed to convert ten of these powerful locomotives into electro-diesels. One duty particularly envisaged for them was the working of the prestige Ocean Liner specials between Waterloo and Southampton Docks on which the last part of the journey had to be made over non-electrified tracks. The 2,500 hp of the locomotive when working full-electric would be needed for the fast running on the main line, up to the standard of the Bournemouth multiple-unit trains, while a relatively small diesel plant would be adequate for the slow running in the approach to the docks and steamer berths.

But to redesign the existing locomotives to

include an additional engine-generator set was easier said than done. Fortunately, so far as space was concerned, the locomotives as built, and described in Chapter 7 of this book, had a flywheel and booster to provide continuity in supply to the traction motors while passing over gaps in the conductor rails. This was not considered necessary on the Bournemouth route, and it was decided to rebuild each booster set with two integral traction-motor blowers which would also cool the booster set, thus reducing weight and saving space. For working over non-electrified lines the Paxman Ventura '6YJXL' diesel engine was chosen, which has a continuous rating of 650 hp. This may not seem much in comparison to the 2,500 hp of the locomotive when working electric; but it was adequate for the slow running on the dock lines at Southampton, even with the heaviest of the boat trains. The weight of the additional equipment needed a re-consideration of the body strength of the locomotive, because as originally designed it did not provide for taking up any main stresses. It was indeed of relatively light and simple construction. To carry the additional weight it was necessary for the body sides to be reinforced and, while the extensive redesign and re-equipment of the electrical parts was in progress, modification to the mechanical parts was carried out at Crewe.

The method of electrical control selected by English Electric was what is termed the 'closed loop' system, and it allowed the driver to select any desired value of accelerating current which was maintained automatically up to the limit of the locomotive performance. This type of equipment provides an important improvement over the normal form of control, stepping through a succession of resistances, in that it is possible to achieve increased tractive effort for any given condition of adhesion. It also gives fine control when working diesel. Normally the driver had to keep the mean tractive effort well below the rail adhesion limit, to ensure that peak tractive efforts would not exceed that limit, and so cause slipping. With constant current control the driver is able to keep the locomotive very close to the limit of adhesion. Improved wheelslip control is also a very important feature. The technology involved in the installation of this system was some of the most advanced that had been applied in a British locomotive, and the ten units converted, later Class '74', fulfilled an important function in the overall motive power set-up of British Railways.

The need for such a function however did not remain for very long. The age of the luxury boat train, whether for oceanic or Continental travel was fast disappearing. One-time patrons of trains like 'The Golden Arrow', and 'The Night Ferry' were by the mid 1970s travelling by air, or using their own cars and the hovercraft service and the great liner sailings from Southampton were dwindling to little more than pleasure-cruise voyages. Boat train services to Folkestone and Dover could be provided by the ordinary multiple-unit formations. Neither the 'E5000' Class electric locomotives, later Class '71', nor the larger electro-diesels, Class '74', were needed. The first of the former, No 71001, formerly E5001, is preserved in the National Railway Museum at York, but the remainder, and all of those converted to electro-diesels Class '74' have now been scrapped.

12. Electric Euston to Glasgow: development and work of Class '87'

The story of ac electric locomotive development must be taken back to the introduction of Class '86' on the West Coast main line, referred to at the conclusion of Chapter 7. These locomotives provided a plethora of brilliant performances on the road, which those who compiled detailed logs of train running found exhilarating to the last degree; but in the intense high-speed service between Euston, Liverpool and Manchester, certain features of their design, in differing from what had been used on the earlier electric locomotives of Classes '81' to '85', proved not entirely satisfactory. The most serious defect was in the bad riding action of the bogies. This was not rough or dangerous riding such as was experienced with the 'Warship' class diesel-hydraulic locomotives as first put into service on the Western Region, but a bouncing action that was not only uncomfortable to the enginemen, but was highly undesirable in the loads it imposed upon the track. It arose from the design feature of mounting the traction motors on the bogie axles. While this made possible some simplification, in that it avoided the need for a flexible connection between motor and axle, it considerably increased the unsprung weight. As was mentioned at the end of Chapter 7, this had been appreciated at the design stage and, following tests carried out at speeds up to 100 mph, it had been accepted by the civil engineer.

But as high-speed mileage rapidly mounted up it was not only that bouncing ride which gave concern. The subjection of the traction motors themselves to all the vibrational effects of being mounted directly on the axles led to bad commutation, or pick-up of current from the motor brushes. This was probably made even more serious by the fact that so much of the braking was accomplished rheostatically, by electrical interaction, rather than by the simple action of brake blocks acting through friction on the wheels. Attention to the commutators was found to be needed more frequently than on the earlier electric locomotives, which had the motors mounted on the bogie frames and which did not have rheostatic braking. In passing it may be mentioned that the earlier electric locomotives Classes '81' to '85' had vacuum braking for the trains as on the standard coaching stock then in use, controlled by a vacuum/air proportional valve on the locomotive. Class '86' were dual fitted so as to be able to work trains fitted either with the vacuum, or the Westinghouse air brake. It was the locomotive brakes on the last-mentioned class that had the rheostatic feature; and as this more than doubled the life of the brake shoes, and so lessened maintenance charges, it was desirable that it should be retained. It is perhaps not generally realised that

Redesigned Class '86' bogie showing prominent flexicoil springs of the secondary suspension (British Railways).

on locomotives engaged on the heaviest and fastest express work, with ordinary friction braking, the shoes have to be renewed about every seven or eight days!

So far as the riding was concerned, one of the Class '86' locomotives was withdrawn from traffic and fitted with a redesigned bogie, with the motor mounted on the bogie frame, instead of axle-hung,

and driving through a flexible connection; while the secondary suspension took the form of a set of three Flexicoil springs on either side of the locomotive, prominently in view, acting between a bearing plate outrigged from the bogie frame, and the under side of the locomotive body, with dampers on each side of the assembly. This modification, applied to locomotive No E3173, was entirely successful. The

Above *The first of the Class '87' electrics, built 1973, and now named* Royal Scot. *The flexicoil suspension of the bogies is seen prominently* (British Railways).

Left *The second of the Class '87' locomotives, No 87002* Royal Sovereign *hauling the Royal Train* (GEC).

bouncing action was eliminated, the commutation greatly improved and these attributes showed no signs of deterioration after no less than 200,000 miles of running. When authorisation was obtained for electrification of the West Coast main line northward from Weaver Junction to Glasgow, with construction of a further 35 high-speed electric locomotives to provide for the additional service, the features included in the rebuilt E3173 had been sufficiently proved to form the basis of the new design, which became known as Class '87'. They were to be geared for a maximum speed of 110 mph, though at that time the line maximum was 100 mph. When authorisation was given for the building of the 35 new locomotives of Class '87', it provided also for a further 51 of Class '86' to be rebuilt with new bogies having the traction motors mounted on the frames, instead of axle-hung, and with Flexicoil secondary suspension. These also were geared for a maximum speed of 110 mph. The rebuilt locomotives were designated Class '86/2'.

In designing the new locomotives particular consideration had to be given to the severe gradients of the West Coast main line north of Lancaster. The future standards of passenger service had, to a large extent, been set by the working of two Class '50' diesel-electric locomotives in multiple unit, which enabled the principal express trains to be hauled up the steepest inclines at speeds of around 80 mph. Such a combination of locomotives had an engine horsepower of 5,400, with the capability of sustaining around 4,000 at the drawbar. The new electric locomotives were designed with a continuous rating of 5,000 horsepower, but while this would have been amply adequate for the heaviest and fastest trains contemplated after electrification, there were also freightliners, loading to around 1,000 tons. The schedule for the daytime passenger trains provided no more than 22½ minutes for the 31.4 miles from Carnforth up to Shap Summit, an average speed of 83.8 mph throughout the climb. There are speed restrictions to be observed intermediately, to 75 mph at Oxenholme, and over the curves between Grayrigg and Low Gill, and, to keep such a point-to-point booking, intermediate accelerations to 90 mph and more are needed on the straighter lengths of line. To attain 90 mph in climbing the Grayrigg bank after observing the speed restriction through Oxenholme needs plenty of power with a gross trailing load of 400–450 tons.

In the night hours the situation is different. The passenger services, such as sleeping car trains and motor-rails, are run at slower speeds, not generally exceeding 75 mph. The only train run at daytime passenger-train speed is the famous West Coast Postal Special. The many freight trains, parcels, and newspaper trains, plus the very heavy freight-liners are however run at night-time passenger-train speed and to conform to the timetable pattern they have to run uphill at about 75 mph. To do this with a 1,000-ton freightliner requires not one, but *two* electric locomotives, and the new Class '87's, unlike their predecessors of Classes '81'-'86' are designed for coupling in multiple. South of Liverpool and Manchester there is no gradient on which a single electric locomotive could not make maximum scheduled speed with any load; but it was another matter with the night freights on the formidable climbs to Shap and Beattock summits. Although the new locomotives had an improved performance characteristic at the high-speed end of the range, and a considerably improved continuous rating in the middle range, to climb the Grayrigg bank at 75 mph with a 1,000-ton freightliner requires a draw-bar horsepower of nearly 6,000, plus the power necessary to overcome the effect of gravity on two 80-ton locomotives—another 550 horsepower.

Following the varied experience with what could be regarded as little more than experimental electric locomotives in the first phase of London Midland modernisation, very careful attention was given in design to the purely mechanical features of Class '87'. In retrospect one can have nothing but the greatest praise for the way in which that first phase was accomplished. It was a rather astonishing achievement to introduce an entirely novel form of motive power, novel not only to those who had to make use of it, and travel at speeds and at a service intensity unprecedented in Great Britain, but novel to the high-ranking engineers who had recommended it, and been responsible for its introduction. If one compares the situation with that of launching a highly accelerated train service with steam traction, using machines developed on principles that had been traditional for 50 years or more, the changeover to electric traction on the London Midland main line and the instant inauguration of a speed-up without parallel and a complete absence of mishap, or delays due to so called 'teething troubles', was little short of phenomenal. That the locomotives undergoing the most intensive utilisation needed certain modification in the light of experience is no more than natural. The wonder is that they did not need more. Class '87' was the outcome.

The new locomotives were mounted on twin-axle bogies having a 10 foot 9 inch wheelbase. There is no connecting linkage between the two bogies, because the routes over which they are required to travel at high speed do not have any sharp curves. The unsprung weight on the bogies has been reduced to 2.6 tons per axle, and the overall weight

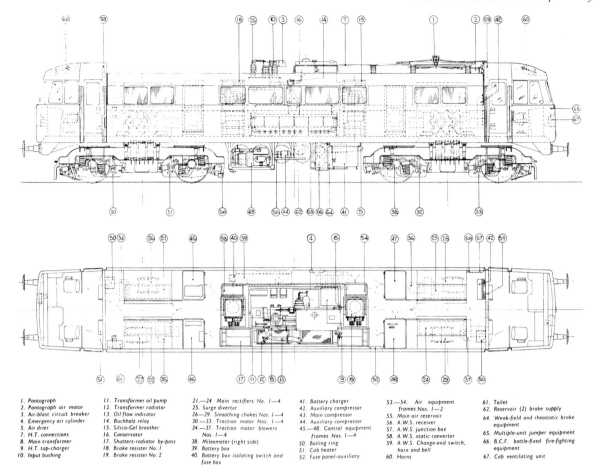

1.	Pantograph	11.	Transformer oil pump	21.—24.	Main rectifiers No. 1—4	41.	Battery charger	53.—54.	Air equipment frames Nos. 1—2	61.	Toilet
2.	Pantograph air motor	12.	Transformer radiator	25.	Surge divertor	42.	Auxiliary compressor	55.	Main air reservoir	62.	Reservoir (2) brake supply
3.	Air-blast circuit breaker	13.	Oil flow indicator	26—29.	Smoothing chokes Nos. 1—4	43.	Main compressor	56.	A.W.S. receiver	64.	Weak-field and rheostatic brake equipment
4.	Emergency air cylinder	14.	Buchholz relay	30.—33.	Traction motor Nos. 1—4	44.	Auxiliary compressor	57.	A.W.S. junction box		
5.	Air drier	15.	Silica-Gel breather	34.—37.	Traction motor blowers Nos. 1—4	45.—48.	Control equipment frames Nos. 1—4	58.	A.W.S. static convertor	65.	Multiple-unit jumper equipment
7.	H.T. connections	16.	Conservator	38.	Mileometer (right side)	50.	Boiling ring	59.	A.W.S. Change-end switch, horn and bell	66.	B.C.F. bottle-fixed fire-fighting equipment
8.	Main transformer	17.	Shutters-radiator by-pass	39.	Battery box	51.	Cab heater	60.	Horns	67.	Cab ventilating unit
9.	H.T. tap-charger	18.	Brake resister No. 1	40.	Battery box isolating switch and fuse box	52.	Fuse panel-auxiliary				
10.	Input bushing	19.	Brake resister No. 2								

of the bogie, fully assembled, is no more than 18.1 tons, including 8.15 tons for the two traction motors and their drive. The roller bearings are of the same type as used in the earlier electric locomotives. Computer analysis programmes, as developed by the Railway Technical Centre at Derby, were used to determine the ideal proportions of the major sections of the bogie frame so as to provide optimum strength per unit of weight. It was designed with the nominal centre of the king-pin connection 2⅜ inches below the axlebox centre line, with the traction and braking forces transmitted through the king pin. The side frames of the bogie pass over the axleboxes and drop down only at the ends to connect with headstocks.

The design evolved to ensure smooth riding of the locomotive under the most severe conditions is very interesting, and illustrative of the highly sophisticated mechanical engineering practice embodied in what I have heard dismissed by certain hard-line purely-steam enthusiasts as 'tin boxes on eight

General arrangement of Class '87', 25kv ac electric locomotive for the Euston-Glasgow service.

wheels'! In Class '87'' the centre transom drops down to receive the king pin connection, and this consists of two laminated-rubber buffers, one fore and one aft, between which a steel bronzed-brushed casting is sandwiched, under a compression loading of about ten tons. This follows the arrangement developed in the modification to the bogies on Class '86'. The transverse stiffness is low initially, to build up a controlled resistance to side thrust, but it is high axially to take the traction loadings. The rotation of the bogie is through these buffers. The torsional stiffness of the bogie when rounding curves is provided by the triple Flexicoil assembly of the secondary suspension, prominent on the outside of the locomotive, which also plays such an important part in controlling the general riding of the locomotive. I came to appreciate from many hundreds

Top *Euston-Glasgow express approaching Preston hauled by '87' Class locomotive No 87005, now named* City of London (GEC).

Above *Glasgow-Euston express near Carstairs, hauled by locomotive No 87020, now named* North Briton (Derek Cross).

of miles at high speed in the cabs of these locomotives how smooth and comfortable the riding was.

Turning now to the electrical equipment, and beginning at the roof, Class '87' differed from the earlier London Midland electric locomotives in having only a single pantograph for current collection, this being of the cross-arm type and mounted immediately in rear of cab No 1. It is fitted with two copper-impregnated carbon rubbing strips and is designed for a static contact thrust of 20 lb. Auxiliary springing is provided in the pan head to allow for rapid response to any irregularities in the

contact wire. The general layout of these compact, but very powerful locomotives can be studied from the accompanying drawings, which are supplemented by a numerical key pin-pointing all the component parts. As an example of the most powerful locomotives that have yet run on the railways of Great Britain, of any type or form of traction, a detailed specification, together with a schematic diagram of the main power circuits, is given at the end of this chapter.

When the electric service to Glasgow was inaugurated on May 6 1974, the remarkable capabilities of the new locomotives were most strikingly demonstrated. It was naturally on the severe gradients of the North Country, both on the Lancaster and Carlisle section and in Scotland that the principal interest was concentrated, because south of Crewe with the line maximum speed remaining at 100 mph the Class '87' locomotives were not able to show any advantage in running times, appreciably greater than that already most

convincingly displayed by Class '86'. In the north, from the inception of the electric service, the 10.45 from Euston, 'The Royal Scot' train itself, was allowed 67 minutes to pass Carlisle from its one passenger stop at Preston, 90.1 miles. The uphill 31.4 miles from Carnforth to Shap Summit, pass to pass, were allowed 22½ minutes, while the exactly similar downhill run to Carlisle was allowed 26 minutes, admittedly with the inclusion of some recovery time. In climbing the Grayrigg bank there were several hampering speed restrictions to be observed, not below 75 mph it is true, but enough to prevent the making of really spectacular uphill times; but on the Shap Incline itself some speeds that would previously have been thought quite sensational were soon regularly being run. It was customary for speed to be slightly eased at Tebay, and then on the 1 in 75 gradient of Shap itself the drivers really showed off what their locomotives could do.

Two performances may be quoted:

Locomotive No	Gross Trailing load (tons)	Speeds (mph) Passing Tebay	On 1 in 75	Estimated edhp
87013	390	90	95	5,230
87026	415	84	88	5,180

An attained speed of 95 mph on Shap was certainly an impressive example of the potentialities of the new power, though on my own first run in the cab of one of these locomotives on the Glasgow service we did not need to go quite so hard in order keep sectional time. Drivers found it a little difficult to pass Carnforth 27.3 miles from start at Preston in the scheduled 18½ minutes, chiefly due to the intermediate speed restriction to 70 mph through Lancaster. Although running at 98 to 100 mph for

more than ten miles on the preceeding level stretch, and attaining 98 mph after the restriction, our time to Carnforth was 19¼ minutes; but then the time for the 31.4 miles up to Shap Summit was 21 minutes 54 seconds—an average of 86 mph—and we passed Summit exactly on time. Sustained speed on the 1 in 75 gradient of the bank itself was 82 mph.

In Scotland itself major interest naturally centred upon ascents of the Beattock bank, ten miles long; of this length the first two miles are at 1 in 88, and the remainder average 1 in 75, as with Shap. A striking example of how the 'Electric Scots' have virtually eliminated the effects of the steep gradients was provided by a run by the afternoon express originating at Birmingham at 14.05, on which good time was made with an 11-coach train, of 390 gross trailing tons, and locomotive No 87009. Scheduled time for the run of 73.5 miles from Carlisle to Carstairs was 52 minutes, and the following times were made:

Distance (miles)	min	Schedule m s	Actual
0.0	CARLISLE	0	0 00
6.1	Floriston		5 54
8.6	Gretna Junction	7½	7 32
13.0	Kirkpatrick		10 36
25.8	LOCKERBIE	19	19 12
34.5	Wamphray		24 27
39.7	Beattock	28	27 53

Above *An '86/2' Class electric locomotive No 86216 (now named* Meteor*) on the 07.04 Liverpool to Euston just south of Bushey (Brian Morrison).*

Below *Euston-Glasgow express crossing the Clyde near Crawford, hauled by No 87015 in June 1974 now named* Howard of Effingham *(Derek Cross).*

49.7	Summit	35½	34 25
57.7	Abington	41	39 58
66.9	Symington		45 46
73.5	CARSTAIRS	52	51 10

This could be regarded as a good timekeeping run, except to note that a minute was gained on the apparently sharp uphill timing of 7½ minutes for the ten miles of the steeply graded Beattock bank. But it is when the average speeds are worked out that the capacity of the Class '87' locomotives

becomes more clearly revealed. It is interesting to take the three clearly defined stages of the journey as follows:

Section		Distance (miles)	Time m s	Av speed (mph)
Floriston–Beattock	Gradual rise	33.6	21 59	91.5
Beattock–Summit	Steep ascent	10.0	6 32	91.6
Summit–Symington	Gradual fall	17.2	11 21	91.0

This shows that it made no difference whether the locomotive was climbing a steep incline, or running downhill, so massive was the built-in power and the skill in handling which avoided excessive speed where the gradients were favourable.

When the service was first introduced, the 'Royal Scot' train was allowed 78½ minutes from passing Carlisle, at slow speed, to arrival in Glasgow Central, 102.3 miles, and I have details of one journey on which the distance was covered in 70½

Above *Locomotive No 87016 at high speed near Abington, in Upper Clydesdale with a London-Glasgow express, in June 1974* (Derek Cross).

Left *One of the '87' Class locomotives at 100 mph on the main line south of Bletchley, with a Euston-Glasgow express* (GEC).

Below *Glasgow-Euston express in wintry weather, January 1982, near Crawford, hauled by No 86257* Snowdon (T.H. Noble).

Traction	Type	Loco Class	Adhesion weight (tons)	Approx max hp	HP per ton adhesion
Steam	4-6-0	LNW 'Claughton'	59	1,500	25.4
Steam	4-6-2	LMS 'Duchess'	66	3,000	45.3
Diesel-Electric	1-Co-Co-1	Class '40'	108	2,000	18.5
Diesel-Electric	Co-Co	Class '50'	117	2,700	23.1
Electric	Bo-Bo	Class '87'	80	5,000	62.5

minutes, with a 12-coach train of 430 tons, at a pass-to-stop average speed of 87.2 mph. On this occasion the average speeds were 98.7 mph from Floriston to Beattock, 88.5 mph up the bank, and 95.8 mph from Summit to passing Law Junction, after which considerably reduced speed was necessary over the concluding 18¼ miles down into Glasgow. At the same time, brilliant as these performances are, particularly in the power displayed in mounting the most severe rising gradients, a potential weakness in these otherwise outstanding locomotives lies in the relatively limited weight available for adhesion. One day, when I was in the driver's cab of the locomotive working this same train, also with a load of 12 coaches, we were climbing the Beattock bank at a steady 88 mph showing approximately 5,000 equivalent drawbar horsepower, when a slight shower of rain caused the locomotive to slip, and speed fell to 76 mph. The ingenious equipment for detecting and arresting

wheel-slip came into operation rapidly and efficiently; but when conditions were stabilised again we had lost about 1,000 horsepower.

The contrast between these locomotives and the diesel-electric and steam types that preceded them is remarkable when set out in tabular form (above).

The 'Duchess' Class steam 'Pacifics' could be distinctly touchy on a wet rail, but the above comparison makes it clear why the Class '87' electrics could be liable to slipping. It was appreciated that, when nearing maximum output, these locomotives would be working very near to the adhesion limit. This led to the construction of an additional unit, No 87101, with thyristor control, which provides better tractive effort characteristics through stepless power control, instead of the normal tap-changing on the remaining Class '87' locomotives. At the time it was feared that the introduction of thyristor techniques would cause interference with signalling and communication circuits, and until the present time locomotive No 87101 has remained the only one of its kind. But the exhaustive trials conducted since the locomotive was introduced in 1975 would appear to have indicated that the problems are not insoluble. In the meantime the thyristor-controlled locomotive was

Two Class '87' electrics, coupled in multiple, Nos 87001 Royal Scot *and 87006* City of Glasgow *at Preston in October 1982 pulling a 700 ton train load of steel coil (C.J. Tuffs).*

proved definitely superior in its capacity for the immediate suppression of wheel-slip conditions.

The working of the night freight trains in the North Country was a very important feature of the 25 kv electrification in the London Midland Region, and I was priviledged to see some of its most interesting facets at first hand. First of all, there are results of observations made during the best part of a snowy November night in 1976 when I was in the panel signal box at Carlisle, and logged the running of 21 fast trains which entered upon the illuminated diagram between 23.13 and 02.57 hours. The average headway was therefore 11 minutes, but at times the succession was much closer. The point of entry was the automatic signal near the site of the one-time Burton and Holme station, and, except for one freight train that seemed to be rather dragging its feet and not doing more than 60 mph, the speeds at that point of entry upon the Carlisle panel varied between 70 and 101 mph. The 21 trains included the following: 6 freightliners; 4 parcel trains; 1 fast ordinary freight; 1 newspaper train; 4 express passenger trains; 4 sleeping car expresses; and 1 postal special. The uphill performances of some of the freight trains that night were extremely good, despite the adverse weather conditions, as the following tabulated details show.

Route	Load (tons)	Carnforth to Tebay (min)	Av speed (mph)
Southampton–Coatbridge	441	21½	72.2
Longsight–Glasgow	1,038*	24	64.7
Wallersole–Larbert	622	30	51.8
Dover–Dundee	461	30½	51.0
Dudley–Glasgow	844*	24½	63.4
Willesden–Glasgow	740*	22½	69.0
Willesden–Glasgow	831*	26½	58.7
Garston Docks–Glasgow	900*	23½	66.2
Willesden–Glasgow	735*	27½	56.6
Parkston Quay (Harwich) –Coatbridge	886*	24½	63.4

*Hauled by two locomotives, coupled in multiple

To supplement these observations, authority was obtained on another occasion to ride in the driver's cab of the Garston to Glasgow freightliner, when a maximum load of 1,067 tons was being conveyed, by a pair of '87' Class locomotives. During the night's observation at Carlisle, while two Class '87's were used on some of the heaviest trains, electric locomotives of Classes '81', '84', '85' and '86' were also used, sometimes coupled in multiple, which had been made possible since their original introduction. The Garston to Glasgow freightliner on which observations were made was diesel-hauled as far as Wigan, and the interesting part of the journey north began after Preston was passed, and speed settled down to the freightliner maximum of 75 mph on the level stretch northwards to Lancaster. We were put into the loop road at Carnforth to allow the West Coast Postal Special to go ahead, but from there we made an impressive run to Carlisle.

The details of the running uphill from Carnforth to Shap Summit are tabulated below, and what this involved in sheer weight-lifting can be studied by a comparison of the speeds with the gradients as shown in the accompanying diagram, remembering that the difference in altitude above sea level is 885 feet between Carnforth and Shap Summit. At the same time, even with a freightliner, limited to a maximum speed of 75 mph, it is not entirely a straightforward run. While there are no curves

Top right *A train of steel coil, southbound from Ravenscraig in March 1984: another 700 ton load, here hauled by locomotives 86320 and 86328 coupled in multiple* (T.H. Noble).

Above right *A Kensington to Perth motorail, near Crawford in Upper Clydesdale, hauled by locomotive No 86205 since named* City of Lancaster—*June 1974* (Derek Cross).

Right *Electric locomotive No 87019* Sir Winston Churchill *in Glasgow Central station in August 1978. On left No 86219, since named* Phoenix (Brian Morrison).

Distance (miles)		Sched* (min)	Actual† m s	Av speed (mph)
0.0	Carnforth Loop north end	0	0 00	—
3.3	Milepose 9½		4 43	—
7.3	Milnthorpe		8 04	71.7
12.9	Oxenholme	11	12 38	73.6
18.0	Lambrigg Crossing		16 53	72.0
19.9	Grayrigg		18 24	75.2
25.9	Tebay	22½	23 18	73.5
31.4	Shap Summit	pass	28 16	66.5

*Schedule from passing Carnforth at 75 mph. †Times from dead start.

requiring a reduction in speed, with a train of this weight the neutral sections in the overhead line can result in a slight drop in the speed during the brief interval when no current is being collected. There is one of these sections near Oxenholme and another one just south of Tebay.

Two ac electric locomotives coupled in multiple, No 86321 and 87019 Sir Winston Churchill *arriving at Warrington Bank Quay in July 1983 with a freight from Ravenscraig steel works. The electric locomotives coupled off at Warrington and were replaced by a Class '47' diesel for the conclusion of the journey over a non-electrified route (C.J. Tuffs).*

Garston–Glasgow freightliner
Load: 20 vehicles, 1,067 tons loaded
Two Class '87' electrics Nos 87010 and 87019

From the dead start, speed had risen to 70 mph at the miniature summit point at Milepost 9½, and we then ran at or near 75 mph until the neutral section near Oxenholme caused a brief drop to 70 mph. Then speed was accelerated to 75–6 mph for the rest of the Grayrigg bank. Negotiation of the neutral section before Tebay caused a slight drop in the average speed from Grayrigg, and on Shap itself, where on the last mile at 1 in 75 we were doing 65 mph, the driver eased the working a little, to avoid too rapid a rise in speed once the summit was topped. The speed was skilfully held not to exceed a maximum of 77 mph anywhere on the descent to Carlisle, and we ran to a stop for adverse signals just outside the Citadel station, 62.3 miles from the start at Carnforth, in 56 minutes—a fine start-to-stop

average speed of 66.7 mph. The running average speed over the adverse 28.1 miles from Milepost 9½ to Shap Summit was 71.7 mph. It should be mentioned that the distances in the accompanying gradient diagram are from London (Euston).

As regards the more spectacular aspects of London Midland electric running, in express passenger service, brief details of three runs will aptly conclude this chapter.

On the last run of the three there were eight individual maximum speeds of 106 mph up to 109 mph, while on the second run the average speed between Carnforth and Shap Summit was exactly 90 mph despite careful observation of the speed restrictions for the curves of the Grayrigg bank.

The descriptive specification of the Class '87' locomotives is as follows:

Route	Gross trailing load (tons)	Distance (miles)	Net time (min)	Average speed (mph)
Crewe–Watford Junction	395	140.5	91½	92.3
Preston–Carlisle	395	90.1	62¾	87.0
Warrington–Euston	395	182.2	123¾	88.6

A striking near-broadside shot of the southbound 'Clansman', Inverness to Euston, near Beattock in October 1983 hauled by locomotive No 87023 Highland Chieftain *(T.H. Noble).*

Transformer and tapchanger. The transformer is electrically identical to that supplied for Class '86' except that, because the Class '87' is a more powerful locomotive, the total rating of the transformer is increased to 5,860 kva, a rise of 20 per cent, and the train heat winding load is also now up to 460 kva to accommodate train air-conditioning requirements. The transformer consists of an auto-transformer which can be tapped at 38 positions by a high-tension tapchanger controlled by the master-controller on the driver's desk.

The secondary-winding of the transformer is split into four parts; one for each traction motor-rectifier smoothing-reactor group. Each of these circuits is self-contained and in case of a fault can be isolated by the driver who can thus proceed on 75 per cent power; a separate winding is provided for the train heat and auxiliary winding. The auxiliary winding is centre-tapped to provide 130–4 v for running auxiliary machines of the capacitor type.

The transformer is totally immersed in oil which is pump-circulated through cooling radiators. Also included in this circuit is a Buchholz relay which gives warning of gas accumulation in the tranformer. The oil conservator accommodates changes in oil volume as the transformer warms up without allowing contact with the atmosphere which

could allow ingress of moisture and consequent reduction of dielectric strength of the oil. All parts of the equipment which are oil filled can be removed from the locomotive together, without the need to break the oil-circuit.

The transformer weight is 11,400 kg, a reduction of 1,000 kg compared with the Class '86' transformer, and has been effected by redesigning the container to reduce the oil volume, using a form-fitted cover, clamping the iron circuit and windings, and using welded instead of bolted-on flanges. The oil cooling radiators are marginally increased in size to allow for the increased amount of heat generated at the higher rating. The transformer compartment is nominally a sealed area, but a bleed of air is draw from the locomotive body by the resistor fans and is allowed to pass through the compartment to scavenge it and prevent excessive accumulation of ionised gases and the possibility of flash-overs above the tapchanger contactors.

The high-tension tapchanger is a similar design to that successfully used on Class '86' and Class '82' locomotives but incorporates minor alterations to improve reliability still further. It consists of three parts: a selector tank which contains the 38 fixed and two sliding contacts; a set of divert switches; and a drive mechanism which powers the sliders and operates the divert switches in sequence. Two sliders are used to ensure that one at least is carrying the load while the other can be moved off-load to another tapping position. Once this is done the load is transferred by divert switches to the slider in contact with the required tap, and the other slider is thus disconnected from the load in order to move it off-tap. The sliders are moved along the slider bars by a roller-chain operated by a Geneva mechanism in the selector tank. The selector tank is in part of the oil circuit.

Low-tension power circuit and rectifiers. The low-tension power circuits are divided into four separate but identical 'power-pack' groupings, each comprising: transformer secondary winding; bridge-connected silicon rectifier assembly; smoothing inductor; traction motor. The grouping technique enables the whole of a circuit to be isolated by the driver without the need for a fault-finding analysis if a component fault arises within one of the groups, and the locomotive can then proceed on reduced power. Each of the four full-wave rectifier units supplies one traction motor and is cooled by the associated traction-motor blower. Every full-wave bridge arm contains two parallel strings of two AE1 type S904 diodes rated at 1,860 A continuously and 1,340 V dc connected in series. Use of forward and reverse polarity pairs permits common heat-sink mounting, and each diode is fitted with two parallel hole storage capacitors. Each rectifier unit incorporates a surge-suppression circuit mounted within the individual cubicle.

Each locomotive has four separate bridge rectifiers (one per motor). The rectifier cubicles have been designed to make use of the higher rated elements now available and to allow easier access for cleaning purposes. The improvement in rating is demonstrated because each rectifier now has only 16 cells whereas the Class '86' rectifiers had 96 cells. An auxiliary rectifier is used to feed dc auxiliary machines and is a completely self-contained unit. It consists of two elements connected in push-pull across the main transformer tertiary winding terminals.

Frame-mounted traction motors. The GEC Type G412AZ dc traction motors have been developed specially for the particular requirements of the BR West Coast main line. These machines are force-ventilated with a one-hour rating of 950 kW, 1,134 V, 885 A. The motor body is a steel fabrication with a partially laminated magnet frame to improve the commutation of the 100 Hz ripple. The motor armature is hollow and is coupled at one end, by a gear-type coupling, to a cardan shaft running through the armature to a resilient rubber-coupling on the pinion. This allows the motor to be directly coupled to the bogie frame and considerably reduces the unsprung weight on the axles. The three-point suspension incorporates three conical rubber mountings, two on the nose and the third on an extension arm at the tail. The pinion and final-drive spur gear are contained in a cast-steel gearbox which is supported on the axle through taper

roller-bearings and from the bogie by a rubber-bushed torque reaction link. The gear ratio is 73/32 and the bearings and gears are splash lubricated.

The G412AZ motors are four-pole, series wound with interpoles and compensating windings. There is a permanent field-divert of 16 per cent with an operational divert of a further 23 per cent in a single stage, to give maximum utilisation of the locomotive performance over the speed range. For the purposes of rheostatic braking, the motor-fields are separately excited and each armature is connected to a resistor bank to dissipate the power.

The motor is of extremely robust design and incorporates many modern features to ensure long life with minimum maintenance. The armature winding is to Class H standards with Kapton polyimide film insulation for both conductor and ground insulation. Glass banding is used to secure the conductors in the slots. The conductors are TIG (Tungsten Inert Gas) welded to the commutator risers, which eliminates the danger of high-resistance joints developing in the event of any abnormal conditions leading to above normal winding temperatures, as can occur with soldered connections. The field windings are to Class F standards with the series and compole coils through-bonded and bonded to their poles with epoxy resin. The through bonding gives extremely good thermal conductivity to the coils so that a very compact as well a robust field system results.

The robust design is maintained for the brush-gear where the cast bronze brush-holders are supported from the commutator chamber by large single mycalex insulated pins with PTFE sleeves to give easily cleaned creepage surfaces. A multiple spring system and three-part carbon brushes help to maintain good contact with the commutator. Two large openings in the commutator chamber give good access to brushes, brushgear and commutator for maintenance purposes.

The frame is of fabricated construction and incorporates laminated bridges between main and commutating poles to assist commutation of the 100 Hz ripple current which is kept to approximately 30 per cent of the mean dc current at the continuous rating. The ripple is kept to this level by a smoothing reactor GEC Type SH152. The reactor is air-cored with a Kapton insulated copper coil on an aluminium framework. The cooling air enters between the turns of the coil and leaves at both ends.

Combined rheostatic and air braking. To provide a clean environment for the items of brake equipment, ep relay and proportional valves, distributors etc, two cubicles have been provided. These are located near to the transformer and adjacent to the rheostatic brake resistance banks. The brake force is about 83 per cent of locomotive weight and may be achieved by rheostatic or air braking, or a combination of both. The driver's air-brake valve automatically brings in the former which can dissipate 2,000 kW and only at very slow speeds or in an emergency does the air brake on the locomotive supplement the rheostatic. If, however, there is any fault in the latter braking equipment, the air brake is used exclusively.

The rheostatic brake has a separate field excitation, the control of which is by the high-tension tapchanger, thus eliminating the need for extra rheostatic brake control equipment. When rheostatic braking is in operation the motor fields are connected in series for separate excitation, the generated power being dissipated in a separate resistor connected across each armature. Compounding is achieved by virtue of resistors common to field and armature circuits which gives a desirable flattening of the brake effort/speed characteristic. Use of the high-tension tapchanger and one of the rectifier bridges for excitation control eliminates the need for additional equipment.

The air-brake equipment has been supplied by Westinghouse Brake & Signal Co Ltd. It is a self-lapping automatic brake capable of graduable application and release under the regulation of brake-pipe pressure which is in turn controlled by the driver's type M8AS automatic air-brake valve at each driving position. Unlike other ac electric locomotives, the Class '87' locomotives are designed for hauling air-braked trains only, but in the interests of standardisation many of the items of equipment are identical to those fitted to a dual-braked locomotive eqiupped with both air and vacuum. In addition, the locomotives are fitted with an anti-wheelslip brake which operates in conjunction with the automatic air brake and the rheostatic brake. The locomotive air brake may be operated independently of the train brake and the locomotive rheostatic brake, if required, by the straight air-brake valve which is also fitted at each driving position. Compressed air for the locomotive and train is supplied from a Westinghouse type 3VC75 pipe-ventilated two-stage three-cylinder motor-driven air compressor with a swept volume of 75 cu ft/min at a speed of 1.570 rev/min.

Control equipment and auxiliaries. The control equipment is housed in four equipment frames adjacent to each rectifier frame. The upper half of each equipment frame is sealed against dust and houses control and auxiliary equipment. The power equipment is housed in the lower half of each equipment frame, left open to ensure adequate ventilation. One of the frameworks also contains the

electronic module developed by BR for controlling wheel-spin. This compares traction motor currents and contains a unique feature which provides automatic sensitivity adjustment to take account of varying machine tolerances. The equipment runs the tapchangers back if the current difference between any two motors is greater than a pre-set value. The speedometer and traction motor overspeed protection equipment are controlled by magnetic probes measuring gearwheel velocity.

The control is similar to that fitted to the Class '86' except that two locomotives can be operated in multiple and that a single-stage of field weakening is incorporated in the motor circuit. In multiple, fault indication is registered in the leading locomotive. Also, because the service requirements do not necessitate both running at full power simultaneously, full automatic synchronisation of tapchangers has not been provided. A notch-indicator for each locomotive is provided in each cab so that the driver is aware of the power being provided by the trailing locomotive. The two locomotives are linked by 36-way plugs and sockets which are deliberately chosen to be non-compatible with the other three types of jumper plugs and sockets on BR.

Towards each corner of the equipment compartment, a combined rectifier-inductor-cooling fan unit is located, the latter being situated immediately above the corresponding traction motor air-inlet ducting. Cooling air required for each of these four units is drawn through two bodyside louvres. To prevent airborne foreign matter or water from entering the rectifier duct, a water separator, comprising baffle plate and screen, is fitted between the louvres and the rear of the rectifier cubicle.

Cooling-air for the transformer oil radiator and the brake resistances is drawn through five bodyside louvres by two dual-speed electrically driven radial-flow fans, one at the base of each radiator stack. The air passes through the oil radiators on to the resistor stack and is exhausted through self-acting roof-mounted louvred outlets.

When rheostatic braking is in operation, the quantity of air required for cooling the brake resistors is far greater than can be drawn through the radiators or be delivered by the fans operating at normal speed. The speed of the fans is therefore increased, using generated voltage from the braking effort, and shutters at each end of the radiators are opened, allowing the majority of air to bypass the radiators. The air is exhausted as already described.

Driving cabs, vigilance system and fault indication. The driving cabs of the locomotives are similar to previous layouts but some changes have been made as a result of experience and developments. Forced ventilation has been introduced to the cab design and the system automatically controls the cab temperature whilst ensuring changes of fresh air. Added driver comfort results from the provision of 'punkah' louvres fitted in the desk console. Trico-Folberth BPM pneumatic windscreen wipers are fitted at the bottom of both windscreens and, in order to meet modern requirements, the motor has two speeds, automatic parking and a travelling water jet for washing purposes. A desk-mounted combined control valve operates the complete cleaning system.

The Class '87' locomotives are fitted with a driver's vigilance system which basically comprises a two-position foot pedal incorporating an electric switch, audible signal device and relay unit. With the master controller in the driving position the pedal has to be kept depressed. After 60 seconds a continuous audible signal commences and, if the pedal is not released and depressed to reset the

system, an emergency brake application will occur after a further period of five to seven seconds. The system can be reset at any time during the cycle convenient to the driver and, to assist with operation of the driving controls, an alternative desk-mounted hand switch is provided. Resetting the standard Automatic Warning System equipment in response to a cautionary signal aspect also resets the time cycle.

A general fault light on the driver's desk of each cab gives warning of all the above fault conditions plus tranformer over-temperature alarm and battery-charger failure. In the event of power-circuit overload, four power-circuit indicator lights on the top of No 2 control equipment frame enable the driver to identify which circuit is faulty and to isolate it before continuing at reduced power.

A thyristor-type battery charger is fitted. It is completely interchangeable with the magnetstat-type battery charger in use on Class '86'. It is powered from the outer taps of the tertiary winding (264 v) and is rated at 110 v 35 a.

13. Freight locomotive development

When, under the great Modernisation Plan of 1955, the total replacement of steam traction by diesel and electric locomotives, railcars, and multiple-unit trains was authorised for the heaviest duties, the original operating philosophy was to have locomotives of a mixed-traffic capability. At the outset it was not expected that, for some time, passenger-train speeds would exceed 90 mph, while the policy of constructing many new fully mechanised marshalling yards was evidence of the continuing practice of operating freight traffic in single-wagon loads, with relatively moderate loads from yard to yard. Rapidly changing conditions however, particularly in freight business, led to a re-appraisal of the motive power situation. The introduction of the nominated freight, and of liner trains, both liable to load up to gross tonnages of 1,000, and required to run up to 75 mph was one factor; another was the 'merry-go-round' coal train, consisting of a block-formation of high-capacity air-braked mineral wagons, and running up to a maximum of 45 mph. A common-user diesel-electric locomotive that might on other occasions be required to work a 90 mph express passenger train was not ideal for the previously quoted freight assignments.

By the early 1970s the British Railways Board adopted a new policy for traction, to provide specialised units for passenger and freight duties, instead of the previous common-user concept. The immediate need was for a purely freight locomotive of high capacity, so urgently indeed that a complete new design could not be prepared by the Board's own resources within the time available. A general specification was prepared and tenders invited from a number of British and foreign manufacturers. The outcome was rather curious, and took the line of development back, oddly enough, to the remarkable *Kestrel* prototype built by the Brush Electrical Company, as related in Chapter 10 of this book. While this locomotive was somewhat before its time, so far as British Railways were concerned, and it was sold to the Soviet State Railways in 1971, considerable interest was shown abroad in certain of its design features, particularly in its use of an ac rather than dc generator; and with potential sales in the Eastern bloc and other countries of similar political minds an agreement was made between Brush and a state-owned manufacturing firm in Romania to develop a high-powered diesel-electric freight locomotive. When Brush received the invitation from British Railways to tender for the new high-power freight locomotive, the joint Anglo-Romanian project was sufficiently far advanced for an acceptable delivery date to be offered; and the contract for the first 30, to be built in Romania, was won in the face of strong American competition.

Before referring to the far from satisfactory outcome of this unusual contract, the design itself must be described. This was entirely British, and this fact coupled with the proposed incorporation of many British-made components, including the diesel engines, led to Government authority being given for the first 30 locomotives to be built in Romania. The body structure, based on that of the Class '47'

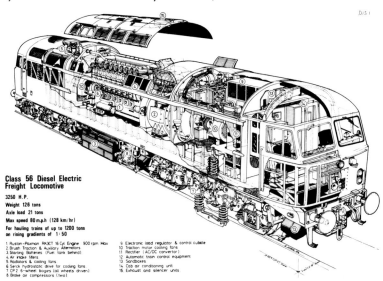

Class 56 Diesel Electric Freight Locomotive

3250 H.P.

Weight 126 tons

Axle load 21 tons

Max speed 80 m.p.h (128 km/hr)

For hauling trains of up to 1200 tons
on rising gradients of 1:50

1 Ruston-Paxman RK3CT 16 Cyl Engine 900 rpm Max	9 Electronic load regulator & control cubicle
2 Brush Traction & Auxiliary Alternators	10 Traction motor cooling fans
3 Starting Batteries (Fuel tank behind)	11 Rectifier (AC/DC convertor)
4 Air intake filters	12 Automatic train control equipment
5 Radiators & cooling fans	13 Sandboxes
6 Serck hydrostatic drive for cooling fans	14 Cab air conditioning unit
7 CP2 6-wheel bogies (all wheels driven)	15 Exhaust and silencer units
8 Brake air compressors (two)	

The Class '56' diesel-electric freight locomotive: perspective part-sectioned arrangement drawing (British Railways).

Left *The Ruston-Paxman 16 cylinder RK3CT engine installed in the Class '56' 3,200 hp mixed traffic and heavy freight locomotive* (British Railways).

Right *Loaded merry-go-round coal train approaching Trowell Junction, hauled by No 56098* (Brian Morrison).

Left *Class '56' locomotives under construction at the famous Doncaster Plant. The body form can be noted* (Brian Morrison).

Below *Southbound merry-go-round coal train on the Midland line approaching Clay Cross Junction hauled by '56' Class diesel-electric locomotive No 56115* (Brian Morrison).

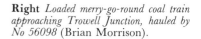

diesel-electric locomotives of British Railways, had stressed-skin body sides, providing maximum rigidity and strength with optimum use of material. The cabs of the first locomotives were of aluminium construction, but later ones have been steel fabricated. Within the handsomely styled exterior two intermediate bulkheads separate the power unit from the numerous items of ancillary equipment. The diesel engine was a 16-cylinder Ruston-Paxman type RK3CT, running at a maximum of 900 revs per minute and rated at 3,250 horsepower. The cylinders were set in two banks in V formation, and there were two single-bank radiator panels, forming the cooling group, to cool separately the engine coolant and that from the lubricating oil and to charge air coolers.

The bogies were of a type used extensively on the Romanian State Railways. The design was derived partly from earlier Swiss practice, and manufactured by a Romanian firm, ICM, Resita. Designated 'CP2' this bogie has a main frame welded up from two box-section longitudinal members, and connected by box-section cross-members. The primary suspension at each axlebox consists of two helical springs and friction dampers mounted either side of the axlebox, to which they are connected through a pivoted beam. The outer axles of each bogie have self-aligning roller-bearings, while the inner axles have parallel roller-bearings which provide for lateral movement within the axlebox, to allow displacement of the wheelset when the locomotive passes round curves. Because the locomotives were required for running up to a maximum of 80 mph with liner and speedlink freight trains, careful attention had to be given to the secondary suspension, and this is provided by triple Flexicoil springs fitted within the body underframe on each side of the bogies. Vertical and lateral damping constraints are provided by hydraulic dampers.

Although ordered in September 1974, it was not until August 1976 that the first of the Romanian built Class '56' locomotives were delivered. The period of commissioning was long and difficult because, despite an essentially sound design, there were surprisingly many defects in manufacturing detail which had to be corrected. It was indeed not until the end of February 1977 that the first locomotive, No 56001, was finally accepted, and the remainder of those built in Romania were accepted in stages until the last one of the 30, in mid-October 1977. An order for a further 30 had been placed with British Rail Engineering Ltd, for construction at the Doncaster Plant; these differed in certain important details from the Romanian batch, though including Romanian-built bogies, and they were not subject to the defects experienced with the imported locomotives. The first of the Doncaster batch, No 56031, was accepted in mid-May 1977. Having regard to the probable use of many of these powerful locomotives on 'merry-go-round' coal trains, referred to as MGR, it had been realised that, with such a high nominal tractive effort, wheel-slip could take place frequently in the relatively poor adhesion conditions of colliery and power-station sidings. In consequence it was important to provide for automatic wheel-slip detection and correction in the equipment. The majority of the earlier '56' Class locomotives were based in the Eastern Region for MGR coal trains, and an interesting comparison of the capacity with other diesel-electric locomotives engaged on freight service in the Region was made in a paper presented to The Institution of Mechanical Engineers by Mr D.F. Russell, Freight Engineer, British Railways Board. From this tabulation (overleaf) it will be appreciated that, although Class '56' was not more than 10 per cent heavier than Class '47', it was very much more powerful in comparison.

When the MGR coal trains were first introduced,

Eastern Region: locomotives used on freight

Class	20	31	37	40	45	47	56
Installed engine (hp)	1,000	1,470	1,750	2,000	2,500	2,570	3,250
Horsepower at rail	770	1,167	1,255	1,550	2,000	2,160	2,640
Maximum permissible speed (mph)	75	80	90	90	90	95	80
Speed at continuous power rating (mph)	11.0	19.5	14.3	20.6	24.8	25.5	16.7
Continuous tractive effort (lb)	24,950	22,200	32,500	27,700	29,700	30,000	52,700
Adhesion weight (tons)	72	73.5	100.3	104	109	112*	124

*Freight service locos, with no train heating equipment

---

working between National Coal Board collieries in the Yorkshire, North Nottinghamshire, and Derbyshire collieries to power stations in the Aire and Trent valleys, the gross trailing loads of the trains were set at about 1,500 tons; but these it was found could not be adequately dealt with by the '47' Class locomotives, and reluctantly the tonnage was reduced to 1,150: 30 wagons instead of 36. The introduction of the '56' Class locomotives, however, has enabled the loads to be increased again to more than 1,500 tons with the new locomotives showing a comfortable margin of power in reserve. Since then, with more locomotives of the class available, they have been put on to the longer runs from the Midland coalfields to Didcot power station, while others have been allocated to the stone traffic from the 'Yeoman' quarries at Merehead in the Mendips. When the ten-year contract between the firm and

British Railways was signed, in 1978, it provided for the conveyance of a payload of 1,400 tons, in 37 high-capacity hopper wagons to Acton yard on four days a week. The trains, which entered upon the West of England main line at Witham Friary, were originally powered by two Class '37' diesels, with a combined engine horsepower of 3,500; but a single Class '56' of 3,250 horsepower could deal adequately with the duty.

Orders for a further 75 locomotives of Class '56' were placed with British Rail Engineering Ltd, for construction at both Doncaster and Crewe, and with more of these powerful locomotives becoming available their activities have been further extended. The heaviest regular freight trains on British Railways, those conveying iron ore from Port Talbot Harbour to Llanwern steelworks and having a gross trailing load of 2,700 tons were, until

Above *Western Region stone train from Yeoman's quarries at Merehead to Acton, near Witham Friary, hauled by locomotive No 56046 (Brian Morrison).*

Below far left *Merry-go-round coal empties passing Trowell Junction, hauled by locomotive No 56069 (Brian Morrison).*

Left *A striking view of a merry-go-round coal empties train from Didcot power station, leaving Southam Road tunnel, near Leamington, hauled by locomotive No 56090 (Brian Morrison).*

Right *Merry-go-round coal empties train from Drakelow negotiating severe subsidence near Moira West Junction, with locomotive No 56083 (Brian Morrison).*

1979, each hauled by three Class '37' diesels having a total engine horsepower of 5,250; but from August in that year this duty was taken over by '56' Class locomotives, working in pairs, and having a total horsepower of 6,500. I rode on the footplate of the leading locomotive of three Class '37's one day in the summer of 1976 when the rail conditions were not too good, and there was a continual tendency towards slipping; and with the full 2,700 tons trailing load we made rather heavy weather of the ascent from Margam Moors to Stormy Siding where the gradient steepens from 1 in 139 to 2½ miles at 1 in 102—94—79—93. Speed fell away from 39 mph to 17 mph before the summit was reached. The train was, of course, air braked, and on favourable stretches we ran up to the maximum permitted, of 60 mph. Schedule time, pass to pass, over the 42 miles from Margam Moors to Newport is 61 minutes, and, but for signal checks prior to passing through Cardiff, this we should have maintained. But there was no time to spare, and use of a pair of '56' Class has certainly improved the working.

Taking all round, Class '56' can be regarded as a successful design, in a field where the wide variety of duties, and range of speeds makes it difficult to achieve an ideal performance in any one of the range. Nevertheless, apart from the initial head-

aches arising from the indifferent manufacturing quality of the imported locomotives, the design as a whole has revealed technical shortcomings that tend to increase the maintenance costs, and which have been largely eradicated in the later development, represented by the '58' Class. On Class '56' there have been troubles with the bogie riding, and persistent maintenance difficulties with the engine exhaust and coolant systems. These are discussed in more detail later, when referring to the great improvements made in the Class '58' locomotives. On the other hand the introduction of ac generation of current, and the use of brushless alternators has resulted in maintenance economies in this respect that have allowed the times for routine depot examination to be considerably extended beyond that of other diesel-electric locomotives, as per the following table.

Above *Western Region iron ore train between Port Talbot and Llanwern on the main line east of Newport hauled by two '56' Class locomotives, Nos 56044 and 56041* (C.J. Marsden).

Above right *Before the introduction of Class '56' a loaded ore train between Port Talbot and Llanwern, triple headed by three Class '37' diesel electric locomotives, passing Newport* (O.S. Nock).

Right *Merry-go-round loaded coal train for Aberthaw power station, passing Barry, hauled by diesel electric locomotives Nos 37204 and 37245* (Brian Morrison).

Below right *Train of steel-coil, southbound, passing Tibshelf Junction, near Westhouses, hauled by locomotives Nos 37101 and 37200* (Brian Morrison).

Routine Examination: intervals in engine hours

Examination Code	A	B	C	D
Engine Classes				
20, 31, 37, 40, 45, 47	45	225	675	2025
Engine Class:				
56	80	400	1200	3600

With the accumulating experience with Class '56' constantly under review, the British Railways Board determined upon the design of a development freight locomotive, to effect reductions in first cost and fuel consumption; to improve accessibility of all parts requiring periodic examination, and attention in maintenance. Although it can be said that Class '58' is a development of Class '56', the former includes so many radical changes as to suggest that the new ensemble is not a synthesis of the existing main features, but an example of avoiding the many that it was not desirable to copy. While

the diesel engine is necessarily the heart of an outstandingly successful development in this case, the radical changes embodied in Class '58' stem from bedrock, the structural build-up.

After the introduction of the first main line diesel-electric locomotives in the early stages of the original Modernisation Plan, it was frequently remarked that the new power seemed very heavy in relation to its tractive effort. The case was quoted of two Class '37' diesels, weighing more than 200 tons between them, being needed to do the same work as a Class '8' steam 'Pacific' weighing about 155 tons. Whether such a comparison was truly fair is not of immediate concern; but in later designs of diesel a sustained attempt was made to reduce weight, and one way of doing this was to use the stressed-skin type of body construction, referred to in earlier chapters. This of course is a highly sophisticated form of design in which not only the underframe but also the entire body takes a share of the traction and braking stresses. Using computerised techniques in

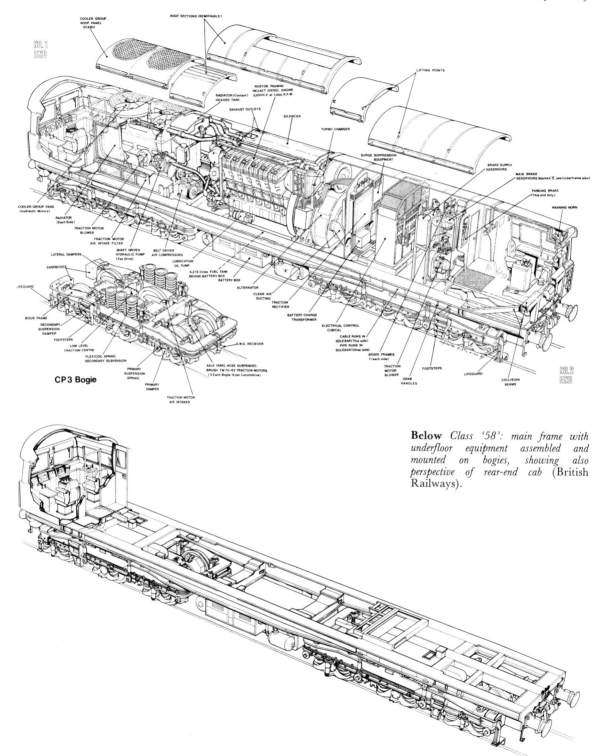

NO.1
END

COOLER GROUP
ROOF PANEL
(FIXED)

ROOF SECTIONS (REMOVABLE)

LIFTING POINTS

RUSTON PAXMAN
RK3ACT DIESEL ENGINE
3,300 H.P. at 1,000 R.P.M.

RADIATOR (Coolant)
HEADER TANK

EXHAUST OUTLETS

SILENCER

TURBO CHARGER

SURGE SUPPRESSION
EQUIPMENT

BRAKE SUPPLY
RESERVOIRS

MAIN BRAKE
RESERVOIRS (Marked 'X', see Underframe also)

MAIN BRAKE
RESERVOIRS (Marked 'X', see Underframe also)

PARKING BRAKE
(This end only)

WARNING HORN

COOLER GROUP FANS
(Hydraulic Motors)

RADIATOR
(Each Side)

TRACTION MOTOR
BLOWER

TRACTION MOTOR
AIR INTAKE FILTER

LATERAL DAMPERS

SHAFT DRIVEN
HYDRAULIC PUMP
(Fan Drive)

BELT DRIVEN
AIR COMPRESSORS

LUBRICATION
OIL PUMP

SANDBOXES

4,215 litres FUEL TANK
BEHIND BATTERY BOX

BATTERY BOX

LIFEGUARD

ALTERNATOR

CLEAN AIR
DUCTING

TRACTION
RECTIFIER

BATTERY CHARGE
TRANSFORMER

ELECTRICAL CONTROL
CUBICAL

BOGIE FRAME

SECONDARY
SUSPENSION
DAMPER

FOOTSTEPS

LOW LEVEL
TRACTION CENTRE

FLEXICOIL SPRING
SECONDARY SUSPENSION

A.W.S. RECIEVER

PRIMARY
SUSPENSION
SPRING

AXLE HUNG. NOSE SUSPENDED.
BRUSH TM 73-62 TRACTION MOTORS
(3 Each Bogie/ 6 per Locomotive)

CABLE RUNS IN
SOLEBAR (This side)
PIPE RUNS IN
SOLEBAR (Other side)

BRAKE FRAMES
(1 each side)

TRACTION
MOTOR
BLOWER

GRAB
HANDLES

FOOTSTEPS

LIFEGUARD

COLLISION
BEAMS

NO.2
END

CP3 Bogie

PRIMARY
DAMPER

TRACTION MOTOR
AIR INTAKES

Below *Class '58': main frame with underfloor equipment assembled and mounted on bogies, showing also perspective of rear-end cab* (British Railways).

Left *The Class '58' diesel-electric freight locomotive perspective part-sectioned drawing* (British Railways).

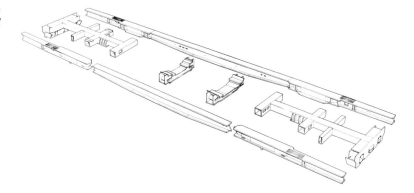

Right *Class '58': the all-welded main frame showing component parts* (British Railways).

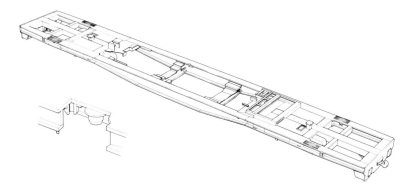

Right *The main frame of the Class '58' completely welded up* (British Railways).

stress analysis, optimum use of material was effected, together with some weight reduction. In the case of Class '56' the body construction was based on that of the successful Class '47', which at the time the new freight locomotives were designed was nevertheless about 15 years old. Although saving some weight, this design was expensive to build, and encasing a large engine resulted in problems with maintenance and air ventilation. The British Railways Board after some experience in running Class '56' decided upon a totally different basis of construction.

The Class '58' locomotive is built on a massive steel underframe, designed to take all the traction and braking stresses experienced in the heaviest traffic. There are no load-bearing members above floor level, in total contrast to Class '56'. There are two fabricated steel girders of I section running throughout from one headstock to the other, the form of which is very clearly shown in the photographs of the first locomotive of the class, with a fish-bellied shape in the centre. It is designed to allow lifting of the complete locomotives at the bogie centre pivots, and will carry all the static loads imposed by the equipment, and also, of course,

those resulting from dynamic forces when the locomotive is in operation. At each end, as will be seen from the perspective drawing, there are 'collision beams' mounted above the buffer beams, and re-inforced by diagonal struts on to the main frames. The entire arrangement has been designed for ease of assembly, and maintenance. First stages in erection of the complete locomotive involve placing the fabricated frame structure upside down on the erecting shop floor, while all the equipment suspended from the underside is assembled and secured. This includes such items as the battery boxes, fuel tank and air reservoirs for the brake system. Then the frame is rotated about its longitudinal axis to its normal position, and suitably supported ready for the equipment to be assembled on its upper side.

As will be appreciated from the perspective drawing, the idea of a completely smooth exterior has been abandoned in the Class '58' locomotive, and an outside platform, being actually the upper flange of the main frame girder, has been provided as a means of ready access to all the internal equipment. The side panels and ventilation grilles can readily be removed for this purpose. The cabs are

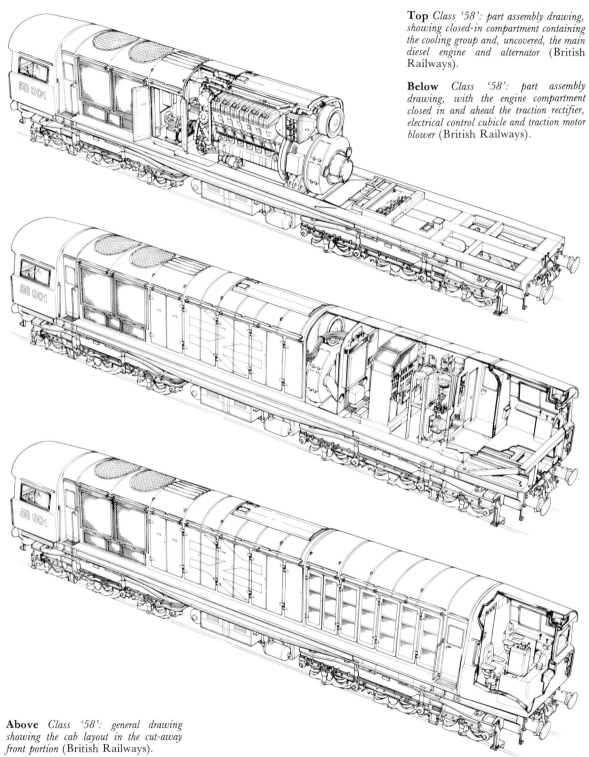

Top *Class '58': part assembly drawing, showing closed-in compartment containing the cooling group and, uncovered, the main diesel engine and alternator* (British Railways).

Below *Class '58': part assembly drawing, with the engine compartment closed in and ahead the traction rectifier, electrical control cubicle and traction motor blower* (British Railways).

Above *Class '58': general drawing showing the cab layout in the cut-away front portion* (British Railways).

First of the new '58' Class 3,200 hp freight diesels, built at Doncaster Plant (C.J. Marsden).

quite separate structures, and can be removed *in toto*; between them there are four compartments separated from each other by bulkheads. All equipment likely to produce fumes and noise, or needing oil, is in the centre compartment, while adjacent is that containing the turbo-charger air inlet, and the main alternator. The electrical control cubicle, brake equipment and rectifier are in a clean-air compartment, while at the opposite end of the locomotive is the compartment containing the cooler group. The layout was indeed dominated by the need to control the large volumes of air needed by a 3,300 horsepower locomotive. The cabs, cooler group, power unit, electrical and braking equipment can all be independently removed for overhaul or maintenance.

Coming now to the engine itself, the installation of a new variety, while of the same generic design as in Class '56' and previously, yet having 12 instead of 16 cylinders and still developing the same horsepower, is one of the most outstanding features of the new locomotive. As a result of experience with Class '56', one of the major requirements of British Railways was an engine that occupied less space, in order to provide greater accessbility to other equipment. The two main options were to change from the traditional medium-speed engine, running at about 850 rpm, to a quick-running type at 1,500 rpm, or to introduce a shorter but uprated version

of the older type, running a little faster, but needing only 12 cylinders. Rustons Diesels Ltd, a company in the GEC group, were close to releasing a 12-cylinder engine of 3,300 horsepower, which had been developed from their standard range, and this was selected, as having the additional advantage that the Class '56' electrical control gear could be used, and a large degree of interchangeability of spare parts between Classes '56' and '58' would be possible. The history of development of the Ruston 'RK' engine, first in collaboration with English Electric and later with GEC, can, in its overall results, be seen from the following table, all the locomotives concerned having the standard 10-inch diameter cylinders. In view of earlier remarks about the weight of the first British main line diesels, some additional ratios have been added.

In studying this table the gradual increase in engine horsepower per cylinder will be noted— gradual that is until Class '58', when there was a remarkable jump from 203 to 275. The Ruston RKC engine, running at 1,000 rpm and still in a prototype stage, was installed in a Class '47' locomotive, engaged on freight duties, and it gave good service, though this experiment served to emphasise the common complaint of all engine users that, while failures of the engine itself were rare, failures of the pipework were a major problem. It is really surprising that, after 20 years' experience with heavy utilisation of internal combustion locomotives of one kind or another, so little attention seems to have been given to what may appear to be no more than a detail, but which can nevertheless result in a

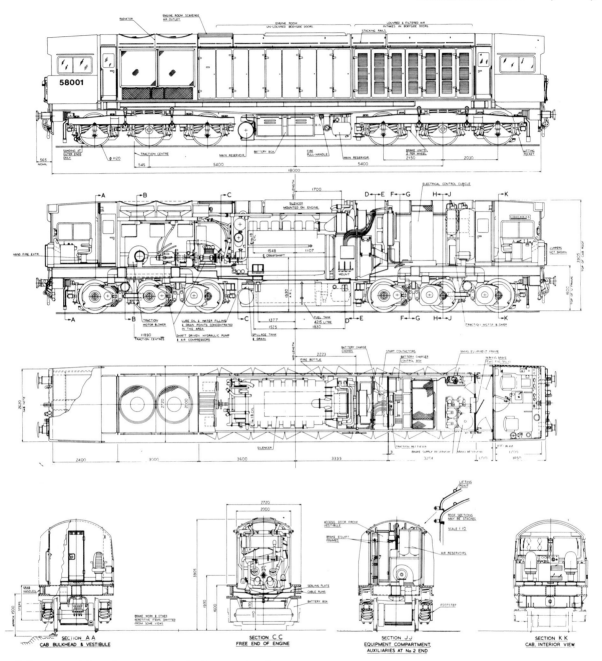

failure requiring the removal of a locomotive from its train. I shall not forget the occasion in 1963 when I was riding a Class '40' diesel on 'The Midday Scot' working through from Euston to Glasgow, and a minor pipework failure compelled its removal from the train at Crewe. It was replaced at a moment's notice by a steam 'Pacific', which was

fortunately in good condition, and was able to regain some of the lost time. With the Class '47' locomotive fitted with the prototype Ruston 12-cylinder engine, in two years there were 16 stops for leaks in the pipework. Of these six were in the exhaust, four in the coolant system, four in the fuel supply, and two with lubricating oil. One is remin-

Left *General arrangement drawing of complete locomotive* (British Railways).

Below left *A number of sectional views showing the cross-sectional arrangements at various points* (British Railways).

Right *A Class '58' diesel under construction at Doncaster Plant. Note the mounting of the engine and other equipment on the massive underframe* (C.J. Marsden).

Below *An unusual duty for a '58': the second of the class, No 58002, hauling 'The 58 Pioneer' rail-tour from Paddington to Matlock and return on September 18 1983, seen here between Ambergate Junction and Whatstandwell on the Matlock branch line* (L.P. Gater).

ded of the humorist who once described the piping of the exhaust system on one diesel locomotive as reminding him of 'a mad woman's knitting'! While Class '56' is not as bad as that, the accompanying diagram showing the difference between Class '56' and '58' is illuminating. The number of pipe-joints has been reduced from 28 to ten.

It is perhaps symptomatic that reference to the troubles with the ancilliary features should have been made before mention of the means by which the marked increase in horsepower per cylinder has been obtained, other than that of the increased running speed. This quantity has been increased by 33 per cent over Class '56', of which only 11 per cent is due to increased speed. The remainder is due to higher pressure in the cylinders: more than 20 per cent. The success with which this enhancement has been achieved is due to a systematic stress analysis by the most modern scientific methods of every part of the engine, both moving and static. These have been applied particularly to the strength of the crankcase and bedplate assembly; to the loadings on the main bearings, and to the crankcase arch, all due to the higher speed and the considerably

Opposite page top to bottom

Returning empties merry-go-round coal train from Rugeley power station to Coalville on the freight only line from Burton to Leicester, near Moira with locomotive No 58006 (C.J. Tuffs).

Locomotive No 58005 setting back train of loaded coal hopper wagons into sidings at Overseal from Moira West Junction (C.J. Tuffs).

Empty merry-go-round coal train Drakelow power station to Coalville, passing Gresley on the freight-only Burton to Leicester line with locomotive No 58002 (C.J. Tuffs).

Beside the cooling towers of Ratcliffe power station locomotive No 58004 leaving with a train of fly-ash for Fletton near Peterborough (C.J. Tuffs).

This page top to bottom

Loaded merry-go-round coal train Coalville to Drakelow, near Gresley. This photograph shows very clearly the construction of the '58' Class, with the open walkway between the cabs, on the massive underframe. The locomotive is No 58003 (C.J. Tuffs).

In the wintry weather of January 1984, locomotive No 58006 is working a train of sheeted steel coil on the Midland main line from Corby steel works to Toton yard (C.J. Tuffs).

Coal train for Garston Docks prior to leaving Rawdon Colliery, with locomotive No 58002. The train is routed via Burton-on-Trent, Wychnor Junction, Lichfield, and under the wires via Crewe to Merseyside in November 1983 (C.J. Tuffs).

Class '58' No 58009 in ex-works condition is seen shunting HAA hopper wagons on Drakelow West Curve in readiness to take a rake of empties to Cadley Hill Colliery on January 4 1984 (C.J. Tuffs).

Evolution of Ruston 10-inch diameter diesel engine

Year	Loco Class	Number of cylinders	Engine speed (rpm)	Horsepower per cyl	total	Loco weight (tons)	Horsepower per ton
1957	20	8VT	850	125	1,000	72	13.9
1957	31	12VT	850	123	1,470	110	13.3
1958	40	16VT	850	125	2,000	135	14.8
1961	37	12VC	850	146	1,750	102	17.1
1967	50	16VC	850	169	2,700	117	23.0
1977	56	16VC	900	203	3,250	125	26.0
1982	58	12VC	1,000	275	3,300	128	25.8

increased firing pressure. In applying the basic RK engine to the '56' Class it had been found necessary to use grey cast iron to a considerably higher grade than in earlier engines, and this grade BS17 was also proposed for Class '58'. But it had to be subjected to a most exhaustive series of stress-strain tests, in the course of which it was found necessary to increase the strength of the crankcase arch. No less intensive were the development testing procedures applied to the one-piece cast aluminium pistons that have been a consistent feature of Ruston engine designs over many years. Before incorporating the improved design in any locomotive the pistons were submitted to a very severe overload test, to simulate low-cycle fatigue,

and tests under high firing pressure to accentuate any high-cycle fatigue damage. This latter test was carried on for a minimum of 350 hours, representing a million operations.

The Class '58' locomotives, like Class '56', have been designed to run at 80 mph to enable them to be used on liner and speedlink freight trains, and special reference is necessary to the design of the bogie. This is a development from the experience obtained with a trial of two 'CP1' bogies mounted experimentally under one of the Doncaster-built '56'

The 'CP3' bogie, perspective drawing (British Railways).

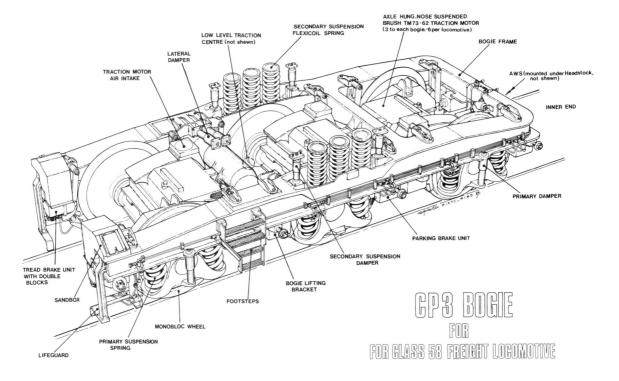

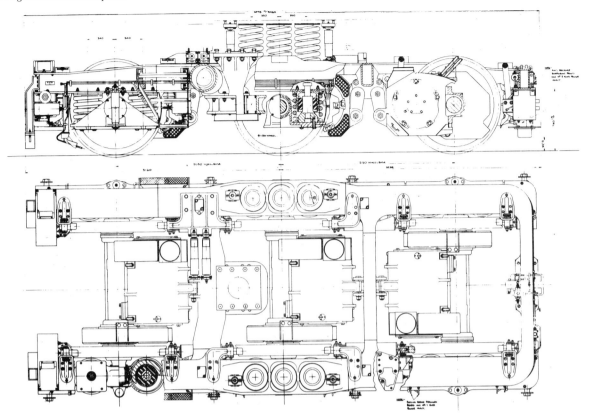

The 'CP3' bogie: general arrangement drawing (British Railways).

Class. The 'CP2' bogie, built in Romania, had certain unattractive features which the experimental 'CP1' hoped to avoid; but this, in turn, revealed other disadvantages, and the new BR 'CP3', illustrated in the accompanying perspective drawing, has been designed to overcome these. One feature which will immediately be noticed is that the all-welded frame is U-shaped and has no cross-member beyond the outer axle at the leading end. The '56' Class locomotive, although designed specifically to

British Railways requirements, was also built by BREL with a view to the export market as well, and the open end of the bogie frame is designed to accommodate the Continental type of centre coupler, if need be. As on Class '56' the primary suspension is by helical springs, while the secondary suspension is by two nests of three Flexicoil helical springs, which fit into pockets in the girder under-frames. Roller bearings are used throughout. The traction motors which are axle-hung are of the Brush TM 73—62 design, and are a derivative of the one successfully used on Class '45' (the 'Peaks'), on the prototype *Kestrel*, and on Class '56'. The motor pinion drives a solid spur gear wheel on the axle.

14. HST: conception and design

By the running of the 25 kv ac electrics on the West Coast route, and by that of the 'Deltics' on the East Coast, the hallmark of speed for a British express passenger train had been advanced to 100 mph. But, while this had been achieved amid a main line traffic density greater than anything found elsewhere in the world, it was appreciated that individual runs at average speeds of 80 mph start-to-stop and overall journey times showing averages of 70 to 75 mph were not enough to meet the competition of internal airlines. An assessment of the market had shown that railways were favourably placed up to a total journey time of about three hours. With the electric service from Euston providing hourly departures through the day to Liverpool and Manchester, and journey times of 2 hours 35 minutes in each case, success was amply explained. On the other hand, when journey times included in this market research extended beyond three hours there was a progressive decrease and loss of business to air. It was of course well known that there were certain weather conditions that gave railways a strong advantage in reliability and punctuality; but the exceptional cases, which were always gratifying to railway supporters, did little or nothing to strengthen the overall case.

Even before the completion of the West Coast main line electrification to Glasgow, consideration was being given to substantial service acceleration on four main arteries of traffic:
a) East Coast main, London to Newcastle and Edinburgh;
b) West Coast main, London to Preston, Carlisle and Glasgow;
c) Western Region, London to Bristol, South Wales and the West of England;
d) the busy North East—South West axis, connecting at its extremities Newcastle and the West Riding cities with South Wales, Bristol and Plymouth.

In this and the next chapter the more conventional ways in which British Railways have moved into this very desirable area of higher-speed passenger trains are described. The collateral project of the Advanced Passenger Train involving techniques that were entirely new is discussed in the concluding chapters of this book. The first stage proposed, and subsequently put into brilliantly successful effect, was to use well-established traction and rolling stock technology to produce a train capable of continuous running at 125 mph and having braking equipment that would provide stopping distances in service conditions no greater than those of existing trains travelling at speeds up to 100 mph. The upper limit of 125 mph was important on two counts: first, it was established that the higher speed did not pass the limit beyond which the enginemen could satisfactorily observe the rapid succession of colour light signals; second, on this account, and on the fact of adequate braking distance, no reconstruction of the signalling would be necessary on routes already equipped for 100 mph continuous running.

With the philosophy of major acceleration on the more important long-distance passenger routes accepted, it was then a matter of giving practical effect to the evolving requirements of the commercial departments. The electrification of the West Coast main line to Birmingham, Liverpool and Manchester had demonstrated, beyond any doubt, the immense advantage of a frequent, regular-interval service throughout the day, and it seemed as though the frequent admonitions of that famous editor of *The Railway Gazette*, John Aiton Kay, for shorter trains and many more of them, was having an echo in the 1970s. It was certainly a revolution from the gargantuan loads of the war years, when the operating people asked that the new high-speed trains should have rakes of no more than seven or eight coaches of the Mark III type, 75 feet long, and providing seats for a total of 96 first-and 288 second-class passengers apart from the accommodation in buffet and kitchen cars. The weight of an eight-car train, fully loaded with passengers and luggage, was estimated at about 300 tons, and the power to pull this had to be sufficient to maintain a speed of 125 mph on level track, in the face of adverse winds. The value of air resistance was of course all important, and so far as British Railways was concerned, above 100 mph it was a matter of guess-work. Since nationalisation a great deal of experimental work had been carried out to obtain accurate values of coach rolling resistance, but these systematic investigations had not proceeded beyond 100 mph.

The tests showed that, in still air, the resistance of one of the latest types of coach would be 14.5 lb per ton at 90 mph; but the resistance was not directly proportional to the speed, and at 100 mph the resistance was 17.5 lb per ton. From measurements made at lower speeds the characteristic shape of the resistance curve could be seen, and by a certain amount of intelligent guess-work and extrapolation, the resistance to a speed of 125 mph in still air was estimated at 25 lb per ton. The earlier experimental work also included the effect of adverse winds, and with a 10-mph head wind blowing, at an angle of about 45 degrees to the track, the resistances at the speeds previously quoted were increased to 17.5 lb per ton at 90 mph, 21 lb per ton at 100 mph, and to at least 30 lb per ton at 125 mph. This meant that with a 300-ton high-speed train the traction resistance of the coaches alone would be about 9,000 lb, and to haul such a resistance at 125 mph would require around 3,000 horsepower. In addition to this, all the resistance and internal friction of the power unit had to be provided for, and the decision was taken to have a total engine horsepower of 4,500, with a power car at each end of the train. In view of what I have written in Chapter 8 about the effects on the track of the London Midland electric locomotives at speeds up to 100 mph, great stress was laid upon the need to have a relatively light axle-load and a minimum of unsprung weight. In the early stages careful consideration was given to the alternative of gas turbine propulsion, as opposed to high-speed diesel engines. To provide the necessary power any variation, or development of the relatively slow-running marine type of diesel used in the great majority of British Railways' locomotives, would have been unacceptable on the grounds of weight.

At this stage it was fortunate that British Railways had some experience with the Paxman-built 'Ventura' engine. This was a quick-running machine working at 1,530 revs per minute, against 850 in the marine-type diesels, and engines of this type were superior in all matters of cost, whether in initial price, fuel or maintenance charges, to any gas turbine then available. In view of the satisfactory

The prototype HST, No 252001, showing the distinctive driving cab, on a test run passing Swindon in June 1976. The test car No 6 is marshalled next to the leading power car (Brian Morrison).

experience with the 'Ventura' engine it was decided to use the same basic design, but in a more powerful form, with 12 cylinders instead of six. A straight doubling-up however would have provided no more than 1,300 horsepower, whereas the HST needed 2,250. This substantial increase was obtained by incorporation of a new design of turbo-charger, having an increased pressure ratio, and by a new design of fuel injection system, giving high injection rates and pressures. The new type of engine which had the cylinders arranged in 'V' form, was named the 'Valenta'. Although the 'Ventura' remained the basis of the mechanical design, much had to be done to accommodate the 75 per cent increase in the power developed. In providing the additional strength the inherent qualities of the original 'Ventura' had to be borne in mind, in that relatively high power had been obtained on a light structure; and in all the strengthening processes applied to the 'Valenta' the need to keep the weight down was essential. The principal changes in design between the two engines lay in the crankcase, cylinder heads, connecting rods, pistons, bearings, strengthening of the crankshaft, cooling arrangements, and redesigned gear train.

In the redesign work everyone concerned was aware that the new and very powerful 'Valenta' engines would be subjected to an intensity of utilisation never previously expected from motive power on British Railways. The high-speed train services had to be provided with the minimum of new rolling stock, while the trains running at a standard line speed of 125 mph would have their engines running at or near maximum output for long periods. So, in addition to requiring an advanced and highly sophisticated design from the viewpoint of the power-to-weight ratio, its reliability must be beyond question. In one respect, however, the contemplated service, including very long daily

The prototype HST running trials at Swindon, showing test car No 6 attached to the leading power car (Brian Morrison).

mileages, gave opportunity for the stringent maintenance work that was so essential. The new trains were being designed for purely daytime service. There were to be no overnight runs, and therefore the whole fleet would be available at stopover points for inspection during the night hours. At some turn-round stations, no facilities for full routine maintenance were available, and it would be purely inspection—yet enough to pin-point any developing defects. Even so, the scrutiny was to be very highly organised and disciplined.

The decision to have two power cars, each of 2,250 horsepower, one at each end of the train, greatly simplified the working at terminal stations. No light-engine movements would be involved, and at Paddington, for instance, a loaded train could arrive from the west, discharge its passengers, be serviced, its buffet car re-victualled, take on a fresh complement of passengers, and be away again in little more than half an hour. Sometimes, if the arriving service was late, the turn-round time could be considerably less. The disadvantage of course was that the trains were irrevocably of fixed formation. It would be impracticable to add extra vehicles to meet the needs of heavier traffic than usual, and there would be the undesirable situation of some passengers having to stand for part or all of their journeys. But, with the introduction of a greater service frequency, at regular intervals through the day, it was felt that this difficulty would be minimal. The provision of a partially streamlined power unit at each end of a high speed train was interesting as it recalled the use of a beaver-tail streamlined observation car on the steam-hauled 'Coronation' express of the LNER from 1937, in eliminating the tail-end eddies in rear of a train of conventional

stock. The power-car at the rear of new high-speed trains had the same beneficial effect.

While naturally a wealth of attention was given to development of the power units of the new trains, the riding qualities of the coaching stock were of equal, if not greater importance. Among travellers on the Western Region in particular the execrable riding of the 'Blue Pullman' trains was still fresh in memory, and any further departure from conventional coaching stock would inevitably be looked upon with the gravest suspicion! But in its likely effects on the track, and the likelihood that any irregular or rough riding at 125 mph could be transmitted back to the train, the riding of the power cars was, of course, of paramount importance. The type of bogie suspension chosen was based on experience with high-speed bogies previously and successfully developed for use with electric locomotives. This development arose out of the need to cure the rodeo-like riding of the Class '86' locomotives on the West Coast main line, and which resulted, as described in Chapter 12 of this book, in a different form of suspension for the class '87' and '86/2' locomotives. In the proposed design for the bogies of the new High Speed Train there would not have been enough room to adopt the Class '87' design suspension in its entirety. This consisted of coil-spring primary and secondary units, with the wheelsets located by four resilient links of the Alsthom type, incorporating lateral restraint rubbers. An initial, although instantly

The prototype HST in revenue earning service in April 1976 working the 15.15 train from Bristol to Paddington (Brian Morrison).

rejected solution, was to make the Alsthom links narrower; but recalling how disastrous such easily made compromises, in analogous cases, had proved in the past, it was decided to refer the problem to computer analysis in the Research Department of British Railways.

A study was made by analog computer of bogie critical speeds, feeding into the computer all the proposed design features of the bogie. It transpired that in the worst conditions that would be acceptable for wheel tyre wear, and so on, the critical speed was no more than 90 mph. This, of course, would have been useless on the schedules planned for the HST and, still on a purely theoretical basis, dampers were introduced to check and limit the yawing action. This had the desired effect, but the theoretical analysis of the design was not finished. Studies were made on a different computer of the vehicle reaction to slight irregularities in the track, both vertically and laterally, with measurement of the related actions of the power car, such as body pitching, bogie pitching, body bounce, and body sway. Such is the capability of modern computer science that the numerous effects could be laid bare before a single piece of actual manufacturing had begun. One looks back a little wistfully to episodes in the history of railway mechanical engineering and ponders upon how the course of development might have been changed had such aids to design analysis been available. It was not, indeed, necessary to go back as far as the steam age: in

Chapter 4 of this book the hair-raising saga of diesel-hydraulic traction in the Western Region is recalled!

Even with all the careful preliminary analysis at Derby, the prototype HST, completed in 1972, was not absolutely right at the outset; nor, indeed, could one expect so revolutionary a development to be. On its first outing, speed was worked up to 125 mph and the riding was completely stable; but, when repeat runs were tried, severe hunting of the bogies developed at only a little over 110 mph. To put the quality of the ride into a quantitative form the technical term 'ride index', and its numbers must be explained. The following indicates the physical effects of the different ride-index numbers:

Ride index	Effect
1	very good
1.5	almost very good
2	good
2.5	almost good
3	satisfactory
3.5	just satisfactory
4	tolerable
4.5	not tolerable
5	dangerous

When first put on trial the prototype HST had a lateral ride index of 3.4 at 125 mph; but when the severe hunting started, at 112 mph it went up to the range 4.2 to 4.8. Even in the most stable conditions, at 125 mph it was no less than 3.2. This was clearly not good enough and on close analysis it was observed that the predominant mode of oscillation was swaying. Being mounted on resilient pads, even in stable running conditions the traction motor tended to roll about its centre of gravity; but, when bogie hunting began, some of the oscillating frequencies synchronised and made things much worse. The meticulous records being kept of the test running enabled the points on the track where rough riding began to be pin-pointed, and they were found to be, without exception, where the rails had recently been transposed. It is standard permanent way practice, when the rail heads have been slightly worn to a coned profile, to change the rails over from the left-hand to the right-hand position. The actual change in railhead profile at such a transposition is very slight indeed, and had always been accepted by rolling stock engineers; but at HST speeds it was enough to initiate some unacceptably rough riding.

The first steps taken on the prototype train to improve riding and stability were to increase the damper rates on the lateral, and yaw dampers—in other words increasing the strength of the springs. Then, to prevent the rolling and swaying tendencies of the traction motors, the mounting on the bogie cross members were made solid, instead of resting on resilient pads. This cured the hunting action of the bogies, and test runs up to a maximum speed of 142 mph were made without any sign of the previous trouble. But, while the hunting was cured, the lateral body oscillation increased, bringing the lateral ride index up to 4.0 at 142 mph. Bogie pitching was still pronounced, and an attempt to cure this by uprating the primary damper had the opposite effect. So the process of experimenting and observation, a combination of theory with practical trials, went on until eventually the prototype train had covered a quarter of a million miles! This trial running took place in both the Eastern and Western Regions. It was a continuous sequence of careful and painstaking mechanical engineering per-

sistence, which was not concluded until the ride index in both lateral and vertical planes had been reduced to 3.0, at the maximum speed at which the train could be run. It is important to appreciate that this was on the power cars, and not on the passenger-carrying vehicles. But, having established satisfactory riding conditions, which were maintained even when the train had run 248,000 miles, there was still the effect of the train on the track to be examined.

When writing of the riding troubles experienced with the Class '86' electrics, reference was made to the effect of unsprung weight, resulting from mounting the traction motors on the axles. The HSTs were to be used on non-electrified routes, and at that time the 'Deltics' represented the most severe effects on the track that were acceptable by the Chief Civil Engineer. These had been the subject of an intensive study, from which it had been determined that the peak effects took place first at less than half a millisecond after passing over a rail joint, and were taken up by rail and sleeper inertia, and second, a few milliseconds later, when they were transmitted to the ballast. Although the maximum unsprung weight per axle in the HST power cars, 2.17 tons, is much less than that of a 'Deltic', which was 3.6 tons, and the total weight of the former is only 67 tons, the much higher speed of the HST resulted in the first peak force as calculated being nearly 20 per cent higher. The second peak was roughly the same. Track measurements at Dinwoodie, Scottish Region, and at Didcot gave fairly close confirmation of the calculated values,

The prototype HST on trials in the Eastern Region, at speed near Hatfield (British Railways).

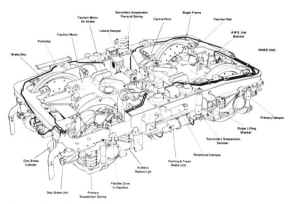

Above *Drawing of HST power bogie* (British Railways).

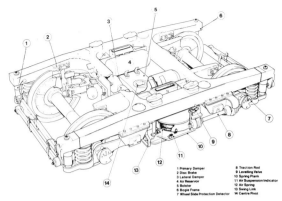

Above *Drawing of HST coach bogie* (British Railways).

and it was speed, rather than unsprung weight, which was causing the higher loading. A study was made of the possible advantages of using a resilient wheel, a proprietary design of which gave promise of a considerable reduction of the initial peak force. But sustained investigation, which had characterised all the research work on the prototype HST, revealed disadvantages, and even dangerous facets in the event of a mishap, so that the use of a resilient wheel could no longer be considered.

The power-car bogie as finalised was a beautiful piece of modern engineering. That it appears complicated, if you look at the accompanying perspective drawing, is perhaps inevitable in view of the many refinements built into it to ensure the most perfect riding. One of the most noticeable features, clearly seen from outside, is that the axleboxes are not contained in fixed horn guides on the frame, but are carried in what is termed a radius link. This is connected to the frame by the primary suspension springs, and the primary dampers are also prominent outside. The bogie frame itself is an outstanding piece of mechanical design. It is entirely of welded steel construction, in which modern computer-aided techniques were used to ensure that the distribution of the metal in the longitudinals and cross-sections was such as to provide the exact strength necessary to resist the stresses set up in high-speed running. It was equally necessary to withstand the loads set up by sudden slight irregularities in the track, and in braking. A prototype frame was then made up and subjected to laboratory testing, with loadings to simulate the conditions experienced in high-speed running. Certain final modifications were made as a result of the prototype testing, before the design was passed for production-line manufacture.

In a book concerned with locomotives, it is naturally the power car that receives the principal attention; though in a train like the HST the close-coupling and fixed formation of power and trailer cars into an integrated set train naturally involves the riding qualities of all the vehicles. In the absence of a good ride by the train as a whole the high speed would not be commercially viable. The bogies of the passenger vehicles are similar to those of the BR Mark III design but adapted to carry the longer vehicles of the HST. The primary suspension is by a trailing arm, pivoted at the end nearest to the centre of the bogie, and having one coil spring per wheel, at the outer end. Lateral control of the wheel sets is by means of rubber-bushed links between the trailing arms and the bogie frame, and the axlebox itself is designed to provide the anchorage points for the vertical, lateral and longitudinal springs. This design ensures accurate alignment of the wheel sets through the principle of a swinging arm. Whereas the secondary suspension of the power car bogies is through four helical springs, two on each side of the frame, the passenger cars have a secondary suspension consisting of an air cushion, at the midpoint on each side of the frame. There are levelling valves to maintain constant height of the car body, while to control body roll there are long pendulum links, with a torsion bar. The bogie pivots on a central pin, which has rubber-bushed guides which transmit traction and braking forces to the bolster. This in turn is connected to the bogie frame by the traction rods. The weight of the car is carried on the bolster by two side bearers of low-friction metal, and these in turn control rotation of the bogie. The overall result was a superb-riding vehicle, the performance of which has in no way deteriorated with age.

Reverting to the power cars, the changes in design from the prototype set were largely confined to the layout of the driving cab. The original arrangement was to seat the driver, who was

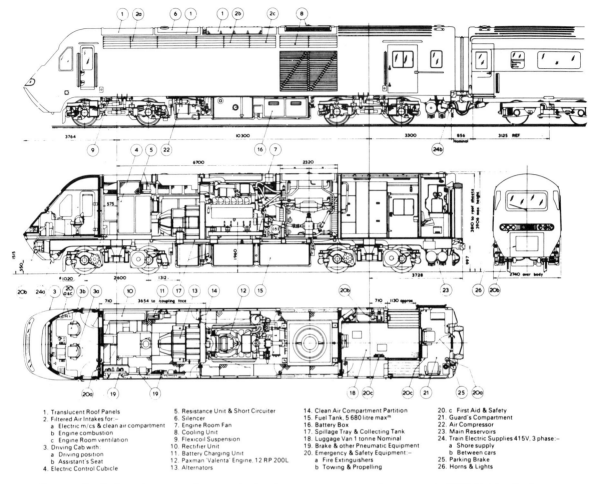

1. Translucent Roof Panels
2. Filtered Air Intakes for:-
   a Electric m/cs & clean air compartment
   b Engine combustion
   c Engine Room ventilation
3. Driving Cab with:
   a Driving position
   b Assistant's Seat
4. Electric Control Cubicle
5. Resistance Unit & Short Circuiter
6. Silencer
7. Engine Room Fan
8. Cooling Unit
9. Flexicoil Suspension
10. Rectifier Unit
11. Battery Charging Unit
12. Paxman 'Valenta' Engine. 12 RP 200L
13. Alternators
14. Clean Air Compartment Partition
15. Fuel Tank, 5 680 litre max^m
16. Battery Box
17. Spillage Tray & Collecting Tank
18. Luggage Van 1 tonne Nominal
19. Brake & other Pneumatic Equipment
20. Emergency & Safety Equipment:-
    a Fire Extinguishers
    b Towing & Propelling
20. c First Aid & Safety
21. Guard's Compartment
22. Air Compressor
23. Main Reservoirs
24. Train Electric Supplies 415V, 3 phase:-
    a Shore supply
    b Between cars
25. Parking Brake
26. Horns & Lights

BR Class '253' power car for HST (British Railways).

actually manipulating the controls, exactly in the middle, with his co-driver on a seat jutting out from the rear bulkhead, and very much to the rear. ASLEF did not like this, and asked for the driver to be positioned a little left of centre and his co-driver abreast of him on the right. They also asked for side windows. The air-conditioning equipment and the horn were accommodated in a more pronounced and out-jutting nose in the production model, as shown in the accompanying drawings. Except for the driving cab, which is a separate unit, the superstructure and underframe form a completely integrated welded unit. It was, of course, necessary to provide for maximum strength with minimum weight and the stressed-skin technique was used, aided at the design stage by computer stress analysis. Constant regard had to be paid in the design to the need for free access to all components requiring inspection or removal in maintenance. Time for such work during the night hours was

going to be limited, and no risk of work being skimped because of difficulty of access or observation could be countenanced.

The separate unit of the cab consisted of plastic materials, which was the simplest way of forming the streamlined nose. This was essential for high speed, but, in view of the relatively small numbers required, as compared with mass-production quantities in the automobile industry, the techniques for production of the air-smoothed shapes of modern car bodies in lightweight sheet steel could not be applied. Instead the body thickness of the cab (2 in) is made up of a sandwich. The outer and inner skins are of glass-reinforced polyester, between which there is a foam core of polyurethane. This form of construction gives a high degree of strength in relation to weight; but an important

Above *Cab of the production HST showing (centre) the seat for the driver and (right) that for the co-driver* (British Railways).

Above right *Building the reinforced plastic cabs for the HSTs at Crewe Works* (British Railways).

consideration was its strong resistance against impact from stones, or missiles. It is a regrettable fact of modern life that public servants and their equipment have to be protected as far as possible from vandalism, and tests made on the material chosen for the HST cabs showed that the sandwich construction was notably successful in resisting high-speed impact from sharp objects travelling very fast. It was found that a dangerous missile might penetrate the outer skin, but would have its effect absorbed by the polyurethane sandwich between the inner and outer skins.

It was indicative of the care being taken in the

development of the prototype HST that, although it was completed in 1972, it was not until a year later that a party of distinguished visitors and the press were invited to a demonstration run, from Kings Cross to Darlington, and back, on August 2 1973. Two months earlier, by way of a culmination to the long period of prototype testing, the train broke the world record for diesel traction by attaining 142 mph in the course of a run from Darlington to York. I was privileged to travel on the invitation run on August 2, when I clocked a momentary maximum speed of 138 mph in the same locality. Between Kings Cross and York, to fit in with other traffic, the special train ran to the normal maximum of 100 mph to which the 'Deltic'—hauled trains were limited; but after a brief stop at York, to pick up more guests, we made a fast run to Darlington. One feature of the equipment that British Railways were anxious to demonstrate was the brake power of the new train, because this represented one of the most

vital operating features of the HST. With disc-type brakes, instead of the conventional brake shoes, acting on the wheel treads it was possible to stop from 125 mph in the same distance that locomotive-hauled trains composed of standard stock took to stop from 100 mph. Because of this no modification to the signalling on high-speed stretches was necessary.

On the northbound demonstration trip, after a slow start over the curves to York Yard North signal box, speed picked up very rapidly. At the fifth milepost we were just topping the '100', while between posts 11 and 26 the average speed was 128 mph. The travelling at this very high speed was so smooth and quiet that one lost almost entirely the sensation of ultra-quick travel. Then, by careful pre-arrangement, and an impressive 'count down' on the public address system of the train, an emergency stop was made from a speed of 128½ mph. The train was brought to rest in 1 mile 260 yards, in 58 seconds from the moment of application. It was a remarkable demonstration. In the train there was absolutely no sensation that a heavy brake application was in progress. There was no disturbance of crockery or glassware, and not the faintest suspicion of a jerk. It was most reassuring to observe that a train travelling at such a speed could be stopped in so short a distance. The four-aspect colourlight signals on this fast-running section are spaced at about 1,300-yard intervals, so that quite apart from any pre-sighting of the signal there would be 2,600 yards, 1 mile 840 yards, from the

'double-yellow' to the signal at which a dead stop would be required. Consequently, even in the almost unthinkable case of the brakes not being applied until the train was actually passing the 'double-yellow', there would still be a margin of 600 yards before the 'red'. As a result of this quick stop we ran the 27.15 miles from York in 16 minutes 23 seconds, an extraordinary average speed of 98.5 mph start-to-stop over this quite short distance.

We went on to Darlington very rapidly, and then started on the return run to York. The immediate start had to be quite slow, as the northbound run had terminated in the down main line platform at Bank Top station, from which the track southwards is very curving. But once past Eryholme, 5.2 miles out, we were really 'going', and between Northallerton and Thirsk we reached the highest speed I have personally clocked on British Railways, one half-mile in exactly 13 seconds—138.4 mph. Six miles between Mileposts 27 and 21 were covered in 2 minutes 41 seconds which is 133.8 mph. There was a slight check down to 123 mph near Pilmoor, but speed was increased again to 131½ mph before the slowing down for York began. The 44.1 miles from Darlington to York took 27 minutes 37 seconds—96 mph. It was an impressive and enjoyable experience and those who travelled on the train that day no doubt looked forward to hearing about an early start being made on the production trains. Actually there were many delays not all of them due to engineering problems.

The drivers' requests for changes in the cab lay-

Above left *Commissioning trials between Darlington and York, prior to going to the Western Region—an HST at maximum speed near Thirsk (British Railways).*

Above *One of the production HSTs before going into regular service, on trial and standing in York station, while the 'Deltic' hauled 'Flying Scotsman', comes slowly through from the south (Brian Morrison).*

Below *Revenue-earning service on the East Coast route: 'The Talisman' leaves Kings Cross (Brian Morrison).*

out brought some headaches. It might have seemed a simple matter to move the driver over to a position just left of centre, and to put his co-driver alongside him on the right; but to give him the necessary look-out from his new position meant enlarging the width of the front window, and this, together with the request for side windows would have so increased the window area that on sunny days the cab would become insufferably hot. At such speeds there could be no question of having windows to open, and so the cabs had to be air-conditioned. Space for the necessary apparatus was found by an alteration to the shape of the nose. Then there was the question of noise. The prototype HST was definitely better than existing diesel-electric locomotives on British Railways up to about 100 mph; but at higher speeds the HST became progressively worse. In this respect it was considered essential to conform to the rules of the International Union of Railways that govern the layout of driving cabs, and which lay down a maximum sound level. When British Railways' engineers were explaining to me that this was not now an amenity for the well-being of the crew, but a definite requirement, I could not help thinking back, not so many years either, to some of the steam locomotives introduced since the end of the Second World War, and to the frightful racket one had to endure when riding in their cabs!

To meet the UIC criteria of sound level in the cab the design was modified in four ways:
a) an improved form of resilient mounting between

the cab itself and the steel frame of the car;
b) a redesign of the floor structure, including a number of layers of acoustically absorbent material as shown in the accompanying cross-sectional drawings depicting 'before and after';
c) an acoustically absorbent trim was added to the inner skin of the cab structure above windscreen level;
d) greater precision was applied to the manufacture of the gears, in an attempt to reduce noise at source. These measures were between them successful and made the production HST cabs extremely quiet and comfortable.

The first production-line HSTs entered revenue-earning service in the Western Region in August 1976. Commissioning trials in the north-east had begun in March, the power cars having been built at Crewe, and the passenger cars at Derby. An interim high-speed service was introduced in October of that year pending delivery of the full allocated compliment of trains; but, even so, from that time there were 11 trains daily scheduled to make start-to-stop average speeds between 90 and 96 mph and another 13 at between 85 and 90 mph. This was only beginning; but the enginemen entered into the spirit of the new timetable with such zest that the running was exhilarating to record. I witnessed a great deal of it at first hand.

HST power car cab: on left the prototype, on right the production cab with air conditioning equipment in the nose (British Railways).

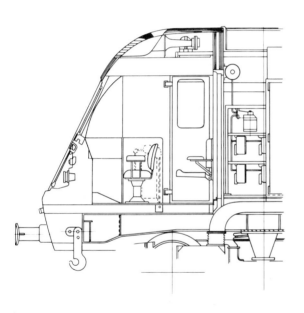
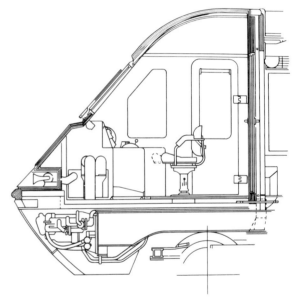

15. HST: The widespread influence

The introduction of the first High Speed Trains into regular service on the Western Region was accompanied by a euphoria of enthusiasm from all those who took a detailed interest in the running of British passenger trains. In the 22 years of my authorship of the 'Locomotive Practice and Performance' feature in *The Railway Magazine* I never remember being the recipient of such a volume of correspondence or of so many detailed logs of individual runs. It was not surprising; because, although Western Region had not then received its full allocation of HSTs, and by no means all sections of the routes they ran which had been earmarked for 125 mph running had been upgraded to that standard, trackwise, the performance of the trains was indeed spectacular—and what was more gratifying it became consistently so. In the course of my ordinary business travelling I made a large number of journeys as a passenger on the Western Region HSTs, in addition to others on which I was privileged to ride in the driver's cab; and apart from the technicalities of performance the overriding impression, always, was of the extreme smoothness of the coach riding. But it is with the attributes of the power cars as 'locomotives' that we are primarily concerned in this book, and the effect their introduction has had in the improvement of train services. In certain areas, surprisingly perhaps where the full 125 mph can *not* be run, the effects are proving most striking.

First of all, however, there is the Western Region on the two routes where they were first introduced:

The first high speed train service at 125 mph—an express for Bristol leaving Paddington (British Railways).

Paddington to Bristol, and Paddington to Swansea. Here full capacity of the HSTs for sustained high-speed running, powerful climbing of moderate gradients and rapid acceleration, was fully displayed from the outset. So far as maximum speed was concerned, in the early days it was evident that 125 mph was by no means the 'ceiling' in ordinary service. In the previous chapter I have told of the exploits of the prototype train on the magnificent racing stretch of the Eastern Region between Darlington and York; and one of my friends in the locomotive department of British Railways sent me details of runs made on the same section of line during the commissioning trials of the production trains destined for the Western Region, on which maximum speeds frequently topped the 130 mph mark. However, in the autumn of 1977 I clocked a run from Chippenham to Paddington at a time when a number of temporary speed restrictions were in operation, but the driver, anxious to keep time despite these, ran hard intermediately, and from Milepost 69 to Milepost 44¾ the time was no more than 10 minutes 57 seconds, an average speed of 133 mph. The maximum was 136 mph and this very fast running was renewed after Reading, with an average once again of 133 mph between mileposts 21 and 11. Despite the checks the 94 miles from Chippenham to Paddington took only 57½ minutes.

I may add that the riding in the train at higher than normal maximum speed was as good as ever, though the engineers felt that it was necessary to restrain the exuberance of some drivers, and a governing device was fitted to the controls to limit the maximum speed to around 127–8 mph.

So far as gradient-climbing at high speed was

Above *A picturesque rear-end view of the 11.15 HST Paddington to Bristol (Temple Meads) approaching the City of Bath* (Brian Morrison).

Above left *A striking view of an HST eastbound from Swansea, with the exit from the east portal of the Severn Tunnel in the background* (Brian Morrison).

Left *An Eastbound HST at maximum speed of 125 mph east of Twyford* (British Railways).

Bottom left *An eastbound HST in the beautiful wooded cutting west of Pangbourne, where the speed is also 125 mph* (British Railways).

concerned, I have a record of one of the South Wales expresses, then booked to run non-stop over the 111.8 miles from Paddington to Bristol Parkway, observing the 75 mph restriction over the diverging junction at Wootton Bassett, attaining 120 mph on the descending gradient to Little Somerford and accelerating on the lengthy continuous rise at 1 in 300 to no less than 128 mph. I noted from the driver's cab on other occasions that considerably less than full power was necessary to maintain the full 125 mph once atained on level track. The margin of power in reserve at these high speeds was notably displayed in this fine uphill acceleration to 128 mph on 1 in 300. So far as normal running was concerned, a journey by the 17.03 departure from Paddington was typical. Apart from the regulation slowing to 80 mph through Reading, there were no checks until nearing Shrivenham, and before that we had passed Milepost 69 in 40¼ minutes from Paddington; the average speed from the start was thus 102.7 mph.

On all the Western Region service runs, for one cause or another, the actual starts from rest had to be made relatively slowly, even on one westbound from Reading; but what the HST sets could do when driven at full power from the start was shown on some of the commissioning trials between York and Darlington. On these the start was made from

Milepost 2, beyond the curving immediate start out of York; and on these runs the trains consistently reached 99 to 102 mph by Beningbrough, 3½ miles from the start. The running afterwards was very consistent on three separate occasions, with three different train sets, and the times on passing a point at Northallerton, given as 27.99 miles from the start were, successively, 15 minutes 20, 27 and 13 seconds—no more than 14 seconds between the fastest and the slowest. The fastest run gave the following times:

Distance (miles)		Time		Speeds
		m	s	(mph)
0.0	Milepost 2	0	00	—
3.54	Beningbrough	3	18	99
9.18	Alne	6	18	125
14.07	Pilmoor	8	38	126
20.24	Thirsk	11	30	128
27.99	Northallerton	15	13	124
37.2	Cowton (stop)	20	02	—

The flying average over 24 miles was 126.1 mph, and that from start to stop 110.8 mph.

The performance of these trains in the public eye was consummated by three runs of which details were widely publicised. The first two were made on May 7 1977 when the Inter-City 125 'Jubilee Special' was the first British train ever, carrying fare-paying passengers, to be publicly scheduled to make a start-to-stop average speed of more than 100 mph, in this case over the 117.6 miles between Bristol Temple Meads and Paddington, via Badminton, with times of 70½ minutes going up, and 70 minutes down. The actual times made were 68 minutes 23 seconds and 67 minutes 35 seconds: respective average speeds of 103.3 and 104.4 mph. Then, in April 1979, the Western Region went considerably better, and on a carefully pre-arranged run with the 9.20 from Paddington they made a start-to-stop run, which was a world record with any

form of traction, by covering the 94.0 miles to Chippenham in 50 minutes 31 seconds, an average of 111.6 mph. The important feature of this run was its very close adherence to the official speed limit of 125 mph. This, of course, was after the speed governors had been fitted; but I could not help calculating how much further time might have been saved had we run at the average speed of 133 mph so easily sustained by these trains in their early history, instead of 125 mph, on the uninterrupted sections—namely Southall to Milepost 35, Goring to Shrivenham, and Mileposts 80 to 91. I estimate that a further 1½ minutes could have been saved on the overall time, to give a start-to-stop average speed of 114.8 mph.

The next introduction of the HSTs came in May 1978, on the East Coast main line between Kings Cross and Edinburgh, but the inaugural run of 'The Flying Scotsman' was not particularly felicitous. It was an open secret that this beginning was not as soon as the Regional management wished; but there were delays in completing some of the engineering work necessary on the track, and the operating department feared that running delays would lead to unpunctuality and give the new trains a bad image at the outset. But such procrastination

HSTs on the East Coast route: the 13.00 Kings Cross to Edinburgh, climbing Holloway bank, just out of Copenhagen Tunnel (Brian Morrison).

was ultimately over-ridden, though not without effects on timekeeping. I was a guest of British Railways on the inaugural run of 'The Flying Scotsman' on May 8 1978, and we experienced no fewer than *thirteen* temporary speed restrictions for permanent way work, and twice we were stopped dead for signals. Our total time for the 392.7 miles from Kings Cross to Edinburgh was 310¼ minutes, instead of the 292 minutes scheduled, inclusive of a two minute station stop at Newcastle. This, of course, was no fault of the train itself, or of its equipment, and on the return run to London, by which a number of the guests travelled, the same HST set had the excellent analysis tabulated below, on the five successive start-to-stop runs.

The scheduled average running speed of 77.5 mph was improved to an actual of 80 mph and the net average was 83.6 mph.

At the time of the introduction of the HST service on the East Coast main line a relatively small proportion of the route had been upgraded to allow 125

Section	Distance (miles)	Schedule time (min)	Actual m s	Net time (min)	Net av speed (mph)
Edinburgh–Newcastle	124.4	104	95 18	93	80.3
Newcastle–Darlington	36.0	31½	30 45	30¾	70.2
Darlington–Peterborough	155.9	112	111 38	104	90.1
Peterborough–Stevenage	48.8	34	33 45	31	94.6
Stevenage–Kings Cross	27.6	22½	24 45	22¾	72.7

Above *Climbing on the northern part of the line: the 10.15 out of Edinburgh passing Cockburnspath and embarked upon the bank to Grantshouse* (D. Haviland).

Below *At the north end of Copenhagen Tunnel: the 09.30 (Sundays) from Kings Cross to Edinburgh is on the slow line, as will be seen by comparing with the picture on page 208* (Brian Morrison).

mph running, but another difficulty was that the inclusion of an additional trailer car in the passenger formation put a tax on the available motive power. While on the Western Region, before the adding of speed controlling devices, drivers were able to streak away to maximum speeds in the region of 135 mph with their seven-coach trains, on the East Coast route, with 'eight', it was often difficult to attain the maximum of 125 mph on level track. Nevertheless, the scheduling of trains booked to make an overall average speed of 80.7 mph between Kings Cross and Edinburgh was a measure of HST capacity on this route. At the same time one cannot help feeling that the basic philosophy behind the introduction of these trains, particularly on

routes liable to heavy peak loading such as the East Coast main, and (later to be discussed) the West of England line of Western Region, has been a little unimaginative. The idea of having fixed-formation trains, permanently coupled to their power units was excellent from the viewpoint of minimising empty stock movements in stations, and similarly lessening track occupation; but at times of peak traffic they could be a sad frustration to passengers. Any approbation of the technical merits of a super-high-speed train is apt to disappear if the coaches are overcrowded and one has to stand all the way; or when all that can be run in the way of a relief train is made up of conventional coaching stock hauled by a diesel-electric locomotive with a maximum speed of 95 mph.

In March 1979 the tragic rock-fall in Penman-shiel Tunnel, north of Grantshouse, and the necessity of constructing a deviation line, postponed the plans to introduce the full HST service between Kings Cross, Edinburgh and Aberdeen, pro-grammed for May 14 of that year, and led to the diversion of some of the through Anglo-Scottish expresses from Newcastle across country to Carlisle, and thence to Edinburgh by the former Caledonian route. While this long detour considerably lengthened the overall time between London and Edinburgh it was interesting in providing examples of performance over routes for which the HSTs had not originally been intended. The cross-country run of 60 miles from Newcastle to Carlisle was scheduled in 74 minutes. In the far-off days of the North Eastern Railway this used to be a fairly fast route for the nightly North of Ireland boat train

from Newcastle to Stranraer; but now, as far as really fast running is concerned, the permanent speed restrictions are crippling. For the first 27 miles to Haydon Bridge, 55 mph is the overall maximum; then it is 60 for the next 20 miles, to near Low Row, and the summit of the line, and finally 50 mph throughout the long concluding descent into Carlisle. That an average speed of nearly 50 mph could be scheduled was dependent on the capacity of the HSTs to accelerate very rapidly from the many locations where much lower speeds than the foregoing line maxima are enforced. It was an intriguing experience to ride in the cab and see trains designed for 125 mph so skilfully handled as to maintain booked time over this difficult route.

The Caledonian line northwards from Carlisle was equally interesting. Here the HSTs were run-ning over a route where 25 kv ac electrics were making such spectacular time, and climbing the once-deadly Beattock bank at speeds of 85 to 90 mph. When I rode HST over this route, again in the cab, one had to allow for our driver not being a regular runner, but one who had learnt the road at the time of the Penmanshiel emergency. He was naturally not prepared to run quite so hard as some of the 'natives', who had been working over it all their lives. Although our man did well to pass Beattock Summit, 49.7 miles from Carlisle and at

The 10.00 Kings Cross to Edinburgh HST in September 1979 on the new diverted line beside Penmanshiel Tunnel. The overbridge across the original may be seen just above the leading power car (D. Haviland).

Top *Beside the Firth of Forth: the 12.15 HST Edinburgh to Kings Cross, approaching Cockburnspath in September 1979* (D. Haviland).

Above *A southbound HST, Edinburgh to Kings Cross rounding the diversion built to circumvent the ill-fated Penmanshiel Tunnel in September 1979* (D. Haviland).

an altitude of 1,015 feet above sea level, in 38½ minutes from the start, despite a permanent way slowing that cost about three minutes in running, not many weeks later one of the '86/2' ac electric locomotives took a train of ten coaches of ordinary stock over the summit in 33 minutes from Carlisle. This superiority was achieved mainly by running up to the full line maximum of 100 mph or a little more on all the level and favourable lengths, whereas the driver of the HST was running mostly at 90 to 95 mph.

There was however little in it in the climb of the Beattock bank itself with its ten miles nearly all

rising at 1 in 75. This was a task unlike anything previously set to the HSTs, and, with the power cars working at maximum, I took very full details of the climb. We passed Beattock station at 91 mph and over the last five miles the average speeds, mile by mile, were 88, 85.7, 83.8, 82.3 and 82 mph with a total time, over ten miles of ascent, of 6 minutes 56 seconds—86.5 mph overall. The electric '86/2' locomotive took 6 minutes 36 seconds. The power units of the HST, working at their maximum, were according to careful calculation developing about 3,400 horsepower at 82 to 83 mph, which was what would be expected in relation to a diesel-engine horsepower of 4,500. The theoretical horsepower at 100 mph is quoted as 3,265. This climb of the Beattock bank was an impressive experience for me personally, and added notably to my build-up of data concerning the performance of the HSTs in general.

When it comes to the difficult East Coast main

Year	Traction	Number of trains	Average overall time (min)	Overall average speed (mph)
1938	steam	4	205	38.2
1973	diesel	6	172	45.5
1983	HST	4	142	55.2

line from Edinburgh to Aberdeen, over the Forth and Tay bridges, and the numerous permanent speed restrictions for curves and difficult junction layouts, it is, perhaps, not entirely fair to compare average train times since the introduction of the HSTs with what had gone before. In the zenith of steam days, which could be represented by the services of 1938–9, the relatively few express trains were very heavily loaded, up to the limit of North British 'Atlantics', Gresley 'Pacifics' and the impressive 'P2' 2-8-2s of the 'Cock o' the North' Class. Neither of the two last-named classes was permitted to be double-headed in cases of exceptional loading, and recourse had then to be made to 'Atlantics' assisted by 4-4-0s. Prior to the introduction of the HSTs, with diesel-electric haulage and generally lighter loads than in steam days, the times of one or two trains were faster, but three hours was still the generally accepted norm over the 130.5 miles from Edinburgh to Aberdeen. The above table shows the comparative times.

The introduction of the HSTs made possible unprecedented journey times between Kings Cross and Aberdeen. Even with 'Deltics' in service south of Edinburgh, the overall time for the 523.2 miles had not been brought below the epoch-marking 520 minutes set up on the last night when the East Coast companies were racing in 1895. The fastest diesel time was 9 hours, 13 minutes—553 minutes—by the then 12 noon express from Kings Cross, appropriately named 'The Aberdonian'. But with the HST sets, two trains—the 10.00 and 15.00 departures from London—were booked to cover the 523.2 miles in 7 hours 18 minutes (438 minutes) at an overall average speed of 71.7 mph. North of Edinburgh, and particularly on the heavy gradients between Arbroath and Aberdeen, it was the ability of the HSTs to accelerate rapidly and climb the steep gradients which underlined their superiority. Over the years I have made an extensive study of running conditions north of Dundee, and it is perhaps in the severe southbound starts from Stonehaven and Montrose that the HSTs showed up their overwhelming advantage. Out of Stonehaven, for example, one normally reckoned to pass the summit point, at Milepost 220¼, only rarely in less than ten minutes, 4.7 miles from the start. The speed would rise to 38 or 39 mph past Dunnottar signal box and fall away to about 35 mph at the top.

Yet on the present 10.02 out of Aberdeen, our time to Milepost 220¼ was 5 minutes 33 seconds, speed having risen to 72 mph(!) on the climb. Overall times were naturally affected through the slowing down and restarting from stops at Stonehaven, Montrose and Arbroath; but now there are several trains booked non-stop over the 71.4 miles between Dundee and Aberdeen that have to average 60 mph over this section.

While the maximum speed that can be run anywhere north of Edinburgh is about 80, and while this may seem very unexciting for an HST, the power of these trains is such that the sharply undulating gradients have been virtually ironed out. Take the case of the short stretch between Arbroath and Montrose, a distance of 13.7 miles: in steam days the time was 21 minutes start to stop, and on a very good run one could note a speed of 27 mph up the bank to Letham Grange, a dash of up to 72 mph at Inverkeilor, and a fall again to 40 mph on the cliffs above Lunan Bay, gaining about a minute on scheduled time. Now, with an HST, the first bank was climbed at 63 mph instead of 27, speed was restrained to no more than 70 mph downhill and the second bank was topped at 65 mph. To anyone who was unaware of the gradients, the HST might have been travelling over a level road, and those 13.7 miles with a saw-tooth profile were covered in just 13 minutes. It is south of Newcastle, however, that the East Coast HSTs make their most spectacular running. There are several trains that run the 188.2 miles between Kings Cross and York at an average speed of 95 mph start to stop, while 'The Flying Scotsman' runs the entire 268.3 miles from London to its first stop at Newcastle at an average of 92 mph.

When further HST sets were available, and they were put on to the West of England services of the Western Region, the entire route between Reading and Exeter was still limited to a maximum speed of 90 mph. While some improvements have subsequently been effected, the non-stop time for the 'Cornish Riviera Express' with seven coaches is still 123 minutes for the 173.5 miles from Paddington to Exeter, an average of no more than 84.6 mph. One is compelled to write 'no more' in view of contemporary scheduling of the East Coast. But it is the line west of Exeter that provides the most significant evidence of the HST presence.

While the Great Western Railway set immense store on its fast running on all main routes, the opportunity for this ceased at Exeter on the West of England line, and over the 131.5 miles onwards to Penzance the 'Cornish Riviera Express' was allowed 3 hours and 37 minutes with five stops, an overall average speed of no more than 38 mph. This had some similarity to the situation in steam days

Below *Western Region: the 09.45 Paddington to Penzance just out of Whiteball Tunnel, on the Somerset-Devon county boundary. The signalling is still semaphore, and the manually operated Whiteball signal box may be glimpsed through the single arch of the Brunellian overbridge* (Brian Morrison).

Bottom *The 09.03 Penzance to Paddington HST at the picturesque Great Western style station of Bodmin Road, in July 1980. The station has now been renamed Bodmin Parkway* (Brian Morrison).

over the East Coast main line between Edinburgh and Aberdeen, thought the gradients and the speed restrictions were if anything still more severe. At that time there was an overall speed limit of 60 mph throughout Cornwall, and there were very few locations on the South Devon line where one could do much more. Today, with eight intermediate stops, the average time by six services operated with HSTs is 2 hours 56 minutes, showing an overall average speed of 44.9 mph and an improvement of nearly 20 per cent.

It is when one comes to analyse the intermediate details that the nature of HST capacity becomes apparent on a route like this. To outward appearances one might question the value of introducing trains of this nature on to a line of such severe gradients and limitation upon maximum speed. Indeed, at the time these trains were first put on, the only part of the 305 miles from Padddington

Left *Western end of the line, Penzance, with two HSTs alongside at a quiet time* (Brian Morrison).

Right *On the Midland line: the 12.55 Nottingham to St Pancras passing Ratcliffe power station* (Brian Morrison).

Below *HSTs on the Midland: St Pancras in June 1983 with the 10.30 for Sheffield (at left) and the 11.10 for Derby* (Brian Morrison).

to Penzance where the full '125' potential could be developed was between Paddington and Reading. It would however have been clumsy operationally to have use the HSTs only between London and Exeter. Their running had to be extended to the furthest end of the line, even though with the hindrances west of Exeter they could show overall average speeds of no more than 62 mph from Paddington to Penzance, compared with the spectacular averages of over 70 mph between Kings Cross and Aberdeen. But in Cornwall, the 'Cornish Riviera Express', in common with all other services worked by HST sets, has to make seven intermediate stops, with lengths of run, westward from Plymouth, of 17.8, 9.1, 7.8, 4.5, 14.5, 9.0, 11.2 and 5.6 miles. The booked running times add up to

97½ minutes for 79.5 miles, equal to a running average of 49 mph, while detailed recordings of a typical journey showed a total running time of 92½ minutes—51½ mph.

As on the Aberdeen route it was the ease with which steep gradients were mounted that proved the most impressive feature of the running. Though the Western Region HST sets contain only seven Mark III coaches weighing 240 tons, the power-cars have between them 4,500 horsepower 'under the bonnet' and it is no more than natural that they should show up to great advantage against a Class '50' diesel-electric locomotive, with 2,700 engine horsepower, when hauling a load of seven or eight ordinary coaches. It is also very interesting to see how the HSTs can tackle the formidable Hemerdon bank,

which, beginning no more than four miles out of Plymouth always constitued a severe task for steam locomotives that were only just commencing their eastward journeys, and starting 'cold'. With diesels, which were often working through from Penzance, it was better; but even so, two miles at 1 in 42 could be a back-breaker. Fortunately, however, the approach to the foot of the bank from the Plymouth is one of the few places on the South Devon line where the alignment is good enough to work up some real express speed, and charge the bank. This is very necessary because the present schedule time demands an average speed of 62½ mph over the 5.2 miles from Lipson Junction to the remote relay cabin on the site of the former Hemerdon signal box.

The comparison between what happened and some previous runs of my own was little short of sensational, even though it was little more than the new timetable required.

The pre-war times suffer through the time involved in changing engines at Bristol from LMS to Great Western haulage, which of course was obviated with the through-working of the 'Peak' class diesel-electrics after nationalisation. The diesel had a further advantage over steam on the northbound run as it did not require rear-end banking assistance up the Lickey Incline.

Prior to the introduction of the HSTs the fastest train from Bristol to Birmingham covered the 89.9 miles in 92 minutes; but with the same maximum speed limit of 90 mph and the slow running in the first 12 miles out of Bristol, as well as the even slower last six miles into Birmingham, I have clocked the run in 80 minutes with an HST, on a day when no fewer than five temporary slowings for permanent way work were enforced, successively to 20, 25, 40, 28 and 15 mph. Between them they cost about five minutes in running. So far as real speeding was concerned, we could not really get going until after Cheltenham; but after that we covered 37 miles at an average speed of 86 mph, including the ascent of the Lickey Incline. One cannot take a full-blooded dash at this because of a slight speed restriction to 75 mph before Bromsgrove; and speed had not been accelerated above 80 mph when the 1 in 37 gradient was struck. Then, in 1½ miles of the exceptional bank, speed had fallen to 63½ mph, but in the last mile only 3½ mph further was dropped and the gradient was topped at exactly 60 mph.

This run had formed part of the lengthy daily odyssey of the 09.15 express from Plymouth to Edinburgh, which covers the 547 miles in 8 hours 49 minutes, a notable average speed of 62 mph. The corresponding southbound train, leaving Edinburgh Waverley at 09.30 is, indeed, extended to Penzance, making the record daily run of an HST of 628 miles in 10 hours 29 minutes, an average of almost 60 mph throughout. In referring to these marathon HST journeys one recalls the famous through service inaugurated in the autumn of 1921 between Penzance and Aberdeen jointly by the Great Western, Great Central, North Eastern and North British Railways. Southbound, the one through carriage ran attached to well-established passenger trains from Aberdeen as far south as York, and from Swindon westwards. In between, the Great Central route was used as far as Banbury, continuing on the Great Western via Oxford, to make up a total mileage 30 miles greater from Edinburgh, for 658 miles, showed an average speed of only 36.8 mph, a striking contrast to the 59.5 mph of the 09.30 from Edinburgh today.

The latest route on which the HSTs have been introduced is that of the former Midland Railway between London (St Pancras) and Sheffield, serving the cities of Leicester and Nottingham intermediately. This took place in October 1982. While

much upgrading of the track had taken place before that date, the maximum line speed had not been advanced beyond 100 mph at any location, and it was interesting to observe what train performance would be necessary to maintain a timing of 72 minutes start-to-stop for the 99 miles between St Pancras and Leicester, or for the southbound run of 68.9 miles from Leicester to Luton in 49 minutes, average speeds of 82.5 and 85 mph. The Midland HSTs, like those on the North East-South West route are like those on the Western Region in having only seven passenger cars; and, while this makes the accommodation somewhat crowded at times, it certainly enables the long adverse gradient to be climbed at maximum line speed. South of Bedford the ruling gradient is 1 in 200 and the only difficulty drivers seemed to face was in keeping down to 100 mph. As for the sharply graded 'peak' between Bedford and Wellingborough, with gradients of 1 in 120 each side, this I saw mounted with minimum speeds of more than 90 mph.

So, what has been the nationwide effect of introducing the HSTs? They have brought some very spectacular accelerations on routes where speeds of 125 mph can be run continuously, as between Kings Cross and Newcastle, and between Paddington and Bristol. But the HSTs have also brought very substantial service improvement in many other directions. The ability to climb severe gradients, like those of the East Coast main line, and those down in the West of England, at little less than line maximum speed has led to notable accelerations of sevice. The limiting factor is, of course, the need to conform to speed restrictions on curves that are essential with conventional types of rolling stock both for comfort and safety in travelling. The introduction of the HSTs was to some extent considered to be an interim stage in the development of high-speed travel in Great Britain, before still more sophisticated projects like the Advanced Passenger Train were sufficiently proved to be put into regular public service. In the meantime, however, the HSTs have proved an outstanding success.

Above *HSTs in the industrial north: the 09.15 Plymouth to Dundee passing Brightside, north of Sheffield, in December 1983* (Brian Morrison).

Below *A remarkable photograph likening BR to the route of the French TGV—the 07.25 Penzance to Edinburgh HST topping the Lickey Incline* (Brian Morrison).

16. Preserving historic locomotives

Amid all the drive for modernisation, for higher speeds, and for the incorporation of the latest and most sophisticated technology so far as finance permits, an overall look at British Railways in the 1980s cannot ignore the intense interest displayed, the scholarship and the disciplined industry devoted to the preservation of important historical records. That a major part of such activity is concentrated upon steam locomotives is perhaps inevitable, because it can be said without much fear of contradiction that none of man's inventions has ever created such a widespread and erudite coterie of admirers, of all ages and sexes, and of all nationalities. Nowhere is this cult more extensive, or better informed than in Great Britain, the birthplace of the steam locomotive; and in a book devoted to the history of the British locomotive in the 20th century it is appropriate, and indeed essential, that more than a passing reference should be made to the remarkable activity in preservation. Nor it it confined to steam. This third volume of the history has naturally been concerned almost entirely with other forms of motive power; and now that some of the earliest and perhaps least successful have been withdrawn, enthusiast regard for them has been manifested with astonishing fervour on various occasions. So this chapter of

nostalgia, if one could aptly call it so, is not entirely concerned with steam.

It would be difficult to give any precise, logical explanation of why locomotives have always exercised such a fascination upon young and old alike. It has been suggested that it is because the steam locomotive is the nearest piece of machinery to possessing human traits, with all their foibles and attributes. They purr along, or roar, making rough music through the loud tattooing rhythm of their exhaust beats; they hiss and scream, and to those whose involvement goes further than lineside 'spotting' and photography—those who had to drive and fire them—they could be as temperamental as a pampered movie star. But how can the present enthusiasm and affection for the diesels be explained? In the earlier designs, certainly, much elegance was shown in styling, with bonnets in front of the drivers' cabs and an aspect that could be likened in spirit to some of the most celebrated private motor cars. Then, however, the Design Panel of the British Railways Board took a hand and changed all that, and many of the die-hard steam fans opined thereafter that no one could be expected to enthuse over 'a lot of tin boxes'. But many people did, and still more continued to do.

One of the most astonishing manifestations of this brand of enthusiasm came at the time when the 'Western' Class diesel-hydraulic locomotives (BR Class '52') were being withdrawn, and many farewell special trips were run. These locomotives were not the most shapely, even among the 'tin-boxes', and in

The restored Southern 4-6-0 No 850 Lord Nelson *leaving Skipton for Carnforth with the 'Cumbrian Mountain' express in September 1980* (John Titlow).

Above *Western tribute—a spectacular but not a very edifying start leaving Paddington for a 'farewell special' run on February 26 1977. The locomotive is No 1023* Western Fusilier *(Brian Morrison).*

Left *A notable North Eastern freight 0-6-0 No 2392, of Class 'P3', here seen outside the shed at Grosmont, North Yorkshire Moors Railway* (Brian Morrison).

Below *One of the Stanier three-cylinder 4-6-0s of the 'Jubilee' Class No 5690* Leander, *now owned by Leander Locomotives Ltd and based at Carnforth* (British Railways).

performance on the road they were far outclassed by the nominally equal-powered diesel-electrics of Classes '47' and '50'. But among Western Region enthusiasts they achieved an extraordinary popularity. *The Railway Magazine* highlighted the situation editorially in its issue of May 1977:

'Undoubtedly, the publicity phenomenon of recent months has been the interest shown in the Western Region's doomed Class '52' diesel-hydraulics. Many professional public relations consultants would give their eye-teeth to know the secret of the appeal of these locomotives, generating as it has enough money to purchase one for private preservation and fill to capacity rail tours headed by them on almost every weekend in the last two months of their active lives. British Railways, a bemused beneficiary of this publicity, may well have been embarrassed to have all this praise heaped on a "non-standard" product, though this very individuality seems to have been part of the appeal . . .'

The special trains carried attractively designed headboards on the locomotive front. Some of these were *Western Farewell, Western Lament, Western Memorial, Western Requiem*. Occasionally, to give patrons their full money's worth, the specials were hauled by two of the Class '52' locomotives, though I fancy some of the past stalwarts of the GWR Locomotive Department at Swindon would have turned in their graves at the sight of the *Western Tribute* leaving Paddington, on February 26 1977, double-headed, and laying such a cloud of dirty smoke as would be more than enough to get any steam-locomotive driver suspended! The most astonishing event in this long succession of farewell appearances came on Saturday November 20 1976 when locomotive No 1023, *Western Fusilier*, worked an excursion from Kings Cross to York, and back. It was the first time one of them had ever been into the former Great Northern terminus, and it was an object of much interest and some curiosity there; but I cannot imagine that any of the enthusiastic passengers, still less the engine crew, can have been prepared for the well-nigh incredible reception awaiting them when they arrived at York. More than a thousand sightseers had gathered; the platforms were six-deep for much of their length and, when the locomotive went on display in the yard of the National Railway Museum, great queues lined up to pay a brief visit to the cab. No fewer than seven of these diesel-hydraulic locomotives have been preserved, three of them privately, while the 'hero' of that famous ride to York, now in the care of the National Railway Museum, is on loan to the Dart Valley Railway and working between Paignton and Kingswear.

Principal interest in the preservation of historic locomotives is naturally devoted to steam, and to those units which have been restored to working order and are used from time to time to haul special trains. The organisation and equipment of the various steam centres has been most efficiently developed, while the actual running, throughout Great Britain, has been carefully coordinated by the Steam Locomotive Operators Association (SLOA). Within certain limits of activity British Railways have been ready enough to co-operate, fully recognising that the private organisations involved are staffed by men not only dedicated to the task but also fully competent professionally in the repair and general maintenance of steam locomotives. Such, indeed, is the confidence that has come to be placed in these private owners of preserved locomotives that British Railways themselves are now running a number of publicly advertised services, definitely earmarked for haulage by preserved steam locomotives, which have to be hired from their present owners. These special trains, which are invariably full to capacity, are patronised largely by enthusiasts, many of whom, begoggled and armed with tape-recorders and cameras spend much of the journeys hanging out of the windows.

The result of this enterprise and dedication is that examples of many famous steam locomotive classes long withdrawn from ordinary traffic may, from time to time, be seen in full action, and in many cases on beautiful scenic routes. There is, however, a distinction in the origins of these steam-hauled trains of today. There are the various privately preserved railways that operate regular advertisied services, of which the Bluebell, the Severn Valley, and the North Yorkshire Moors are notable examples, and there are the 'steam centres', in direct connection with the regular routes of British Railways, where preserved locomotives are housed, and serviced, and from which they are chartered to haul special trains on British Railways' tracks. Of these latter Carnforth Steamtown, the National Railway Museum at York, the establishment of the Great Western Society in the former Western Region running shed at Didcot, and the premises of Messrs H.P. Bulmer, the cider makers of Hereford, which is the base of some of the largest and most powerful preserved steam locomotives, must be specially noted.

While locomotive preservation in its most evoctive form its naturally represented by the working examples, invariably maintained in a condition of immaculate cleanliness rarely seen in earlier days, even on locomotives allocated to the most prestigious of express passenger trains, there is immense historic importance in the numerous static exhibits within the National Railway Museum, and

Above *One of the most famous of all preserved locomotives, the Gresley Class 'A3 Pacific' No 4472* Flying Scotsman *on the 'Cumbrian Coast' express at Ravenglass in August 1978* (Derek Cross).

Left *The first of the British standard 'BR7 Pacifics' No 70000* Britannia *now preserved on the Nene Valley Railway, Peterborough, in June 1980* (John Titlow).

Below *The celebrated Southern 4-cylinder 4-6-0 No 850* Lord Nelson *crossing Eskmeals Viaduct with the 'Cumbrian Coast' express in August 1980* (John Titlow).

Above *The preserved Caledonian 'racer' of 1888, No 123, working a special train of two preserved Caledonian coaches between Perth and Edinburgh. This engine is now in the Glasgow Museum of Transport* (W.J.V. Anderson).

Right *Two preserved Scottish locomotives, now in the Glasgow Museum of Transport, working an exhibition special from Largs to Glasgow in 1963: the Great North of Scotland 4-4-0* Gordon Highlander *leading and the* Jones Goods *4-6-0 of the Highland Railway next to the train* (W.J.V. Anderson).

Below *The ex-LMS 'Pacific' No 46229* Duchess of Hamilton, *the chassis and machinery of which went to the USA in 1939, disguised as the* Coronation, *climbing southbound from Carlisle to Aisgill with the 'Cumbrian Mountain' Pullman near Kirkby Stephen in February 1982* (David Eatwell).

the smaller establishments at Swindon, Glasgow, the Midland Railway Centre at Butterley, Derbyshire, and elsewhere. The preserved locomotives are not the easiest of machines to maintain in the kind of condition that is essential for main line running. Furthermore, at the time of their withdrawal from ordinary service, few of them were in really good condition; and while any of them selected for subsequent running with chartered specials would be subjected to the most stringent examination before taking the road, the intermittent utilisation, and the natural deterioration of any machinery take their toll. Their remaining working mileage became necessarily limited. As museum pieces, particularly after restoration of the original pre-grouping liveries, they are priceless. One thinks particularly of those three at York, representing constituents of the Southern Railway. One could hardly find finer examples of British locomotive practice engaged in heavy passenger work at the turn of the century than the Adams 4-4-0 of the London and South Western, Stroudley's immortal *Gladstone*, representing the Brighton railway, and the massive, elegantly proportioned Wainwright 4-4-0 of the South Eastern and Chatham.

Towards the end of the steam era, largely through the interest of Mr James Ness, then General Manager of Scottish Region, certain representative locomotives of pre-grouping origin were set aside for preservation, repainting in their old colours, and were completely overhauled for working special trains, mostly in Scotland. The famous Caledonian 4-2-2 'single' No 123, and the Jones Goods 4-6-0 had been preserved since the mid-1930s, but they were then joined by the North British 4-4-0 *Glen Douglas*, one of the most successful of all locomotives to work over the very severe gradients of the West

The rebuilt 'Merchant Navy' Class 4-6-2 No 35028 Clan Line, *which attained a maximum speed of 104 mph on an ordinary service run with the 'Atlantic Coast' express* (British Railways).

Highland line, and one of the very handsome 4-4-0s of the Great North of Scotland Railway. These four locomotives in their magnificent and distinctive colours powered many excursions in Scotland, working mostly in pairs, in the early 1960s. It was a pity that there was not a passenger engine of the former Glasgow and South Western Railway to complete the quintet of pre-grouping Scottish railways; but, when the brilliant foursome was finally withdrawn and accorded an honoured place in the Glasgow Museum of Transport, it was joined by a Drummond 0-6-0 tank engine, which had been beautifully restored to its original condition and livery. There these splendid examples of Scottish locomotive engineering may be studied at leisure.

Restoration work of any kind can have its pitfalls, and if one went a little further afield in Scotland, to the Falkirk Steam Centre of the Scottish Railway Preservation Society, the visitor carrying in mind the sky-blue livery of the Caledonian 4-2-4 No 123, in Glasgow, might be faced with an apparent poser. At Falkirk there is a magnificently restored 0-4-4 tank engine No 419 in dark Prussian blue; and yet if one asked which was the correct Caledonian colour, the dark, or the sky-blue, the answer could truly be 'Both!' The dark one was the true 'official' colour, but, around the turn of the century, one works where locomotives were repaired found that by mixing white with it—white being free issue!—the rich dark colour could be made to go further. The effect was so beautiful that sky-blue, although not the official colour, was generally accepted and

The Flying Scotsman, *climbing the last mile of the long ascent to Aisgill with the 'Cumbrian Mountain' express in April 1980* (David Eatwell).

recognised as 'Caley blue'. In the Glasgow Museum the Jones Goods of the Highland Railway carries the bright-yellow livery, that on the Brighton railway became known as Stroudley's 'Improved Engine Green'. It was the standard colour scheme of the Highland Railway while Stroudley was there, but David Jones eventually changed it to a delightful apple-green, still retaining all the elaborate lining out. The first of the big goods 4-6-0s, however, arrived from Sharp, Stewart's works in Glasgow, in the 'yellow' livery, and as such it now reposes in preservation.

Before nationalisation, the London and North Eastern Railway, and particularly its North Eastern Area, centred at York, was the most preservation-minded of all British railways. Its heritage, dating back to the opening of the Stockton and Darlington Railway in 1825, was much cherished by its top management, and at the time of the Railway Centenary, in 1925, there was a notably high proportion of ex-North Eastern Railway locomotives on display. Now three very celebrated NER passenger engines are in the national collection. The strikingly ornate Fletcher 2-4-0 No 910, and the 'racing' 4-4-0 No 1621 of 1895, are at York, while the neat and efficient Tennant 2-4-0 No 1463 is in the North Road Museum at Darlington. This latter engine dates from 1885. But the North Eastern Railway was primarily a mineral hauler, and it is certainly appropriate that no fewer than five examples of heavy freight locomotives should be preserved, three in full working order. Of the highly embellished 0-6-0 No 1275, at Darlington North Road, I am old enough to have photographed her as a working engine at Whitby, in 1923, before she was restored to her original condition and gorgeously painted for the pageant of 1925. I have also pleasant memories of that later generation of NER 0-6-0s, the Worsdell 'C' class, of which No 876 is in the North of England Open Air Museum, at Beamish, County Durham. Examples of three generations of mighty mineral haulers, the 'P3' 0-6-0, the 'T2' 0-8-0, and the three-cylinder 'T3', all featured in the first volume of this work, are in active service on the North Yorkshire Moors Railway, where their tractive power is invaluable in getting the loads from Grosmont up to Goathland.

While the North Yorkshire Moors was both territorially and sentimentally an activity closely linked with the North Eastern, the Severn Valley was by no means an exclusive Great Western preserve. The extent and expertise of its workshops at Bridgnorth has led to many preserved locomotives from 'foreign parts' being sent there for attention. These included the very famous London and North Western 8 foot 6 inch 2-2-2 single *Cornwall*. The Torbay section of the Dart Valley Light Railway is more nearly 100 per cent Great Western, even to the extent of having one of the 'Western' Class diesel-hydraulics; but it is 'light' only in name, because in its heyday as a Great Western branch line it carried the 'King' Class 4-6-0s, and in its preserved state welcomed the ex-LNER 'Pacific' engine *Flying Scotsman*. The Didcot Railway Centre is of course the main gathering point and display ground *par excellence* of preserved Great Western motive power, and the popularity of the GWR with steam enthusiasts is evidenced by there being no fewer than 18 examples of Swindon design attached to the depot. These include two

'Castles', three 'Halls', and one 'Manor'. The Society also acts as host to a very distinguished visitor of Southern Railway origin, the Bulleid 'Battle of Britain' Class 4-6-2 No 34051, *Winston Churchill*, with the original air-smoothed casing and chain-driven valve gear.

Among the working preserved railways, the Bluebell, the first of them, has a notable collection of vintage ex-Southern Railway types, ranging from Stroudley 'Terrier' 0-6-0 tank engines of the Brighton, to an Adams 'radial' 4-4-2 tank of the London and South Western, and the sturdy Wainwright designs of the South Eastern and Chatham. But the Bluebell management shows a very catholic taste so far as locomotive lineaments are concerned,

by including among the more modern designs one of the unspeakably ugly Bulleid 'Q1' 0-6-0s. They also have a number of working locomotives of Maunsell origin, and a highly prized Bulleid air-smoothed 'Pacific' of the 'West Country' class, the *Blackmore Vale*. Though derided by enthusiasts whose sentiments lie elsewhere, and sarcastically dubbed 'spam-cams', the fact that so many of them have been preserved in their air-smoothed condition is a sure sign of the popularity they achieved, among Southern supporters. In addition to the *Blackmore Vale*, and the *Winston Churchill* mentioned earlier in this chapter, three other 'West Country's—*Wadebridge, City of Wells*, and *Swanage*—have been preserved, and one further of

Left *The pioneer Midland three-cylinder compound 4-4-0 as restored and based at the National Railway Museum though often used on special trains* (British Railways).

Below *The preserved 'A4 Gresley Pacific' No 4498* Sir Nigel Gresley *in April 1967 leaving Kingmor yard, Carlisle, with an enthusiasts' special bound for Crewe but over the Settle and Carlisle line* (Derek Cross).

the 'Battle of Britain' series, *92 Squadron*. As if this were not enough, there are also five others of the rebuilt variety.

While the privately preserved railways, despite their limited route mileage, have generated an immense amount of interest, and have gathered to themselves almost as many historic locomotives as they have miles of route to run, the greatest appeal as far as steam locomotives are concerned undoubtedly lies in the steam-operated rail tours which are organised with the ready co-operation of British Railways, and which have enabled so many who were not old enough to see steam in full action on the main line to witness the undoubted thrill of a big locomotive, in immaculate condition, doing a fine job of heavy train haulage. To older enthusiasts also it is gratifying that examples of so many famous designs dating from the grouping era, and even earlier, have not only been preserved, but have been restored to a working condition acceptable for haulage of passenger trains on those routes of British Railways where steam locomotives are permitted. All the four groups are well represented in this category though structural clearances preclude the use of most ex-Great Western classes on other than their parent system. It must be added, however, that in pre-electrification days engines of the 'Castle' Class worked as far north as Carlisle, over both the West Coast main line, over Shap, and by the Midland route via Settle and Aisgill summit.

Right *The preserved North British 4-4-0 No 256* Glen Douglas, *formerly used on the West Highland Line working on an enthusiasts' special on the Glencorse branch* (W.J.V. Anderson).

Below *The Great Western four-cylinder 4-6-0 No 7029* Clun Castle, *passing Durran Hill Junction at the northern entry point to the Settle and Carlisle line with a special train* (Derek Cross).

The most powerful of all Great Western passenger locomotives, the *King George V* has a relatively active life, for a preserved veteran, working on Western Region routes attainable from its base at Hereford.

The death of R.A. Riddles, at an advanced age, at the end of 1983, recalled his vital association with the second of the famous locomotives based at Hereford, the LMS 'Pacific' No 6201 *Princess Elizabeth*. It is fairly safe to assert that, but for his personal work on the engine, through two successive nights, the record-breaking non-stop runs between Euston and Glasgow on November 16 and 17 1936, on which the present fame of the locomotive largely rests, would not have been possible. The preliminaries to these two epic performances involved the replacement of one of the coned joints in the main steam pipe, at Willesden shed, during the night of November 15–16, and then the remetalling of the bearing face of the left-hand outside crosshead slipper, which had run hot on the northward record run, at St Rollox Works, Glasgow, on the night of November 16–17. How, following this repair, and a second sleepless night for Riddles, the special train was taken back non-stop from Glasgow to Euston at an average speed of 70 mph, was an achievement no less epic than the repair during the night that had made the *Princess Elizabeth* engine fit for such a terrific run. It was typical of the spirit of the steam era that a man so senior as to be principal assistant to the Chief Mechanical Engineer would take off his coat, work through the night with the fitters, and ride the engine on a 400-mile non-stop run—not only once but two nights in succession! A sister engine, the *Princess Margaret Rose*, maker of one of the most brilliant runs I have ever logged personally south of Crewe, is also preserved, but leading a rather sedentary existence at the Midland Railway Centre at Butterley, Derbyshire.

It is from Carnforth, Lancashire, that many of the most popular steam-locomotive workings of today originate. The depot is certainly placed strategically at the junction of three main routes, and is on a site formerly occupied by running sheds of the former London and North Western, and Furness Railways. The relatively small shed of the Midland Railway was also not far away. But, since electrification of the West Coast main line, steam locomotives have not been permitted under the wires. Even with this embargo, however, the Furness and Midland lines are available, and they lead to some of the choicest routes in the north of England for steam-hauled special trains. Apart from those privately chartered, which are many, there have been the extremely popular workings sponsored by British Railways, but including in their circuits some lengthy sections powered by privately owned steam locomotives. These include the 'Cumbrian Coast Express', originating further south on the London Midland Region, and steam-worked from Carnforth over the Furness line to and from Sellafield. Then there is the 'Cumbrian Mountain Express', to and from Carlisle, travelling in one direction electrically hauled over the West Coast main line over Shap Summit, and in the other over the famous Settle and Carlisle line of the Midland Railway; with steam haulage with one locomotive between Carnforth and Skipton, and a second locomotive between Skipton and Carlisle. How long this choicest of steam excursion workings will continue is unhappily now in the balance, and not for the first time in its history the line, as a through route, is under threat of closure.

Even in the most prosperous days of the Midland it is doubtful whether a detailed financial analysis of the receipts from passenger and freight traffic carried would have revealed that they covered maintenance costs, a high proportion of which must have been borne by the far more profitable lines farther south; and now with far less staple traffic, and faced with the ever-increasing maintenance costs of the 100-year old viaducts and other major works, the future prospect is disturbing. In the meantime, however, it has provided the scene for some of the most enjoyable railway enthusiasts' activities imaginable. It can truly be said that in its 70-mile length there has been something for everybody. Fortunately its roadbed and major structures enable the largest and heaviest steam locomotives to be used, and whether emanating from Carnforth, or the National Railway Museum at York, these have been seen in great variety. Photographers from all over Great Britain, and even from overseas, have sought out every conceivable vantage point, often taking advantage in their pre-planning of advertised stops of the train to proceed by car from one point to another so as to photograph the same train twice in the same journey.

Equally, travelling by the trains has for some developed into a highly organised and strenuous occupation, using sound-recording equipment to register the exhaust beats of the locomotives, while fellow enthusiasts compile the most detailed logs of the running times, with individual maximum and minimum speeds recorded by stop-watch. But while all this is in progress, with participants in varying degrees of personal discomfort through continuous vigils at open windows, their less documentary-minded friends are content to sit back and enjoy the varied and magnificent panorama of mountain scenery, which begins on the cross-country line from Carnforth soon after crossing the River Lune.

Right *The preserved Great Western 4-6-0 No 6000* King Geoge V *on the first leg of the historic four-day round trip in October 1971, the first time steam had been allowed on British Railways metals since 1968. Leaving Severn Tunnel from Hereford, en route for Birmingham, via Oxford* (R.O. Coffin).

Right *The Great Western 'Manor' Class 4-6-0 No 7819* Hinton Manor *approaching Bewdley on the privately owned Severn Valley Railway* (John Hunt).

Right *The preserved 'K4' Class three-cylinder 2-6-0.* The Great Marquess, *survivor of a class of six very powerful engines built specially for the West Highland line* (British Railways).

Left *The Great Eastern 0-6-0 No 564 (LNER Class 'J 15'), as restored and working on the North Norfolk Railway in May 1978, with the author on the footplate* (Brian Fisher).

Right *This engine, now preserved at Bressingham, near Diss, is a 1945 renewal of the engine that made a tour of North American railways in 1933. It was not the original 'Royal Scot' of 1927, but one of the later batch built at Derby in 1930, No 6152. The plaque carried below the nameplate commemorates the 1933 tour, but the 'renewals' were virtually new engines* (British Railways).

Below *The remarkable scene at York on arrival of the 'Western Talisman' special, November 20, 1976, hauled by No 1023* Western Fusilier (L.P. Gates).

Passing through Melling tunnel it continues thenceforward without a break to the outskirts of Carlisle. It is nevertheless the preserved locomotives themselves that provide the most absorbing interest, and to no one more so than myself, from an acquaintance with the Settle and Carlisle line and its cross-country connection to Carnforth which goes back now for nearly 70 years.

In its normal workaday guise, and particularly after the incorporation of the Midland Railway in the great London Midland and Scottish system, the Leeds–Carlisle section was never favoured with the cream of the available motive power. Running foremen had to make do with locomotives displaced from duties elsewhere; and, although when the general modernisation of the LMS fleet in the Stanier era took place new 4-6-0s were allocated to the Midland Division, very often there were not enough of them for all the most important duties, and on accelerated train schedules there was a considerable amount of double-heading. It would have been difficult then to look forward to a time when express trains over the Settle and Carlisle line would be hauled, on occasions, by the largest, and most prestigious express passenger locomotives, not only the LMS, but of the Southern and London and North Eastern Railways also. They have indeed been halcyon days for locomotive enthusiasts, and if

now these days are numbered one can certainly be glad that they have been so comprehensively documented.

The locomotive designs concerned have all featured prominently in the earlier volumes of this work, but in view of the attention and affection they have aroused in their preserved state a few notes on the individual units involved will be appropriate.

Below *A great South Western veteran: the Adams 6 ft 7 in 4-4-0 No 563, now in the National Railway Museum at York* (British Railways).

Taking the Southern first, it is perhaps not generally known today that it was the completion of the four-cylinder 4-6-0 No 850 *Lord Nelson* at Eastleigh, in 1926, and its claim to be the most powerful express passenger locomotive in Great Britain, that sparked off the development at Swindon resulting in the production of the 'King' Class of the Great Western. Today, the *Lord Nelson* has the multiple-jet blastpipe and large diameter chimney that was the result of the Bulleid developments, and also his malachite-green style of painting; but an earlier generation of Southern locomotives, on the Settle and Carlisle, is represented by the 'King Arthur' Class 4-6-0 No 777 *Sir Lamiel*,

in the Maunsell livery of dark green. There was a major point in choosing this particular engine for preservation, because in the 1930s, when the 'King Arthurs' were still providing the backbone of the motive power responsible for the working of the West of England train service, *Sir Lamiel* made what is believed to be still the record run with steam traction from Salisbury to Waterloo. In recovery of time after a late start, the 83.8 miles were run in the astonishing time of 72¾ minutes, start to stop, including an average speed of 80.2 mph over the 54.4 miles from Andover to Surbiton, and a maximum of 90 mph. No such performance is required, or would indeed be permitted, with the preserved engine, but it is a locomotive with a noble record.

The Bulleid 'Pacifics' which run the mountainous Settle and Carlisle road, the air-smoothed *City of Wells* and the rebuilt 'Merchant Navy' Class *Clan Line*, provide ample opportunity for enthusiasts to make comparison with the famous 'Pacifics' of other lines: the ever-famous 'Gresleys', *Flying Scotsman*, and *Sir Nigel Gresley*; and the massive LMS *Duchess of Hamilton*. The last-mentioned could be regarded as a locomotive with a dual personality. In 1938, following the success of the streamlined 'Pacifics' built in the previous year for the 'Coronation Scot' service, authority was given for construction of ten more engines of the class, only five of which were to be streamlined. The last of the streamlined set, No 6229, was named *Duchess of Hamilton*, and it was out-shopped from Crewe works in October 1938; in the meantime it had been arranged that the LMS should send a locomotive

and train for exhibition at the New York World Fair to be held in 1939, and naturally one of the latest streamlined 'Pacifics' was chosen. In view of the widespread American interest in the British Monarchy, the *Coronation* engine of 1937 was the natural choice; but by that time the pioneer LMS streamliner had amassed a considerable mileage and it was felt that one of the latest would be desirable. So to meet this situation engines 6220 and 6229 exchanged names and numbers, and it was actually No 6229, as 6220, which made the American tour. In the meantime the one-time 6220, retaining the original blue streamlined style, although named *Duchess of Hamilton*, perplexed some lineside observers. I had two runs behind her while in this state, one on the Merseyside Express, from Euston to Liverpool, in January 1939, and the second, a short one from Crewe to Shrewsbury, in 1940.

The exhibition engine, stranded on the far side of the Atlantic when war broke out, was brought back early in 1942, and returned to LMS traffic in March of that year. It was still numbered 6220, painted red and carrying the name *Coronation*; but just over a year later, when under general repair at Crewe, it was renumbered back to 6229, and given its original, and real name, *Duchess of Hamilton*. One can speculate as to how much of the locomotive that crossed the Atlantic actually remains on the preserved locomotive; certainly not the boiler! The records show that between 1943 and 1950, engine No 6229 carried in succession boilers that previously had been on 6233, 6222, 6252 and 6237.

The Southern engines *Sir Lamiel* and *Lord Nelson* are not the only 4-6-0s to take turns in working the steam-hauled trains over the Settle and Carlisle line, or over the Furness line from Carnforth to Sella-field. A total of 14 examples of the splendid Stanier 'Black Five' 4-6-0s have been preserved in various parts of Great Britain, and of these three are based at Carnforth. At the time of writing two other very famous engines of the class are at Grosmont, on loan to the North Yorkshire Moors Railway. These are No 5428, named after the late Bishop Eric Treacy, the celebrated railway photographer, and No 4767, the only one of the class to have the Stephenson link motion, mounted outside the frames. This latter engine is appropriately named *George Stephenson*, and is reputed to be the strongest of the entire class in getting away from rest and climbing a severe bank. Of the Carnforth trio, No 5407 has done much first-class work over the heavy gradients of the Settle and Carlisle line, sometimes

in partnership with another Stanier celebrity, stationed at Carnforth, the three-cylinder 'Jubilee' Class 4-6-0 No 5690 *Leander*.

From considerable footplate experience with the 'Jubilee' Class engines when in their prime, I became deeply impressed with their qualities as mountain climbers. They were introduced as 'second-line' express passenger units to be used all over the LMS system, except on the Highland; and, while on level and favourable stretches they would run freely up to 85 or even to 90 mph, it was in pounding their way up the heavy banks of the North Country that they excelled. They used to work through on the double-home turns between Leeds and Glasgow St Enoch, and with the heavy wartime loads there was plenty of hard slogging over the Settle and Carlisle line. In her present phase of activity *Leander* is sometimes piloted; but those occasions are usually for the pleasure of having a second preserved engine on display rather the load being too much for a single engine. Twelve-coach trains have regularly been taken without any assistance over the Settle and Carlisle line by the preserved 4-6-0s, whether of the 'Black Five' or the 'Jubilee' Class, not to mention the ex-Southern Railway stalwarts.

17. Advanced Passenger Train: conception and development

In 1966, when the full augmented and accelerated service between London (Euston), Birmingham, Liverpool and Manchester was introduced, following completion of the electrification of the route, it was accompanied immediately by an almost spectacular increase in passenger business. Previous market surveys had predicted that railways as a means of inter-city travel were favourably placed where the journey time did not exceed three hours; and this was fully borne out in the case of Liverpool and Manchester, to both of which the accelerated time from London was 2 hours 35 minutes. Even at that early date however, before the extension of the electrified system to Glasgow had been authorised, British Railways was giving active consideration to developments into higher ranges of speed. On the most favourably aligned routes in Great Britain the line maximum speed was no more than 100 mph and, with regard to the many places where speed would have to be reduced well below the '100' because of track conditions, this limitation virtually put all centres of population and industry lying more than 200 miles apart beyond the limit for successful competition against air travel.

On certain routes where the track alignment is relatively straight general upgrading has permitted the introduction of the diesel-hauled High Speed Trains running up to a maximum of 125 mph, and the high ratio of power in relation to total weight built into these trains has enabled some notable acceleration of service to be made additionally on sections of line where the full maximum speed cannot be run, as described in earlier chapters of this book. But so far as the overall main line railway network is concerned, the impact of the HSTs is really no more than the tip of the iceberg. The far greater problems remain untouched. The collateral development of the Advanced Passenger Train, which has so far progressed no further than the construction of three prototype trains has unfortunately been the subject of much adverse and ill-informed publicity. For this it is not only the popular press and the media that have been responsible. Railways generally have long since passed beyond the time when their equipment and working were matters of interest to the 'man in the street'. Nationalisation, at a stroke, killed the interest of investors. Technical and semi-technical journals dealing with transport are far more concerned with aviation and nuclear power, and the ever-increasing army of amateur enthusiasts in railways appear to be concerned with hobbyist rather than professional aspects.

The attitude towards the APT held in some professional circles was exemplified by a recent conversation with a close personal friend, a senior engineer of no mean eminence in his own particular field, who until his retirement was a frequent traveller on the HSTs. Conversation switched to the APT, and he remarked that it seemed a much simpler job to increase the super-elevation of the

The prototype APT 370002 on test near Lockerbie in September 1979. Note the speed indication board to the left of the line (D. Haviland).

rails on curves rather than to go in for this elaborate tilting mechanism, which did not seem to work very well anyway! Like most professional men whose life's work had not involved an in-depth study of railway operation, and all its manifold complications, he had no conception of the extraordinarily mixed nature of the traffic that had to be conveyed at different times, on the same pair of rails. The 'Berks and Hants' line of the former Great Western Railway, over which this friend travels occasionally, is a striking example, with business ranging from the local passenger service to stations like Aldermaston, Thatcham, Newbury and Hungerford, through the West of England HSTs, up to the heavy end of the loading scale in the Foster Yeoman stone trains from Mere headquarters to Acton Yard. The super-elevation on the curves has to be a compromise to suit them all. In these crowded islands there could be no case for building new railways, purely for super-high-speed trains, even if the finance could be made available.

The APT is an ingenious solution, and as Mr Ian Gardiner said at the time of his installation as Chairman of the Railway Division of the Institution of Mechanical Engineers: APT continues to be central to British Rail's Inter-City strategy and is expected to provide 60–70 per cent of the passenger service on the planned electrified network we are all so anxiously awaiting. Coming from Ian Gardiner, Director of Engineering at the British Railways Board, this was an expression of confidence in the future of the APT, even though it is now evident that it will probably not reach the stage of full production in the form demonstrated by the proto-type sets. The final chapter of this book embodies some of the latest thinking on the subject of high-speed passenger travel generally on British Railways, not only with the Advanced Passenger Train but also with the HSTs, which in any case were originally introduced as an interim stage on certain favourably aligned routes, while the development of the APT principle was passing through the vital experimental and prototype stages. In this chapter it is necessary to review the hopes, aspirations, and no less the frustrations experienced since the building of the first gas-turbine powered experimental train for running up to 155 mph.

The over-riding aim in the conception and development of the APT was to make running round curves at much higher speeds possible, without any decrease in the standards of safety or passenger comfort. In launching the development British Railways certainly set their sights ace-high, with the objectives listed below. At the time of launching the APT programme, the highest previous achievements were represented by the 'Electric Scots' on the West Coast Main Line, and the 'Deltic'-hauled trains on the East Coast. Beyond these, the aims were set out thus:

a) maximum speed 50 per cent higher;

b) to negotiate curves at up to 40 per cent faster;

c) to run on existing track with existing signalling;

d) to maintain standards of passenger comfort at the higher speeds;

e) to be efficient in energy consumption;

f) to maintain existing levels of track maintenance.

From the commercial point of view, one of the most important objectives set to the team of engineers which had been built up to develop this

APT test train at Lockerbie station in 1979 prior to a high-speed run northwards to Beattock (D. Haviland).

was formed of tilting the coach body further, to a degree corresponding to the lateral accelerations experienced by the passengers. It was essential that the response to any such experience should be automatic, very rapid and sensitive, and to measure the effect the experimental train was fitted with separate sensing devices on every vehicle, and to activate an electro-hydraulic servo mechanism. At the same time the process of transition from straight track to a circular curve of constant radius had to be provided for, taking account of the transition curves that are laid in to give a smooth passage from straight track to a constant-radius curve. On the transition curve the cant of the track is gradually reduced from nil to the full amount necessary for the circular curve. The transition is necessarily short, and in the case of high-speed running the time is equally short, so that it is essential for the tilt system to respond very quickly. The parameter set for the development engineers to achieve was a response rate of 5 degrees of cant deficiency per second–this being the angle to which the coach had to be tilted beyond the cant of the track itself.

From the outset it was established that the maximum cant deficiency that could be accepted was nine degrees. In such circumstances purely theoretical considerations gave the following comparisions between the maximum speed that could be run on curves of various radii by a conventional locomotive-hauled train and the proposed APT as follows:

project was that the overall cost of operation expressed in terms of passenger-seat mile, should be no greater than on the existing locomotive-hauled trains running at a maximum of 100 mph. In other words, no higher fares would need to be charged, for the higher speed to be provided. Having regard to the substantial supplements charged on some luxury services in Europe and farther afield, this was a very important consideration.

The programme of development authorised in 1968, jointly by the British Railways Board and the Ministry of Transport, was a massive one. It included the building of an experimental train, gas-turbine powered, and a magnificent new laboratory at Derby, including hydraulic test equipment, a brake dynamometer, a mechanical transmission dynamometer, and a six-axle roller rig. The control tower within the building housed the controls and instrumentation, and included a mini-computer.

To negotiate curves at a higher speed than that provided by the cant angle of the track the concept

Radius of curvature		Maximum speed (mph)	
		Conventional	APT
Km	Chains		
0.5	25	65	77½
1.0	50	93	115
1.5	75	110	140
2.0	100	121	153

One could take as an example the curves on the electrified West Coast main line limited to 70 and 80 mph with conventional trains, where with the APT the corresponding speeds could be 90 and 100

Above left *A striking rail-level shot of the second of the prototype APTs at Shields depot, Glasgow in August 1979* (T.H. Noble).

Left *Broadside view of a bogie and pantograph on an APT power unit at Shields, March 1982* (T.H. Noble).

Right *Close-up of the APT pantograph in the raised position* (D. Haviland).

Some vehicles from the first APT prototype at Shields which took part in the Rocket 150 cavalcade in 1980 (British Railways).

mph. But while the APT development had in mind maximum speeds of 155 mph, the immediate objective was to plan for accelerated service without exceeding the 125 mph currently being provided for in the introduction of the diesel-electric-powered High Speed Trains. An increase beyond 125 mph would involve questions of signal sighting, enginemen's reactions, and other factors not yet resolved. Even with no higher maximum than 125 mph, however, it was estimated that with the faster negotiation of curves which the APT made practicable, safe, and comfortable to passengers, the journey time between Euston and Glasgow, 401 miles, could be reduced to about four hours, from the five hours of the fastest trains worked by conventional stock.

Passing from theory to experimental running it was fortunate that there existed, relatively near to Derby, a section of line which had been closed to ordinary traffic: that of the former direct line from Nottingham to London via Melton Mowbray and Manton, which joined the principal main line to the south near Kettering. The northern part of this line, between Nottingham and Melton, was ideal for APT testing, because it included a considerable amount of curvature, which had been in no way inhibiting to the fastest steam and diesel passenger train services formerly operated over it, but which would have severely handicapped any attempts to introduce really high-speed trains. The 12 miles of single line test track included a variety of permanent way, much of it consisting of continuous welded rail on concrete sleepers; but there were some lengths of old-style joined track on wooden sleepers that would provide some bad-condition running. There was a good deal of curvature, and four tunnels. From the experience gained in running on the line, authority was obtained to build three prototype trains, which could be formed in three alternative versions, tabulated at the top of the next page.

In all these formations the power cars were in the centre. There was no case of connecting-corridors, so that the two halves of the train had to be entirely self-contained, with separate catering facilities. Even granting that the trains were prototypes, one is at something of a loss to know why this should have been done when it would have involved doubling up on staff, at a time when the general trend has been to cut down. Despite the successful introduction of propelling at high speed on the Southern Region Waterloo to Bournemouth and Weymouth service, one can understand some innate reluctance to adopt propelling of lengthy

Duty	No of power cars	No of trailer cars	Tare weight (tons)	Max speed level track (mph)	Seats 1st	2nd
Low power	1	11	364	133	144	376
High power	2	12	455	167	144	448
High power stretched	2	14	500	158	144	592

trains on routes involving much reverse curvature at speeds considerably higher than those run on the Bournemouth line. The APT prototype trains as run have included the propelling of six trailer cars from the central power unit. On the prototypes the tilting principle has been applied to the entire train, and on the power cars a differential mechanism had to be applied to the pantograph mounting, because, if this had moved with the tilting of the car body, the pantograph would have moved sideways out of contact with the overhead current line. It had to be retained in its normal position central to the track. The four traction motors of each power car, each having a continuous rating of 1,000 horsepower, made each of the power cars roughly equal in capacity to a Class '87' electric locomotive at speeds of 80 to 100 mph, though those of the APT power cars were geared for higher speeds.

The application of the tilting principle to the power cars of the prototype trains involved some interesting problems in mechanical design. In the experimental train tried out on the Nottingham–Melton Mowbray line, the main object was to test out and indicate the tilting principle. To avoid complications in the transmission drive, the traction motors were axle-hung, even though it did considerably increase the unsprung weight. In the

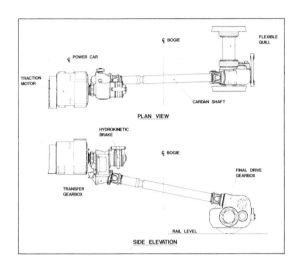

prototype sets, however, designed for maximum-speed running on the West Coast main line, it was considered important to keep all weights to a minimum, and in view of earlier experience on that route from the original Class '86' electric loco-

Above *The prototype APT: details of the flexible drive mechanism* (British Railways).

Left *The prototype APT: drawing of the power bogie* (British Railways).

Flexicoil spring and damper

Pantograph anti-tilt linkage

Lateral damper and bump stop

Secondary yaw damper and linkage

Secondary traction linkage

Bogie frame

Primary lateral link

Wheelset with final drive gearbox

Tilting bolster

Primary traction rods

Tilt jack

Auxiliary friction brake

Primary suspension

Above right *General arrangement of APT-P power car.*

Right *APT-P power car, major elements.*

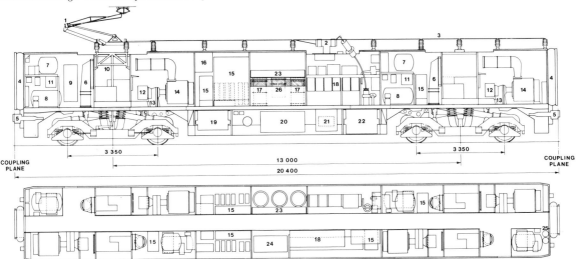

1   PANTOGRAPH.
2   CIRCUIT BREAKER.
3   H.T. BUS–BAR.
4   GANGWAY CONNECTION.
5   DRAWBAR.
6   HYDROKINETIC BRAKE RADIATOR & FAN.
7   HYDROKINETIC BRAKE AIR RESERVOIR.
8   HYDROKINETIC BRAKE WATER RESERVOIR.
9   DOOR.
10 PANTOGRAPH ANTI–TILT MECHANISM.

11 HYDROKINETIC BRAKE CONTROLS.
12 HYDROKINETIC BRAKE.
13 TRANSMISSION GEARBOX.
14 TRACTION MOTOR & BLOWER.
15 ELECTRIC CONTROL EQUIPMENT.
16 AIR COMPRESSOR.
17 COOLING FAN FOR TRANSFORMER,CHOKE,
    THYRISTOR & TILT SYSTEMS.
18 THYRISTOR CONVERTORS.
19 CHOKE.

20 RADIATORS FOR TRANSFORMER,CHOKE,
    THYRISTORS & TILT SYSTEMS.
21 THYRISTOR COOLANT TANK & PUMP.
22 TRANSFORMER.
23 BATTERIES.
24 TILT SYSTEM CONTROL PACK.
25 FIRE EXTINGUISHER GAS BOTTLES.
26 VENTILATION FAN.

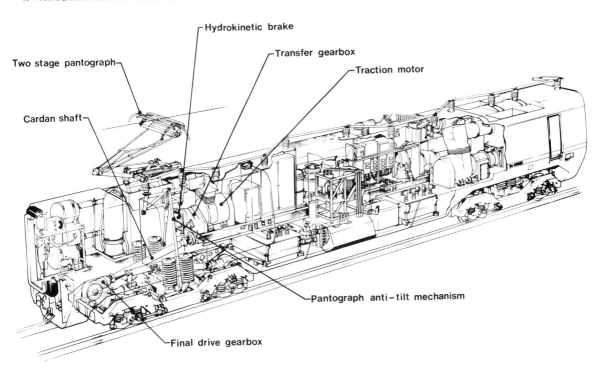

motives, essential to minimise unsprung weight. So, the traction motors were mounted on the body frame, and power transmitted by the flexible drive mechanism shown in the accompanying drawing. From a transfer gearbox mounted adjacent to the motor, the drive was applied through a universal coupling to a cardan shaft and, thence through a second universal coupling to the final drive gearbox which was mounted on the axle. It proved successful in prototype running, though for reasons to be discussed later the titlting principle will not be applied to the power cars of the production APTs.

Except at the leading and trailing ends, all the passenger cars in the prototype trains were articulated in their suspension. This principle is attractive in the weight reduction it makes possible. In a prototype train of 'high power' formation in the two six-car trailer sets on either side of the central power cars there are only 14 bogies, instead of 24 if there had been two under each car, and this not only reduced the rolling resistance through there being many fewer axle boxes, but the bogies themselves contributed not a little to the air resistance of the train itself. The bogie of an articulated connection between two trailer cars had to provide independent suspension for each body, while the tilting principle had also to be incorporated. The mechanism for the latter is quite independent, and, although each coach body responds to the lateral acceleration forces experienced by the passengers, the difference in the tilt angle when entering upon a curve between adjacent coaches has been found so small as to be unnoticeable. It is another matter so far as the train as a whole is concerned. The overall length of a train of the high power formation, with 12 trailers and two power cars, is 321 yards, and at a speed of 100 mph there would be a difference of about seven seconds between the time of entry upon a curve by the front and rear end of the train. It was thus essential for the tilt mechanism on every bogie in the train to react independently. There is a remarkable photograph of one of the prototype trains on trial in Upper Clydesdale, rounding a section of reverse curvature, in which the leading end of the train is seen to be tilting one way while the rear end is tilted the opposite way!

In introducing the prototype trains, even before the first demonstration runs on October 3 1980, to which the Press and media were invited, there had been quite an amount of adverse criticism of the entire tilting concept, arising from rumours leaking abroad that it gave a queasy ride. But whatever was said in that respect, and in due course proved to be quite unfounded, once could have nothing but praise for the passenger accommodation generally. Where weight reduction is a major consideration in

lessening the energy consumption at high speed, and the maintenance of that speed on the heavy adverse gradients of the North Country, there is always a temptation to curtail the space allocated to individual passengers. The airlines have set a pattern, on oceanic as well as domestic flights, and with the prospect of the London–Glasgow journey time being reduced to about four hours and the traditional amenities of a British long-distance railway journey called in question, there could well have been glances across the Channel to what French coaching-stock designers were doing with the new TGV sets. There, SNCF have not only gone the whole way to airline confines of space, but in applying them to railway usage have had to set half the accommodation with passengers sitting back to the direction of travel. This to my mind takes away all the pleasure of railway travel, though probably the great majority of those who travel by TGV are merely anxious to get to journey's end as quickly as possible. The British prototype APTs fortunately have the seats arranged in groups facing fore and aft in the conventional manner.

While it is now known that the production APTs, when construction is eventually authorised, will differ in many respects from the prototypes, these three trains, although doing a negligible amount of revenue-earning service, have between them now run upwards of a million miles, and have provided the British Railways Board with a huge bank of operational data on which the production trains can confidently be based. In the meantime the overall project of the APT can already be seen as a phase of outstanding historic and scientific importance in of the development of the British locomotive.

Before the prototype trains had even been built one could appreciate the force of the remarks of Mr Ian Gardiner, quoted at the beginning of this chapter, from the results of a test run made from St Pancras to Leicester with the experimental gas turbine train. At that time, and before the upgrading of parts of the route to permit HST running at 100 mph, the fastest time over the 99 miles was 80 minutes, after deduction of the recovery allowance in the schedule. This timing was operated by Type '4' diesel-electric locomotives with the line maximum speed at 90 mph on the most favourable sections of line. The experimental APT made the run in 58 minutes, a very striking improvement of 22 minutes in a journey of 99 miles. Since the HSTs were introduced, with certain sections upgraded for 100 mph running, the overall time has not yet been brought below 72 minutes.

The demonstration run of October 3 1980 which I had the privilege of attending, was an impressive

Right *The second APT prototype 370002, standing in the siding at Lockerbie, during the 1979 trials* (D. Haviland).

Below *A prototype APT southbound at maximum speed between Beattock and Lockerbie. Its high speed passage does not seem to disturb the grazing cows!* (D. Haviland).

experience. The original intention was to run from Euston to Crewe and back; but the outward journey was delayed by a signalling failure at Bletchley, and so as not to delay the programme organised after our arrival back in Euston, the trip was terminated at Stafford. The official maximum speed was to be 125 mph on sections where 100 mph was the normal maximum with the electrically hauled trains; and this was only slightly and briefly exceeded, with intermediate maxima of 128, 131, 128 and 127 mph on the down run. By that time, of course, maximum speeds of this order were no novelty on British Railways, with the increasing prowess of the HSTs familiar enough to many regular travellers; but it was a novelty on the London Midland line. Apart from the evergreen pleasure of logging a very fast run, the principal interest lay in observing the behaviour of the train under tilt conditions. Speed

restrictions below the line maximum of 100 mph between Willesden and Stafford are few and far between, being 80 mph at Berkhamsted, Linslade Tunnel and Weedon, 60 mph through Rugby, and 70 mph at Atherstone. North of Rugeley the line maximum then becomes 80 mph until after Stafford. But there are other curves over which 100 mph may be run with ordinary trains where the riding of the APT was of interest.

The first example came on the long curve between Bushey and Watford Junction. Here the speed was 126 mph and the coach in which I was riding tilted over gradually, and with perfect smoothness. A definite reduction in speed had to be made for the Berkhamsted curve rounded at 109 mph instead of the normal 80 mph. It can be said that without a previous and intimate knowledge of the road and an anticipation of the curve negotiation, at nearly 40 per cent higher speeds than normal, would have passed entirely without notice, so smooth was the ride, and so imperceptible the action of the tilt. It was the same at Linslade Tunnel, traversed at 112 mph and at Weedon. At Rugby a temporary speed restriction for track repairs to 50 mph was in force, but later we took the Atherstone curves at 100 mph, while beyond Rugeley we ran at 110 to 111 mph continuously until we began to slow down for the stop at Stafford. The two stages of the run down from Euston were covered as follows: to the stop at Milepost 46 (just short of Bletchley) in 28 minutes 58 seconds, and from the restart to Stafford, 87.6 miles, in exactly 55 minutes. The respective average speeds were 95.3 and 95.6 mph, even though the latter included a 15-mph slowing for track work near Castlethorpe, and the aforementioned restriction just north of Rugby. Allowing for these temporary restrictions and for the effect of slowing down and restarting from the extra stop at Bletchley, the net running time for the 133.6 miles from Euston to Stafford was no more than 75½ minutes, a notable average speed of 106 mph start to stop. The return journey was equally satisfactory, with a net time of 76 minutes.

After this very successful demonstration it was hoped that, prototype or not, the APT would soon go into regular revenue-earning service between Euston and Glasgow. This was not to be however, and more than a year was to pass before a prototype APT made its first passenger-carrying run. Troubles were experienced, which were not readily eradicated. Engineering technology of the highest and most advanced order has been involved in the design and construction of the new trains technology in which Great Britain is leading the world. It is necessarily expensive, though a mere 'widow's mite' compared to what is being spent elsewhere on nuclear-powered exploratory flights into outer space! But with relatively limited resources, the problems in resolving technical difficulties with so novel and advanced a concept as APT necesarily take time, and it was not until December 1981 that a run from Glasgow to Euston and back was made on which fare-paying passengers were carried. This yielded some exceptionally interesting data concerning the performance of the APT on the mountain gradients. There was nevertheless a superabundance of power available on this occasion because, although there were two power cars, only one six-car passenger carrying set was included. The train was completed by one driving trailer, and one trailer brake-car for testing-staff at the opposite side of the power cars to the passenger set. There was thus 8,000 horsepower available for a total tare weight of only 360 tons, as compared to the 455 tons of the full 'high-power' formation train which had conveyed us just over a year earlier.

There was a scheduled stop at Motherwell, after which the 179.5 miles to Preston were booked to be covered in 109 minutes, 98.8 mph, though, allowing for the recovery time included, the average speed expected was 106.8 mph. On that particular morning they needed all the eight minutes of recovery time, and more. Delayed by a track circuit failure near Carluke, the train was nine minutes late on passing Beattock summit, and despite making an average speed of exactly 120 mph over the ensuing

Below *October 1983: pantograph tests with the APT at very high speed between Beattock and Quintishill—instructions were given that speed was not to exceed 155 mph!* (T.H. Noble).

Below right *A rearward view of the 155 mph flyer speeding north during the trials of October 1983. The set was numbered 370006* (T.H. Noble).

41.1 miles to Gretna Junction, the APT passed the latter point still seven minutes late. Schedule time over this length, 22½ minutes, includes four minutes' recovery time, so that an average of 133 mph was apparently expected. But a minute was gained in the approach to Carlisle, and from there to the stop at Preston, 90.1 miles, 56 minutes were allowed, including another four minutes recovery time. Over the mountain section the average speeds scheduled for this prototype run were 93.3 mph from Carlisle (passed at 20 mph) to Penrith; 114.5 mph thence over to Shap Summit to Tebay; 92 mph for the sinuous 13 miles down to Oxenholme, and 119 mph on to Carnforth. This total of 36½ minutes for 62.8 miles from Carlisle involved an average of 103 mph and seemed likely to be the most difficult to maintain on all the run south.

At the same time it seemed as though the full 40 per cent increase over existing speed restrictions on curves was not to be used to advantage on the Carlisle–Carnforth section. For the 'Electric Scots', the speed limits were then 70 mph through Penrith, 75 mph on the Bessie Ghyll curves, 70 mph on various curves between Low Gill and Oxenholme, and 80 mph through Oxenholme itself. The APT was slowed to 90 mph at both Penrith and in Bessie Ghyll, 87 mph at Grayrigg and 92 mph before Oxenholme. Whether there was any significance in these speeds I do not know; but while the aggregate effect of such a succession of restrictions may not have been very great, in view of the rapidity with which the built-in power of the train enabled full speed to be regained, the negotiation of these curves at less than the rated maximum would, in effect, raise the fuel consumption. It is, of course, certain that the drivers responsible for the working of the train on this public occasion would not have been new to the job. The train had been running regularly over the route for some time previously,

and it may be that experience in its handling had led to more moderate speed than the 40 per cent excess over existing speed limits over certain sections of line. A temporary speed restriction to 20 mph north of Shap station caused some loss of time, about 2½ minutes, but the overall time from Motherwell to Preston, 113¼ minutes, included the out-of-course stop south of Carlisle, which was taken care of by the two amounts of recovery time: eight minutes. The late arrival of 4¼ minutes at Preston was not entirely accounted for by the slack at Shap. There was a slight debit against the train on this first half of the journey to London, reflecting perhaps the nature of the route.

The continuation, after a crew change, was a remarkable exposition of high-speed running. Scheduled time for the 209.1 miles to Euston was 129½ minutes, and this was cut to 122½ minutes, a start-to-stop average of 102.3 mph. This included no fewer than four temporary speed restrictions, two to 50 mph and two down to 20 mph which between them cost nine minutes in running; this left a net time of 113½ minutes, and a net average of no less than 110.4 mph. The usual severe speed restrictions to 30 mph at Crewe and 60 mph at Rugby, observed by ordinary trains, were not exceeded but the Trent Valley Junction, south of Stafford, was taken at 85 mph, exactly the 40 per cent excess over the normal 60 mph. This fine run included a maximum speed of 138 mph between Blisworth and Castlethorpe which it was thought might be the highest speed yet attained by any British train carrying fare-paying passengers. But I have logged 136 mph myself on one of the Western Region HSTs between Swindon and Didcot in the course of an otherwise ordinary run, and it is quite likely that speeds approaching, if not surpassing the 138 of the APT were attained before the speed-limiting device was added to these trains.

On the return run in December 1981 Preston was reached in 125¼ minutes, after a run complicated by two temporary speed restrictions for track repairs, and a signal check to 20 mph at Stafford. It was after leaving Preston that trouble occurred with the tilt mechanism, and between there and Gretna Junction the train had to be stopped four times for adjustments to be made. Intermediately, however, there was some very spectacular running, particularly in the ascents of the Shap and Beattock inclines. In referring to the speeds run on the southbound journey earlier on that same December day I emphasised the inhibiting effect of the curves. Above Oxenholme for 1.4 miles leading to the Hay Fell location the limits for ordinary trains and the APT are respectively 80 and 95 mph; for the rest of the Grayrigg bank they are 90 and 115 mph. Then comes the curving section into the Lune Gorge, where for three miles the ordinary limit is 75 mph and the APT is restricted to 90 mph for the part of the way and then 100. Through the straighter part of the gorge the APT can run up to 120 mph and it is only when approaching Tebay and up the Shap Incline itself that the full 125 mph is permitted. On the run of December 1981 the train observed a 20-mph permanent way restriction before Oxenholme,

but accelerated to 100 mph on the upper part of the Grayrigg bank. Then came a slowing to 88 mph round the Low Gill curves, and the attack on Shap itself was begun at 119 mph. The 5½ miles up from Tebay to Summit took no more than 2 minutes 56 seconds; it might have been even faster had there not been a speed limit for the APT of 95 mph over the summit.

The last of the out-of-course stops had to be made just north of Carlisle, but from that a magnificently clear run was possible to the outskirts of Carstairs, through which junction a reduction to 86 mph was made. The average speed over the 65 miles from Gretna Junction was 114.5 mph, including the ascent of the Beattock bank. On three sections the averages were:

Gretna to Beattock station	121.5 mph
Beattock to Summit	120.3 mph
Summit to Carstairs (downhill)	103.5 mph

The speed had to be restrained for part of the downhill run through Upper Clydesdale, but at one point, on a favourable alignment, a maximum of 135 mph was registered. On the continuous 1 in 77 rising gradient of the Beattock bank a speed of 118 mph was sustained. Despite these repeated demonstrations of the power potential of the APT, it was nevertheless obvious that it was not clear of troubles, and the severe weather of the 1981/2 winter brought more, in directions that were not anticipated. As this book goes to press one train has begun a limited amount of revenue-earning service. The experience gained with this unique form of vehicle suspension has, in the meantime, been valuable beyond all words, and the fruits of this experience, and hopes for the future, are discussed in the concluding chapter of this book.

18. Into the future

With my references to the introduction and early working of the '58' Class diesel-electric heavy freighters in Chapter 13 of this book, the history of the British railway locomotive is brought up to the very time of writing; and having reached that stage the reader may well ask, what of the future? In certain contexts it could well be a 'loaded' question. Technologically, the prospect is limitless. The parameters, however, are likely to be set by economic and political considerations. This, of course, is doubly unfortunate at a time when British achievement in the ever-widening diversity of all engineering skills involved in the running of trains is still unsurpassed anywhere in the world.

There was an epoch, some little time before the period covered by Volume 1 of this work, in which there was contested the 'Battle of the Brakes', in which the protagonists were the compressed air and the vacuum systems. Today it could be said that a different form of braking is causing British Railways to be apparently dragging their feet. I need not say any more. The symptoms are unfortunately all too well known, and they manifest themselves in obstructive tactics in a diversity of ways. But it would be wrong and wholly inappropriate to end the majestic saga of locomotive development which, with recollections of Trevithick's adventures, now takes us back nearly 200 years, on a pessimistic note. In my own family circle I have the reputation of being an insatiable optimist, and I like to think that the 'Age of the Train' will soon take us into new developments worthy of the engineering potential constantly on hand.

Following the introduction of the '56' and '58' Classes of freight locomotive, the next step has been the ordering of a new prototype high-powered electric locomotive of the Co-Co type, for 125 mph running, which will be by far the most powerful locomotive yet introduced on British Railways. It is stated to be in readiness for the now authorized electrification of the East Coast main line; but the interesting point about this development is that it suggests a return to individual locomotive haulage rather than a continuance of the practice of running fixed-formation trains, as exemplified by the HST. At the same time notices in the railway press concerning the likely ordering of some electric HST power cars gave the impression that the operating philosophy of the future still contained some uncertainties, although in this respect the overall term 'operating' nowadays has a many-sided application. There is sometimes a distinct cleavage of attitude between that section of the activity which is actually concerned with the movements of locomotives and coaching stock and, of course, with the increasing number of fixed-formation trains, and that which has to try and meet the fluctuating demands for seats from the travelling public.

To the running section the fixed-formation train is a very attractive proposition, providing its reliability is assured; and in the case of the HST the facilities provided for routine examination and servicing have, all in all, proved a very effective back-up to the intense utilisation that the high capital cost of these trains has demanded. At terminal stations the quick turn-around times enabled the set-trains to arrive and depart from the same platform, eliminating all empty stock and pilot engine movements, and simplifying the traffic working generally.

Left *Airport express (on right) Gatwick to Victoria, in Clapham Cutting, propelled by electrodiesel locomotive No 73113 (Brian Morrison).*

Right *Gatwick Airport express, southbound near Clapham Junction and hauled by electrodiesel locomotive No 73105 (Brian Morrison).*

The classic example is that of Paddington. Not so many years ago, close students of railway operation would have found it difficult to imagine that a station handling such an amount of main line traffic would have been worked successfully from a signal box three miles away, in which the only indication of the whereabouts of locomotives and rolling stock was on the illuminated panel diagram. It is true that this modernisation of control was installed before the coming of the HSTs, but with them came a great simplification and improvement. Today there is often not a single locomotive in the once-congested locomotive yard at Ranelagh Bridge, on the down side of the line, about three-quarters of a mile outside the terminus.

From the passenger viewpoint, and to those sections of the railway management concerned with the marketing of travel, the fixed-formation train has certain very definite disadvantages. Passenger travel on the railways of Great Britain has always been subject to considerable fluctuations in volume, not only in the summer holiday season, but in connection with social, cultural and sporting activities. To those who have studied train running over the years, the Glasgow portion of the 10:00 am Anglo-Scottish express from Euston in LNWR days, north of Crewe, will always be an example of extreme fluctuation of traffic. Its normal formation consisted of five coaches, including restaurant car, from Euston, and a single through carriage from Birmingham attached at Crewe; yet at really busy times this train has been known to load to 14 vehicles, including full restaurant facilities from Birmingham, and still be worked punctually by a single locomotive. With the fixed-formation HSTs the total investment has provided just enough sets to operate the advertised service, with the requisite number of sets to cover those temporarily out of use for regularly scheduled maintenance work. Any relief trains to meet exceptional increases in traffic have to be furnished with a separate locomotive and ordinary coaches. This, of course, entails considerably slower running than with an HST.

The policy of offering slower than normal transit times on occasions of exceptional traffic is not new in Great Britain, and does indeed go back to the 1930s when, on certain routes, there were separate timetables for Saturdays in the height of the summer holiday season, in which considerably slower speeds were scheduled than from Monday to Friday. The fast, highly competitive trains were run for the benefit of business travellers, while on Saturdays at that time of the year the clientele was mostly of the once-in-a-way holiday nature. Considerably larger coach formations could be run to cater for peak traffic, without the likelihood of time being lost en route, or the need for double-heading at a time when locomotive power was in any case at a premium.

A train like the HST cannot, unfortunately, be 'strengthened' to meet additional business, and any relief trains have to be of ordinary stock. Quite apart from seasonal holiday rushes, though, British Railways always has predominantly in mind, top class express passenger service, the year-round Inter City business travel market. Since the original conception of the fixed formation HST (and also the APT), this market has changed significantly.

Over the years, British Railways have found that the principal market for Inter City business has been the West Coast Main Line, including, of course, the electrified services to Liverpool and Manchester, and to Birmingham and Wolverhampton. Second to this is the East Coast Main Line, with its very important offshoots to the West Riding cities and to Humberside. For both West and East Coast routes it has been determined that the fixed-formation train with its built-in power units, dedicated to high speed passenger service, is no longer commercially viable, and all future planning is now in the direction of locomotive-hauled trains. The prototype Co-Co electric locomotive already on order is a first move in this direction, particularly aimed at future requirements on the East Coast Main Line. This project has an increased significance and urgency since the authorisation of electrification through to Edinburgh. With the completion of the prototype Co-Co (Class '89') programmed for 1985, there will be ample opportunity for trial running on the West Coast Main Line, and elimination of teething troubles before the need arises for quantity production for the East Coast route.

There are no half measures about the power-potential to be built into this new prototype, because the total continuous rating of its six traction motors, 4,300 kva (5,700 hp), puts it about 15 per cent ahead of the Class '87' 25 kv electric locomotives of the West Coast Main Line and at a considerably higher speed. The new Class '89' is designed for running at 125 mph and it is evidently intended that it will be able to haul at that speed the heaviest loads the traffic department like to hang on to it. East Coast traditions die hard! During the First World War new records were set for maximum tonnages to be hauled by an unassisted British steam locomotive, and the fast schedules developed during the inter-war years were occasionally worked by Gresley 'Pacific' engines with loads up to 600 tons. This, of course, did not apply to the special high speed streamlined trains. But spectacular as has been the speed-up on this route since the introduction of the HSTs, there must have been many times when the traffic department felt gravely inhibited at the restriction to no more than eight-coach trains. This restriction will be eliminated by the restoration of locomotive-hauled electric trains.

As to speed, the progressive quickening of the end-to-end times on the East Coast route since the HSTs were first introduced is a measure of the extent to which additional stretches of the line have been cleared for full 125 mph running. The 'Flying Scotsman' now runs between Kings Cross and Edinburgh in the level 4½ hours — an average speed of 88½ mph. Since the opening of the Selby avoiding line, for example, I have enjoyed a non-stop run from Kings Cross to York at an average speed of exactly 100 mph (189 miles in 113½ minutes). Elsewhere, on routes where the alignment is suitable for continuous running at, or near to 125 mph, one can note still higher start-to-stop average speeds, such as on a recent run from Reading to Bath, on which the 70.9 miles were covered in 39 minutes 48 seconds, an average of 106.8 mph.

Reference has been made earlier in this book to the spectacular accelerations in train service that have been made possible by the introduction of HST sets on routes where the maximum speed potential cannot be realised because of the track alignment; and now, in the summer service of 1984 there has come what is perhaps the most striking example of all, by extending one of the East Coast HSTs to Inverness. The 12:00 noon service from Kings Cross, having reached Edinburgh in 4 hours 47 minutes, after stopping at York, Darlington, Newcastle and Berwick, continues to Perth, and thence over the Highland line to complete the 570.2 miles to Inverness in the remarkable time of 530 minutes, an overall average speed of 64.7 mph. The

corresponding southbound train leaving Inverness at 07:20 is even faster, being due to arrive in Kings Cross at 16:00 hours, 520 minutes overall 65.9 mph. This train takes the former Caledonian line between Edinburgh and Perth, via Falkirk (Grahamstown) and Stirling in both directions.

This new service, happily named 'The Highland Chieftain', in addition to providing the fastest-ever time between London and Inverness, makes some unprecedented speed over the Highland line itself. Unlike some other routes in mountain country, this one has, from its very inception, been essentially a *main* line and has always witnessed some of the fastest running to be found in such territory. But the occasional maximum speeds of 65 to 70 mph in steam days, and entirely on the favourable gradients, bear not the slightest resemblance to the HST performance of today. Could one have imagined, for example, a time when speed would rise to 70 mph on that gruelling initial 1 in 60 climb out of Inverness, or of topping Drumochter Summit, 1,484 ft above sea level, at 77 mph? It is the overall speed between Perth and Inverness, however, which is so revealing of the potentialities of the HST positively to 'iron out' the most severe gradients. On the Highland line, the results are perhaps more spectacular even than those now established in Cornwall, because the straighter alignment of the track permits considerably higher maximum speeds.

The northbound HST, leaving Perth at 18:20 hours, makes eight intermediate stops in its 2½-hour run over the 118 miles to Inverness; but this schedule includes some margin for recovery at the end of the long run from Kings Cross and, on the occasion of my travelling, after leaving Perth 13 minutes late, the arrival in Inverness was 5 minutes early, despite three out-of-course restrictions en route. The total running time was 123½ minutes, showing an average speed of 57.3 mph. The southbound train has only three regular stops as far as Perth, and has a sharper allowance of 2 hours 8 minutes. It was on this train that, from the privileged position of the driver's cab, I noted a remarkable performance.

There were two sections of restricted speed to be observed because of engineering works; a 'stop' order to take up a party at Dalwhinnie, and a signal delay prior to crossing a northbound sleeping car express at Kincraig loop. In addition to this, the station stopping time at Pitlochry was exceeded by nearly three minutes while a large party was entrained. Yet the arrival in Perth was exactly on time. An overall analysis of the run is given at right.

With the HST sets in general, the capacity for rapid acceleration from the rest and for high sustained maximum speed, is nowadays taken for granted

Section	Distance (miles)	Booked time (min)	Actual time		Net time (min)†	Net start to stop average speed (mph)
			m	s		
Inverness to Aviemore	34.7	36	35	25	34½	60.3
Aviemore to Kingussie	11.7	11	12	22	9½	73.8
Kingussie to Pitlochry	43.1	44½	43	40	40	64.7
Pitlochry to Perth	28.5	31½*	28	40	26	65.7

*Includes some recovery time.
†Taking account of time lost by delays.

---

although, of course, the latter attribute cannot be exercised to anything approaching its full extent on the Highland line. It was, nevertheless, something of a novelty to witness speeds of 85 and 90 mph on certain sections in this area. In this connection it should be mentioned that, on many parts of the line, higher speeds are permitted with the HSTs than with ordinary locomotive-hauled trains. It is, of course, the HST's ability to climb the severe gradients at high speed which has made possible the introduction of such enterprising new schedules, in which the attaining of speeds of 68-69 mph on the 1 in 60 gradients provides the outstanding example.

The log of the actual running of the 07:20 train from Inverness to Perth on the occasion of my travelling gives a good impression of the timetable requirements, and of their fulfillment.

Distance (miles)		Schedule (minutes)	Actual time		Actual average speed (mph)
			m	s	
0.0	Inverness	0	0	00	—
0.6	*Millburn Junction*	2	1	42	—
6.7	Culloden Moor	9½	8	00	58.1
14.9	Moy	17½	16	04	61.3
19.0	Tomatin	21½	19	51	65.1
22.6	*Slochd Crossing*	25	23	18	62.7
28.0	Carrbridge	30	28	20	64.4
—		—	pw slack		
34.7	Aviemore	36	35	25	56.7
—		—	sig check		
5.9	Kincraig	6	6	53	51.4
11.7	Kingussie	11	12	22	63.2
2.9	Newtonmore	3	3	13	54.1
13.0	Dalwhinnie (pass)	13½ arr	13	15	60.6
—		— dep	14	00	—
27.0	*Dalnacardoch Box*	25½	26	39	66.0
36.3	Blair Atholl	36½	35	17	64.4
43.1	Pitlochry	44½	43	40	48.6
4.9	Ballinluig	7	4	42	62.5
—		—	pw slack		
12.9	Dunkeld	13½	13	15	56.5
18.2	Murthley	18½	18	15	63.6
21.3	*Stanley Junction*	22½	21	05	65.8
28.5	Perth	31½	28	40	56.3

The overall net running time of 110 minutes shows an average speed of 64.4 mph from Inverness to Perth.

At the various crossing points on the single line sections such as at Moy, Tomatin, Carrbridge and Newtonmore, speed restrictions to 60 mph had to be observed, while there were more severe restrictions to 40 mph at Culloden Moor, Blair Atholl and Dunkeld. It was significant of the care taken to restrain speed on those steeply downhill sections which include much curvature, that the average speed descending the long incline between the Drumrochter Summit and Blair Atholl, where the gradient is mostly 1 in 70, was no more than 71 mph over the 11.2 miles between the sites of the former stations at Dalnaspidal and Struan. By contrast, this same train set, later in the journey south, covered 36 level miles on the unrestricted length between Darlington and York at an average speed of 119 mph.

Turning now to the Advanced Passenger Train, in January 1982 a paper was read to the Railway Division of the Institution of Mechanical Engineers, by Dr D. Boocock and Mr B.L. King. This described the development of the prototype train. While confirming that the technical proving trials had demonstrated successfully that the required advanced performance could be achieved within the constraints of the existing track and infrastructure, it also stated that a reassessment of the business requirements of the West Coast main line had led to a considerable change in the make-up proposed for the production trains, referred to as the APT-S. Instead of the original formation of two separate six-car sets on each side of the two centrally placed power units, it was concluded that a ten-car rake with only one power car, at the end, would be adequate. Experience on the Bournemouth line of Southern Region had shown there were no disadvantages from the high-speed propelling of long and heavy trains, and in the paper the joint authors proposed that the APT-S trains should consist of nine articulated cars with a non-articulated driving van trailer at one end and a driving power car at the other.

Even though the train proposed was to be reduced from the original maximum of 12 cars to ten, the intention to use only a single power car would limit the maximum speed to 140 mph (though this was considered adequate for commercial requirements on the West Coast main line in the immediate future). The nine-car passenger-carrying rake was to be articulated throughout, because this would not only minimise design changes between APT-P and APT-S but also because it would maximise train performance by reducing the total weight, and by reducing the air resistance of the train at speed. At the same time it has to be pointed out that having the entire passenger accommodation in a single articulated rake would mean that, in the event of any defect developing in one car, necessitating attention in the shops, the whole set would have to be taken out of service. For this reason it has now been decided that the production sets will have non-articulated passenger stock. Again, while tilt is fundamental to the APT, it has been decided that this feature will not be applied to the driving power car or to the driving van trailer, neither of which will convey any passengers. The new locomotives, which have already been designated Class '91' will be of the Bo-Bo wheel arrangement and will not be confined to hauling the tilting passenger trains. They are designed for a maximum speed of 140 mph and the high speed service they will operate will be known as IC225, which will supersede the initials APT. This latter will therefore have been used only for the experimental and prototype versions of the tilting train conception. The Class '91' locomotives will have cabs at each end. They will be in the nature of a general-utility electric type, but for a higher range of speed than the existing Class '87', which, with the improved pantographs are now rated for a maximum speed of 110 mph. The design of the new Class '91' will make it available for liner trains, nominated freights and other duties when not engaged on IC225 trains, and thus increase its availability and potential utilisation.

The potentialities of the APT principle glimpsed during the first demonstration running in the autumn of 1980, and again in the brief public journeys in December 1981, have now been thoroughly established. In more than eight months of regular running between Glasgow and Euston earlier this year, 2,400 miles every week of high speed performance, one of the three prototype trains has amassed an impressive mileage of steady service, while a further trains has been subjected to shorter special workings to iron out incidental and occasional troubles that inevitably still remain. But while the IC225 trains will differ in many important respects from the prototypes, it must nevertheless be stressed that the basic conception, as first embodied in the gas-turbine-powered experimental train, and developed in the prototypes, has proved remarkably successful — as an engineering project. One hopes that the time is now not far distant when the results of all the painstaking and unremitting work expended upon it during the past four or five years will be rewarded by authorisation of production of the service trains.

In June 1984, by courtesy of the British Railways Board, I had the privilege and pleasure of a journey from Euston to Glasgow on one of the prototype APTs; but at the outset I must emphasise that this was not a special occasion. It was one of the regular routine runs, the northbound leg of the round trips that have been made three times a week for several months previously. There were a number of

passengers, railway staff, but not connected with the
design and operation of the train. I had the pleasure
of the company of Mr John Mitchell, the APT
Project Manager (Engineering); and as might be
expected he proved a mine of information, not only
on the history of the development so far, but also on
the forward thinking towards the ultimate
introduction of the APT into regular public service.
I was interested to find that in view of the number of
passengers travelling on this occasion, a full
restaurant car service was provided; and in view of
all the biased fabrications about 'queasy rides' and
other adverse publicity that the APT has suffered in
the past it was impressive to see the aplomb, and
quiet efficiency with which the young Scottish
waitresses served an excellent dinner, while we were
running at high speed and while the tilting action of
the train was frequently called into play.

On the earlier part of the journey, when Mr
Mitchell was bringing me up to date with the design
features of the future programme, our actual
running was delayed somewhat by signal checks,
and we were not able to make a better time than 93¾
minutes for the 133.6 miles from Euston to Stafford,
our first scheduled stop. Our most impressive burst
of speed was to cover the 20.7 miles from Tring to
Wolverton at an average of 122 mph, including, of
course, the reduction of speed on the curve through
Linslade Tunnel.

I reserved my detailed logging for the section
north of Lancaster, where Mr Mitchell had
arranged for me to ride in the driver's cab. I have
been familiar with this line from my boyhood, and
shall always remember one of my first journeys over
it in a stopping train, and how at one station in
particular, Low Gill, the extent to which the
carriage was canted over as we stood at the plat-

form! Mr Mitchell brought with him charts showing
the curves in the line, and the reductions that even
the APT has to make over some of them. Through
his kindness I am able to have them reproduced
herewith, though such a prosaically factual display
of the conditions could not possibly convey the sense
of thrill and exhilaration that the actual ride through
from Carnforth to Carlisle engenders.

Before we are finished with overall facts, however, I cannot resist setting down the time of our
ascent of that 31.4-mile section, with its vertical rise
of 885 feet, against certain other notable ascents in
West Coast history, to emphasise the almost sensational impact of the APT. The first two runs were

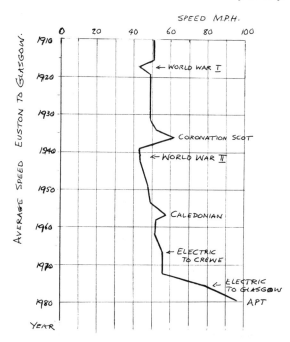

both exceptional efforts, certainly not to be expected in normal service. We were certainly thrilled when the use of Class '50' diesels in pairs enabled the pre-electrification schedules to be put into effect in 1969, though when electrification was completed five years later the times that were possible with the Class '87' locomotives were shown to be more a result of the limitations of the track alignment than of locomotive capacity. Even today, when speed restrictions on certain parts of the line have been relaxed to permit maximum speeds of 110 mph with the Class '87' locomotives, an excellent recent run on the southbound 'Royal Scot' train showed an average speed of no more than 89 mph between mileposts 67 and 38 on the ascent to Shap.

The best that I have known northbound with Class '50's and Class '87's were made to look positively pedestrian beside the lightning performance of the APT, and it was all done in such supreme comfort. Another guest of the British Railways Board rode in the 'second man's' seat while Inspector Tweedie of Scottish Region, and I, stood. I was thus in a good position to appreciate the efficacy of the tilting mechanism, and in negotiating the almost continuous succession of curves between Carnforth and Plumpton its response was superb. The weather also was very bad, with a strong westerly wind and heavy rain; but other than lessening one's personal appreciation of the majestic scenery of the route, it had little effect. The detailed log of that portion of the run between Carnforth and

Penrith makes impressive reading, but I have extended it to show the times made from the dead start at Preston, even though a little time was lost as far as Lancaster, because of local restrictions.

Distance (miles)		Schedule (minutes)	Actual time m s	Speeds (mph)
0.0	Preston	0	0 00	—
21.0	Lancaster	12½	14 25	—
27.3	Carnforth	15½	18 13	120
31.8	Burton		20 25	125
34.5	Milnthorpe		21 41	110
40.1	Oxenholme		24 34	115
43.6	Hay Fell		26 27	110/115/95
45.2	Lambrigg Crossing		27 29	115
47.2	Grayrigg		28 33	90
48.9	Low Gills		29 52	100
53.2	Tebay		32 00	121/118
56.2	Scout Green		33 43	120
58.7	Shap Summit		34 57	92
60.7	Shap		36 05	105
—	Bessie Ghyll		—	90/122
72.2	Penrith	42½	42 57	90
—	Southwaite		—	125
90.1	Carlisle	61	56 20	20 (passing)

Between Burton and Shap, with the exception of Oxenholme, the locations at which times were taken were those of the sites of the previous passenger

Far left *APT Glasgow-London test train passing through Nuneaton station, March 1984* (Brian Morrison).

Left *Chart showing improvements in Euston to Glasgow times over the years 1910-1980.*

Right *New look for the LM Class '87's: No 87006* City of Glasgow *on arrival at Manchester Piccadilly from Euston* (Brian Morrison).

Right *One of the Class '87' electric locomotives No 87012* Coeur de Lion *in the new executive livery* (Brian Morrison).

Below *Speed diagram of APT.*

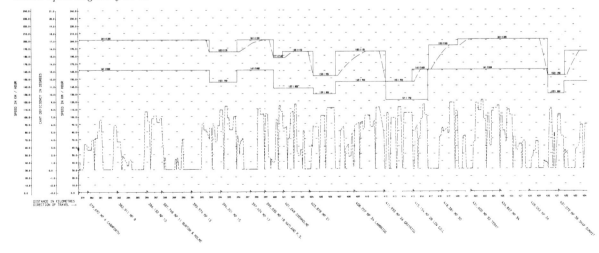

Carnforth—Shap Summit: 31.4 miles

Date	Traction	Occasion	Locomotion	Time		Average
				m	**s**	speed (mph)
1895	Steam	Race to the North	2-4-0 *Hardwicke*	31	15	60.3
1936	Steam	Euston-Glasgow trial	*Princess Elizabeth*	26	45	70.5
1969	Diesel-electric	Accelerated schedules	Class '50'	22	00	85.5
1974	Electric	Electric to Glasgow	Class '87'	21	15	87.6
1984	Electric	Trial running	APT-P	16	24	115.0

stations, or at Hay Fell and Scout Green the relay huts that mark the sites of previous signal boxes. Between Milnthorpe and Low Gill the speeds quoted are those to which the APT is limited, and it is only when one enters upon the relatively straight length of the Lune gorge before Tebay that the '125' can be approached. Going up Shap itself on the 1 in 75 gradient we sustained 120 mph until required to slacken off over the summit. it will be noted that over the 5.5 miles between Tebay and Shap Summit we averaged 111.7 mph. The riding on the curves of the Grayrigg bank, between Oxenholme and Hay Fell, was wonderfully smooth; and it was no less so sweeping through the Bessie Ghyll ravine, at 90 mph descending from Shap towards Penrith.

North of Carlisle the climbing of the long adverse section to Beattock Summit was even more impressive so far as pure speed was concerned, because from Kingmoor Yard cabin to the summit we averaged 117 mph. This, however, can be attributed to the straighter alignment of track, where the only appreciable reduction called for is to 95 mph on the curves between Castlemilk siding and Lockerbie. The comparison with previous fast running is again deeply revealing (above).

Gretna Junction—Beattock Summit: 41.1 miles

Engine	Caledonian 4-2-2 '123'	*Princess Elizabeth*	Class '87' electric	APT
Average speed (mph)	56.7	73.0	96.5	119

The first of the four runs was the fastest made by the now preserved Caledonian 4-2-2 No 123 during the race of 1888, when Edinburgh was the goal. The fast average speed was equalled, or nearly so, on one or two occasions by the Aberdeen 'racer' in the contest of 1895, and averages of 55 mph over the same section of line were frequently made in 1896 by engines of the first 'Dunalastair' Class of 4-4-0 in running the 1:54 am 'Tourist Express'. The performance of the *Princess Elizabeth* in 1936, with a relatively light load, was something quite apart from ordinary daily running. One of the fastest steam runs that I have ever noted personally was on 'The

Midday Scot', when I was on the footplate of the *City of Leicester,* hauling a load of 12 cars; in regaining time after a late start from Carlisle the average speed from Gretna Junction to Beattock Summit was 61 mph.

Now, over this same section of line, the climbing speed is being all but doubled. The schedule time for the northbound APT-P requires an average speed of 114.5 mph and on the occasion I travelled this was stepped up to 119 mph. This seems the point above all others to be emphasised in discussing the potential of this remarkable train. On the run I experienced, the speed between Gretna Junction and Beattock Summit lay between the narrow limits of 95 and 125 mph; as on Shap, the sustained speed on the steepest part of the Beattock bank was 120 mph. In the train the riding was at all times beautifully smooth and comfortable. For the record we passed Carstairs, 163.6 miles from Preston, in 96½ minutes, six minutes inside schedule time; but a very severe slowing for permanent way work caused the last 5.4 miles from Law Junction to the stop at Motherwell to take eight minutes. Even so, we were two minutes inside the total scheduled running time of 112 minutes for the 179.5 miles from Preston. Allowing for the final delay, and two lesser checks earlier in the run, the net time from Preston was 104 minutes, showing an average speed of 103.3 mph.

And so, at midsummer 1984, the fascinating and ever evolving saga of British locomotive history has reached a critical, and brilliant milestone. Thirty years ago, when the great modernisation plan for British Railways was about to be launched, and certain influential management executives felt that acceleration of passenger train service beyond the somewhat mediocre levels that had been attained in post-war recovery was not really necessary, the upward surge that had started even before the diesel revolution had begun to take effect, and which has led us on to the APT, would have been almost unbelievable. In conclusion I cannot do better than show graphically the overall average speeds between London and Glasgow, from the standard eight hours of the pre-1914 'midnight' from Euston through the various vicissitudes to the electric

'Scots' of the 1970s, and finally the target set for the APT. It is an impressive demonstration.

There was to be a brilliant postscript to the story; for on August 30 1984, in connection with the ceremonial naming of one of the HST cars *Top of the Pops* at Bristol Temple Meads, arrangements were made for a fast run down from Paddington by the special train conveying the guests of British Railways and of the BBC. Favoured with an invitation, I was charged with the task of acting as official timekeeper. Apart from the gay social and musical accompaniments that one naturally expected on such an occasion it proved a notable event in British locomotive history, and marked the notching up of yet another world speed record.

The fastest previous non-stop time from Paddington to Temple Meads, via Badminton, stood at 67 min 35 sec made by the 'Jubilee' special on May 7 1977, and in the publicity literature issued to guests on the train of August 30 1984 the schedule time was quoted as 67 min 12 sec, a very modest topping of the existing record. But my friends on BR showed me a confidential document relating to a computer-based schedule built around the potentialities of a special train of only five, instead of the usual seven, trailer cars, in which the overall time was cut to 66 min 18 sec.

In the working notices, which in their insistence upon the 'Special' being given an absolutely clear road reminded me of some of the documents issued to the staff at the time of the Race to the North in 1895, it was hinted that with line speed limits being slightly exceeded (at the discretion of the senior traction inspector, who would be riding in the driver's cab), signalmen and others should be prepared for a gain on the scheduled time and allow a margin in advance. With the advantage of having five trailer cars instead of the usual seven, time was gained at once by an exceptionally fast start out of Paddington, and as early as Slough the train was a minute ahead of the computer-based schedule.

On the open road speed was not allowed to exceed 130 mph and careful regard was paid to the permanent speed restrictions of 80 mph at Reading, 100 mph at Swindon and 70 mph over the junction at Wootton Bassett. Within these parameters time was steadily gained, and Bristol Parkway was passed in 56 min 47 sec, 3 min 55 sec ahead of the computer-based time, having made an average speed of 121.7 mph over the 107.55 miles from passing Acton. Over the concluding 5.8 miles, at greatly reduced speed, the train was beautifully and smoothly handled. We made unusually fast time down the Filton bank—though very slow compared to what had gone before and were at rest in Temple Meads in 62 min 33 sec, to a vociferous welcome from the thousand-odd 'Top of the Pops' fans who were waiting for us.

So far as the locomotive performance was concerned, that arrival, 4¾ minutes earlier than the publicly advertised time, and 3¾ minutes better than the computer, represented a start-to-stop average speed of 112.95 mph, a notable advance upon the previous British best of 111.5 mph from Paddington to Chippenham made on April 10 1979, referred to in Chapter 15 of this book. This was particularly so when one considers the enforcedly slower running at the finish of the Bristol trip. This can be appreciated from a comparison of the speed run from Paddington up to the point where high power was shut off, at Milepost 92¾ in the earlier case, and at Parkway on August 30. These averages were 113 and 118.3 mph. At the time it was made the Paddington-Chippenham run was claimed as a world record for any form of railway traction; but the subsequent inauguration of the French TGV, with start-to-stop runs at 128 mph, precludes any such claim for the latest HST performance. It can, I think, be safely claimed as the world's fastest, on any general purpose railway, with any form of motive power.

HST Special: Record run, August 30 1984

Distance (miles)		Time m s	Average speed (mph)
0.0	PADDINGTON	0 00	—
2.0	Milepost 2	2 21	—
4.25	Acton	3 46	95.5
6.25	Milepost 6¼	4 54	105.5
9.0	Southall (MP 9)	6 16	120.4
13.25	West Drayton	8 18	125.4
18.5	SLOUGH	10 45	128.7
24.2	Maidenhead	13 26	127.0
31.0	Twyford	16 38	127.4
35.0	Milepost 35	18 30	128.7
36.0	READING	19 12	85.5
41.5	Pangbourne	22 20	105.0
48.5	Cholsey	25 39	126.7
53.1	DIDCOT	27 49	127.0
60.5	Wantage Rd (MP 60½)	31 14	129.2
69.0	Milepost 69	35 12	128.0
76.0	Milepost 76	38 29	128.0
77.3	SWINDON	39 14	104.0
83.0	Wootton Bassett	42 20	110.3
94.2	Hullavington	48 16	114.1
107.2	Westerleigh Junc	54 23	127.3
111.8	PARKWAY	56 47	115.0
116.9	Dr Day's Bridge Junc	61 20	67.2
117.6	TEMPLE MEADS	62 33	—

Bibliography

Technical Papers

Institute of Locomotive Engineers

1956 Evolution of the Internal Combustion Locomotive, J.M. Doherty

1969-1970 Whither Motive Power, Captain W.A. Stewart CBE RN (Retd)

1968-1969 The Presidential Address—All Change, A.E. Robson MBE

1962 Design and Construction of the Gas Turbine Locomotive GT3, J.O.P. Hughes

1965 Propelling of High Speed Electric Stock on the Southern Region, W.J.A. Sykes

Locomotive Magazine

1959 Specification for 2,500 hp Bo-Bo Electric Locomotives for the Southern Region

Books

A lifetime with Locomotives Roland C. Bond, Goose & Son, Cambridge, 1935

Two Miles a Minute (Second Edition), O.S. Nock, Patrick Stephens Ltd, Cambridge, 1983

Index

Northbound APT approaching Crewe.